NIMBLE TONGUES

COMPARATIVE CULTURAL STUDIES
ARI OFENGENDEN, SERIES EDITOR

The series examines how cultural practices, especially contemporary creative media, both shape and themselves are shaped by current global developments such as the digitization of culture, virtual reality, global interconnectedness, increased people flows, transhumanism, environmental degradation, and new forms of subjectivities. We aim to publish manuscripts that cross disciplines and national borders in order to provide deep insights into these issues.

OTHER TITLES IN THIS SERIES

Imagining Afghanistan: Global Fiction and Film of the 9/11 Wars
    Alla Ivanchikova

The Quest for Redemption: Central European Jewish Thought in Joseph Roth's Works
    Rares G. Piloiu

Perspectives on Science and Culture
    Kris Rutten, Stefaan Blancke, and Ronald Soetaert

Faust Adaptations from Marlowe to Aboudoma and Markland
    Lorna Fitzsimmons (Ed.)

Subjectivity in 'Aṭṭār, Persian Sufism, and European Mysticism
    Claudia Yaghoobi

Reconsidering the Emergence of the Gay Novel in English and German
    James P. Wilper

Cultural Exchanges between Brazil and France
    Regina R. Félix and Scott D. Juall (Eds.)

Transcultural Writers and Novels in the Age of Global Mobility
    Arianna Dagnino

NIMBLE TONGUES

STUDIES IN LITERARY TRANSLINGUALISM

Steven G. Kellman

Purdue University Press · West Lafayette, Indiana

Copyright 2020 by Purdue University. All rights reserved.
Printed in the United States of America.

Cover image: iStock/Getty Images Plus via Getty Images

Cataloging-in-Publication Data
Names: Kellman, Steven G., 1947– author.
Title: Nimble tongues : studies in literary translingualism / Steven G. Kellman.
Identifiers: LCCN 2019029010 (print) | LCCN 2019029011 (ebook) | ISBN 9781557538727 (paperback) | ISBN 9781612496009 (pdf) | ISBN 9781612496016 (epub)
Subjects: LCSH: Multilingualism and literature. | Language and culture.
Classification: LCC PN171.M93 K44 2020 (print) | LCC PN171.M93 (ebook) | DDC 404/.2—dc23
LC record available at https://lccn.loc.gov/2019029010
LC ebook record available at https://lccn.loc.gov/2019029011

These essays were previously published as listed below:
"Alien Autographs: How Translators Make Their Marks." *Neohelicon*, vol. 37, no. 1, 2010, pp. 7–19.
"Hugo Hamilton's Language War." *Critical Multilingualism Studies*, vol. 7, no. 1, 2019, pp. 51–63.
"*Incubus* and the Esperanto Movie Industry." Published as "Curse of the Spurned Hippie." *The Believer*, vol. 7, no. 3, Mar./Apr. 2009, pp. 33–36.
"An Italian in English: The Translingual Case of Francesca Marciano." *Papers on Language & Literature*, vol. 52, no. 2, 2016, pp. 177–93.
"Jhumpa Lahiri Goes Italian." *New England Review*, vol. 38, no. 2, 2017, http://www.nereview.com/vol-38-no-2-2017/jhumpa-lahiri-goes-italian/.
"Omnilingual Aspirations: The Case of the Universal Declaration of Human Rights." *Critical Multilingualism Studies*, vol. 4, no. 1, 2016, pp. 5–24.
"Promiscuous Tongues: Erotics of Translation and Translingualism." *Neohelicon*, vol. 40, no. 1, 2013, pp. 35–45.
"Translingual Memoirs of the New American Immigration." *Scritture migranti: rivista di scambi interculturali*, vol. 3, 2009, pp. 19–32.
"Writer Speaks with Forked Tongue: Interlingual Predicaments." *Multilingual Currents in Literature, Translation and Culture*, edited by Rachael Gilmour and Tamar Steinitz, Routledge, 2018, pp. 16–33.
"Writing South and North: Ariel Dorfman's Linguistic Ambidexterity." *Orbis Litterarum*, vol. 68, no. 3, 2013, pp. 207–21.

Contents

Preface	*VII*
Does Translingualism Matter?	*1*
Writer Speaks with Forked Tongue: Interlingual Predicaments	*16*
Promiscuous Tongues: Erotics of Translingualism and Translation	*33*
Writing South and North: Ariel Dorfman's Linguistic Ambidexterity	*46*
Alien Autographs: How Translators Make Their Marks	*59*
Translingual Memoirs of the New American Immigration	*77*
Incubus and the Esperanto Movie Industry	*89*
An Italian in English: The Translingual Case of Francesca Marciano	*100*

Hugo Hamilton's Language War	*113*
Jhumpa Lahiri Goes Italian	*126*
Linguaphobia and Its Resistance in America	*134*
Omnilingual Aspirations: The Case of the Universal Declaration of Human Rights	*146*
Glossary	*167*
Works Cited	*169*
Index	*189*
About the Author	*203*

Preface

The motives for literary translingualism—the practice of writing in more than one language or in a language other than one's native tongue—are varied, but its history is long, dating back to the infancy of verbal art. However, war, disease, famine, tyranny, terrorism, natural disaster, and economic hardship have contributed to an unprecedented movement of human beings in recent decades. According to a report released in 2017 by the United Nations Department of Economic and Social Affairs, "there are now an estimated 258 million people living in a country other than their country of birth—an increase of 49% since 2000" ("International Migration Report"). Migrants now constitute 3.4 percent of the world's population. Many of them adopt the language of their new host nation. Not all migrants are writers, and not all translinguals are migrants, but unprecedented mobility is surely a factor in the burgeoning of translingual literature discussed in this book.

And where literature leads, analysis follows. A Google search of "translingualism" yields more than twelve thousand entries. A search of "translingual literature" yields more than three thousand. Internet search engines were still quite primitive in 2000 when I published *The Translingual Imagination*. And when I edited *Switching Languages: Translingual Writers Reflect on Their Craft* in 2003, Google had not yet developed its "universal search" algorithm. However, it is safe to say that the explosion of interest in translingual literature during the past two decades is not simply a function of more inclusive search engines. Books, articles, dissertations, conferences, and special issues on the subject have proliferated. Natasha Lvovich and I assembled a partial bibliography of primary and secondary sources when we co-edited a special issue of *L2 Journal* in 2015 ("Selective Bibliography"). Because no one can be fluent in the thousands of languages that authors have switched to and from, no single scholar can claim mastery of the field, and it has been enlightening and inspiring to interact with many others in many countries who have taken up the subject. The study of authors who write in more than one language or in a language other than their primary one intersects with many vital disciplines, including literary history, stylistics, biography, psycholinguistics, sociolinguistics, postcolonial studies, and immigration studies. It is a microcosm of the entire field of comparative literature, the discipline that examines literature in ways that transcend the boundaries of language and nationality.

My study of translingualism has continued beyond *The Translingual Imagination* and *Switching Languages*. It has taken me to presentations in Amherst, Edmonton, Kuwait City, Los Angeles, Moscow, New Orleans, Oslo, Paris, Uppsala, and Utrecht and to the discovery of how nimble-tongued authors have explored the spaces, links, and barriers between languages. If the phenomenon of translingual writing is anything more than just a quaint curiosity, it has to be because of the power of language to shape—if not determine—perception and identity. The adoption of a particular language has profound implications for social justice and geopolitics.

Although the chapters in this volume originated as discrete essays or presentations, they form a continuous discussion of how linguistic choice is fundamental to the way we present ourselves and who we are.

Over the years, my thoughts about the nimbleness of tongues have been enlarged and enriched by the global community of translingualism scholars, including Michael Boyden, Rachael Gilmour, Julie Hansen, Eugenia Kelbert, Natasha Lvovich, Ania Spyra, Ilan Stavans, Tamar Steinitz, Adrian Wanner, and Elaine Wong. I am grateful to Justin Race, director of Purdue University Press, and Katherine Purple, editorial, design, and production manager, for the hospitality of their publishing house. I am especially indebted to Kelley Kimm for her astute and meticulous copyediting. And no language can express my gratitude—and love—to my wife, the poet Wendy Barker.

Does Translingualism Matter?

When Swedes speak English, evidence of their primary language often peeks through via vocabulary or intonation. A Stockholmer who asks, "What's the clock?" is probably inquiring about what time it is. Since Swedish lacks the affricate /dʒ/, usually represented in English by the letter "j," a Swede who is confined to jail might sound as if enrolled at Yale. The layering of languages was also common in early European manuscripts. Because of the scarcity of writing material, medieval scribes often recycled precious parchment by scraping away earlier texts before inscribing anything new. The result, a palimpsest, might bear faint traces of lower layers, but the practice sometimes eradicated the only copies of important works. However, except for the fact that it is a translation, one of the treasures of the Carolina Rediviva Library at Sweden's Uppsala University lacks any marks of an earlier text. A sixth-century manuscript of a fourth-century translation of the Bible into Gothic, the Codex Argenteus offers one of the few surviving specimens of the Gothic language. Scholars are able to study it because its parchment somehow escaped the fate of other medieval manuscripts—use as a palimpsest. Its Gothic text was not scraped away to make room for another document. Palimpsest, the layering of texts, is an apt metaphor for literary translingualism—the phenomenon of writers who write in more than one language or in a language other than their primary.

During the course of articulating a theory of translation in his 1813 essay "Ueber die verschiedenen Methoden des Uebersetzens" ("On the Different Methods of Translating"), Friedrich Schleiermacher casually denies the possibility of translingual literature, declaring that it is not possible to write something of artistic merit in a foreign language—"es nicht möglich ist etwas der Uebersetzung, sofern sie Kunst ist, würdiges und zugleich bedürftiges urspränglich in einer fremden Sprache zu schreiben" (77). Schleiermacher concedes the possibility of writing in an adopted language, but dismisses it as a rare and wonderful anomaly—"eine seltene und wunderbare Ausnahme" (77). As the numerous examples adduce throughout this book, from the earliest texts to the present, translingual literature is possible and even plentiful, as well as wonderful. While systematic study of translingualism was rare before the twenty-first century, it has proliferated during the past two decades. In numerous books, dissertations, articles, entire journals, conference sessions, and entire conferences, scholars have examined particular authors and texts as well as more general considerations of literary multilingualism, translation, and autotranslation. My own contributions have included two books: *The Translingual Imagination* (2000) and *Switching Languages: Translingual Writers Reflect on Their Craft* (2003). But because no one scholar can master more than a handful of languages, the study of translingualism must be a collective enterprise.

Thus far, scholarship on translingualism has tended to concentrate on literature of the past 150 years and in Western languages, though Yoko Tawada, who writes in Japanese and German, has called attention to what she calls *exophony*, traveling out of one's native tongue, among Asian writers (Tawada). Much attention has, deservedly, been devoted to the modernist trinity of Samuel Beckett, Joseph Conrad, and Vladimir Nabokov. And the fact that postcolonial authors such as Chinua Achebe, Léopold Sédar Senghor, and Raja Rao wrote in the languages of European empires has not been ignored. In addition, the global profusion of refugees, migrants, and travelers in recent years has produced a rich body of translingual writing and of scholarship on that oeuvre. Notable contemporary authors who have migrated into English include André Aciman, Rabih Alameddine, Daniel Alarcón, Julia Alvarez, Louis Begley, Edwidge Danticat, Junot Diaz, Ariel Dorfman, Cristina García,

Olga Grushin, Ursula Hegi, Aleksandar Hemon, Ha Jin, Andrew Lam, Li-Young Lee, Yiyun Li, Shirley Geok-lin Lim, Hisham Matar, Dinaw Mengestu, Téa Obreht, Luc Sante, Gary Shteyngart, and Charles Simic. Though the French are so proud of their language they enforce its purity through diktats from the Académie Française, they have nevertheless bestowed glittering prizes on linguistic interlopers such as Vassilis Alexakis, Tahar Ben Jelloun, Hector Bianciotti, Hélène Cixous, Assia Djebar, Romain Gary, Nancy Huston, Milan Kundera, Jonathan Littell, Amin Maalouf, Andreï Makine, Alain Mabanckou, Irène Némirovsky, Atiq Rahimi, André Schwarz-Bart, Jorge Semprún, Dai Sijie, Henri Troyat, and Elie Wiesel. Germany even created a special award, the Adelbert von Chamisso Prize (named for the nineteenth-century German poet who was born in France), for translinguals—such as Zehra Çirak, Emine Sevgi Özdamar, and Yoko Tawada—who write in German. (Because of concerns that it stigmatizes translinguals instead of honoring their contributions to literature in German, the Chamisso Prize was discontinued in 2016.) Translingual literature has proliferated not only in such widely spoken languages as English, French, and German, but even in Swedish—in work by, for example, Mehmed Uzun (first language Kurdish), Guilem Rodrigues da Silva (Portuguese), Theodor Kallifatides (Greek), Azar Mahloujian (Farsi), and Fateme Behros (Farsi). Modern Hebrew literature was created by writers—including S. Y. Agnon, Yehudah Amichai, Aharon Appelfeld, Chaim Nachman Bialik, Yosef Chaim Brenner, and Shaul Tchernichovsky—who came to Hebrew from Yiddish, Russian, Polish, German, and other European languages. With his 1992 novel *Seijouki no kikoenai heya* (*A Room Where the Star Spangled Banner Cannot Be Heard* [2011]), Hideo Levy established his reputation as the first American to write fiction in Japanese.

However, translingual texts have an ancient pedigree, predating even Sir Isaac Newton's *Principia Mathematica*, René Descartes's *Meditationes de prima philosophia*, and Sir Thomas More's *Utopia*—all written in Latin. Translingual writing may well have developed as a practical matter shortly after the invention of writing itself. It is quite possible that Etruscans, Anatolians, Carthaginians, and other peoples of the Mediterranean basin and Asia Minor appropriated the newly devised alphabet brought by the seafaring Phoenicians not only by adapting it to their own unlettered tongues but also by writing in Phoenician—probably not epic poetry, but at least invoices for their commercial transactions with the Phoenicians. Even earlier, as far back as the twenty-third century BCE, the first poet history knows by name, Enheduanna, the only daughter of the powerful Akkadian King Sargon, composed her poetry in Sumerian, though her first language was probably Akkadian. Within the far-flung empires of antiquity, citizens wrote in the imperial language—Greek, Latin, Persian, Arabic, Chinese, Sanskrit—regardless of what they spoke at home. Indeed, Yasemin Yildiz argues persuasively that what she calls the "monolingual paradigm" (2) first emerged in late eighteenth-century Europe, about the time that Schleiermacher was beginning to use it as a prism through which to (mis)understand literary creation. Throughout the rest of history, multilingualism has otherwise been the norm.

Charting that history requires the talents and energies of generations of scholars. No one researcher possesses the linguistic equipment to take on the task alone. If there are approximately 5,000 languages in the world, the number of translingual possibilities would equal $5,000 \times 4,999 \div 2 = 12,497,500$. And that is only calculating the number of *bilingual* translingual possibilities; authors who, like Kamala Das, Vladimir Nabokov, and George Steiner, move among three or more languages add even more possibilities to the challenge of mapping out the universe of translingual literature.

I do not presume to take on that task in this chapter. Instead, I would like to pose some fundamental—even elementary—questions about the translingual project, the kinds of basic questions that arose in an undergraduate seminar on translingual literature that I have taught in Texas. Before we begin, for example, to juxtapose details of Isak Dinesen's *Out of Africa* (1937) with those of her own version of it in Danish, as *Den afrikanske farm* (1937), it is appropriate to ask: Why is such an analysis important? I do not necessarily mean that as an ethical or political challenge—that is, Why should we be studying literature at all as long as human beings are suffering war, famine, disease, and injustice? This is not the occasion to address that important question, though I trust that each reader in one way or another believes that a world devoid of literary studies is a world that has surrendered to the primitive forces of war, famine, disease, and injustice.

Instead, I would pose this question: Given that the study of literature is a worthy, even edifying and civilizing, endeavor, what difference does it make that a given text was written in an adopted language—in L2 (a speaker's or writer's first acquired language), or even L3 or L4, what John Skinner dubbed "the stepmother tongue" (Skinner)? We can break that down into two questions: what difference does translingualism make to the author and what difference does translingualism make to the reader? Is a translingual text inherently distinguishable from a monolingual one? Is it inherently superior?

As a preliminary caveat, it is necessary to recognize that languages are dynamic continuums, not discrete, static entities. To enter into a particular linguistic community is to jump into a rushing current that is not entirely isolated from other flows. All languages are mongrels and carry echoes of the babel from which they emerge. And, as Rebecca L. Walkowitz observes, it is a mistake to pigeonhole many contemporary texts within a single linguistic category. Numerous works are, as she puts it in the title of her 2015 book, "born translated," existing simultaneously in more than one language. Because genocide and assimilation had eliminated most of the readership for his primary language, Yiddish, Isaac Bashevis Singer wrote to be read in translation, though he stubbornly continued to compose his fictions in his *mame loshn*. Furthermore, if we consider that even the most obdurate xenophobe who refuses to learn anything but L1 (his or her first language) negotiates several registers (slang, formal, intimate, regional, standard, etc.) of just L1 each day, we are *all* multilingual, and all texts are translingual. Nevertheless, Samuel Beckett's *Molloy* (1953), written in the Irish author's adopted French, is a different kind of creation from, say, *Candide* (1759), which, on its title page, Voltaire flippantly claimed was "traduit de l'allemand de Mr. le Docteur Ralph" 'translated from the German of Doctor Ralph' but which he in fact composed himself in his native French. Is the difference an important one? Or is the category of "translingual literature" an arbitrary, pedantic contrivance?

To answer the question of whether writing in an adopted language makes much difference to the writer, we can turn to a large body of translingual memoirs, interviews with translingual writers, and empirical studies in socio- and psycholinguistics. The Indian novelist Raja Rao dismissed the whole subject. "The important thing," he contended, in

English, not in his native Kannada, "is not what language one writes in, for language is really an accidental thing. What matters is the authenticity of experience, and this can generally be achieved in any language" (147). Most other translinguals disagree. They are implicitly, or even explicitly, Whorfians, for whom each language entails a unique Weltanschauung. Otherwise, if languages were perfectly interchangeable, there would be little reason to undertake the arduous task of switching languages.

Many translinguals describe a sensation of split personalities, as if each language embodied a different self. An extreme example is Louis Wolfson, who was diagnosed as schizophrenic and whose 1970 memoir, *Le Schizo et les langues*, is a curious amalgam of French, Hebrew, Russian, and German—anything but English, the mother tongue he detested in part because of a strained relationship with his biological mother. Rosario Ferré, the Puerto Rican author who writes alternately in Spanish and English, contends that "a bilingual writer is really two different writers, has two very different voices, writes in two different styles, and, most important, looks at the world through two different sets of glasses. This takes a splitting of the self that doesn't come easily and can be dangerous" (138). Ariel Dorfman, split between a South American and a North American identity, signals the same truth in the very title of his 1998 memoir, *Heading South, Looking North: A Bilingual Journey*. After completing his book in English, Dorfman, a self-proclaimed "bigamist of language" (*Heading South* 270), immediately reconceived it in Spanish as *Rumbo al sur, deseando el norte* (1998). Luc Sante, who grew up in Belgium speaking French, finds the English language inadequate to recall his earlier self. "In order to speak of my childhood," he notes, in English, in his 1998 memoir, *The Factory of Facts*, "I have to translate. It is as if I were writing about someone else. The words don't fit because they are in English, and languages are not equivalent one to another" (261). For Eva Hoffman, the title of whose 1989 memoir declares that she is *Lost in Translation*, there is an insurmountable chasm between Polish-speaking Ewa Wydra and English-speaking Eva Hoffman that she attempts to overcome by staging dialogues between the two. Wistful over her inability to recover her Polish self, Anglophone Eva invokes a Polish word, *tęsknota*, to convey her nostalgia, sadness, and longing, even while noting that those English words are incommensurate with the Polish (4).

Nevertheless, translingual authors do not always conceive of their condition in terms of loss. "I see no reason to give up one language if I can help it," declares Rosario Ferré. "Having two different views of the world is profoundly enriching" (138). For Anton Shammās, a Palestinian Arab, writing in Hebrew was an act of liberation: "You cannot write about the people whom you love in a language that they understand; you can't write freely. In order not to feel my heroes breathing down my neck all the time, I used Hebrew" ("My Case" 48). Jerzy Kosinski, who wrote in English rather than his native Polish, recalled, "It was a great surprise to me, one of many surprises of my life, that when I began speaking English, I felt freer to express myself, not just my views but my personal history, my quite private drives, all the thoughts that I would have found difficult to reveal in my native tongue" (125). Speaking French rather than his native German is similarly emancipating for Hans Castorp in Thomas Mann's *Der Zauberberg*. It enables him to overcome his inhibitions about flirting with the married Clavdia Chauchat. As he tells her, *en français*, using the intimate *tu*, though he would not have dared to address her as *du* in German, "Moi, tu le remarques bien, je ne parle guère le français. Pourtant, avec toi, je préfère cette langue à la mienne, car pour moi, parler français, c'est parler sans parler, en quelque manière, sans responsabilité, ou, comme nous parlons en rêve" 'As you've surely noticed, I barely speak French. All the same, I would rather speak with you in it than in my own language, since for me speaking French is like speaking without saying anything somehow—with no responsibilities, the way we speak in a dream' (*Zauberberg* 407; *Magic Mountain* 401).

For Oscar Wilde, writing his play *Salomé* in French rather than in his native tongue was an additional way to shock and offend the English, the colonialist usurpers whom he, as a proud son of Ireland, despised. There are almost as many reasons to switch languages as there are writers who adopt another tongue. Every translingual is happy or unhappy in his or her own way. But whether they view the switch positively or not, almost all acknowledge that switching languages makes a profound difference in what—and certainly how—they write.

More significant than the way that translingualism makes a difference for the writer is the way that it makes a difference for the text, which means the difference that it makes for the reader. Does it really matter whether a novel, story, poem, or play was written in L1, L2, L3, or L4? I would like to suggest a thought experiment. Let's apply a blind test. Could we take an unknown work and tell merely from textual evidence whether it was or was not written in the primary language of its author? If we could tell, would the fact of its translingualism mean a profound difference in style or content or quality?

One way to pursue this inquiry is to take a work by a patently monolingual writer and compare it to a work by a translingual. We can of course easily name hundreds, if not thousands, of important translinguals writers, from Chinua Achebe, who wrote in English rather than Igbo, to Feridun Zaimoğlu, who writes in German, not Turkish. But it is much more difficult to identify a writer who is completely monolingual. Jacobean England was separated from and suspicious of the rest of Europe. However, though Ben Jonson famously wrote that William Shakespeare had "small Latin and less Greek" ("To the Memory of My Beloved Master" 263), the speech in *Henry V* in which Alice, the lady-in-waiting, tries to teach Catherine, a French princess who is to marry Henry, the English words for parts of the body is conducted in French (Act 3 Scene 4). Nor did John Milton, a few decades later, restrict himself to English only. Though Samuel Johnson, impatient with the polyglot, polymath John Milton, would complain that he "wrote no language" (442), the author of *Paradise Lost* in fact wrote poetry in Greek, Italian, and Latin, in addition to English.

There are probably some monolingual writers in North Korea, perhaps the most insular and isolated nation in the world, where writers are reportedly constrained to employ their talents extolling the supreme leader. Kim Il-sung and Kim Jong-il themselves both published books, and, according to his official—and incredible—biography, the current supreme leader of the Democratic People's Republic of North Korea, Kim Jong-un, wrote fifteen hundred books during his three years at Kim Il-sung University. In any case, before assuming power, each of the Kims lived abroad and no doubt acquired some knowledge of languages other than Korean. Japan is a notoriously insular culture, though studying English has become fashionable there. And the best-known Japanese writer, Haruki Murakami, knows English well enough to have translated Truman Capote, Raymond Carver, and F. Scott Fitzgerald into Japanese.

So perhaps it is to the United States, the nation of immigrants where the second and third generations strive to assimilate to English-only, that we must turn to find the best specimen of monolingual writing. According to one report, "less than 1 percent of American adults today are proficient in a foreign language that they studied in a U.S. classroom," and "only 7 percent of college students in America are enrolled in a language course" (Friedman). However, monolingualism is not conspicuous among major American writers of the nineteenth century, most of whom were educated in Latin and Greek. If we are looking for a monolingual author, it would certainly not be the polyglot poet Henry Wadsworth Longfellow, who translated from French, Italian, and Spanish and was a professor of modern languages at Harvard. Nor would it be Washington Irving, who spent twenty years as a diplomat in Spain. Nor Herman Melville, who traveled widely as a sailor before settling down to write. Mark Twain wrote vivid accounts of his travels abroad, and in an 1880 essay titled "The Awful Language," described his struggles learning German. Though he recalled, approvingly, a Californian who "would rather decline two drinks than one German adjective," Twain was conversant enough in the language to deliver a humorous lecture in Vienna in 1897 titled "Die Schrecken der deutschen Sprache." And of course much has been made of Twain's mastery, in *Adventures of Huckleberry Finn*, of vernacular English and of what has come to be called Ebonics. The ventriloquism of American speech that Twain orchestrates in his novel led Shelley Fisher Fishkin to hear the echoes of African American voices (Fishkin). Henry James, Ezra Pound, T. S. Eliot, Edith Wharton, Ernest Hemingway, and Saul Bellow were certainly not monolingual. Even Emily Dickinson, who rarely strayed outside her home in Amherst, Massachusetts, studied Latin, and the quantitative prosody of Latin poetry was a model for her own work (Cuddy).

The Jim Crow South was probably the most isolated part of the United States, and its bard was William Faulkner, who concentrated almost all of his fiction in rural Yoknapatawpha County in Mississippi. Faulkner himself never finished high school and, aside from training as a pilot in Canada, had no experience abroad until after he won the Nobel Prize. Creolization—the mixture of cultures, races, and languages—is the ultimate horror for the characters in the Yoknapatawpha cycle. Yet even

Faulkner's Anglophone Mississippi bears traces of French—in names such as Lucas Beauchamp and Charles Bon. In *Absalom, Absalom!*, when Thomas Sutpen brings a cargo of African slaves back from Haiti to work his plantation, we are told "the negroes could speak no English yet and doubtless there were more than Akers who did not know that the language in which they and Sutpen communicated was a sort of French and not some dark and fatal tongue of their own" (Faulkner 27). Thus is another language, in this case Haitian Creole, inscribed into Faulkner's monolingual text as an object of dread.

To find a genuinely monolingual control against which to test the difference made by translingualism, we might have to turn to the isolated Pirahã people of the Amazon. However, as studied by Daniel Everett, their language, unrelated to any other extant language, lacks an alphabet and thus any written texts to compare to those of Beckett, Conrad, and Nabokov (Everett). Moreover, if Proust is right and "les beaux livres sont écrits dans une sorte de langue étrangère" 'beautiful books are written in a sort of foreign language' (*Contre* 305; *Against* 93), then *all* literature aspires to translingualism.

So, for a clearer test of whether translingualism matters, we might instead turn to the antithesis of writers who switch languages—those writers who cling to their primary language despite living in an environment where another language dominates. Lars Gustafsson wrote much of the poetry and fiction that secured his reputation as a leading Swedish author during the twenty years he lived in Austin, Texas. Witold Gombrowicz continued writing in Polish during the twenty-four years he spent in Argentina, and Aleksandr Solzhenitsyn persisted in using Russian to expose the Soviet gulags during the twenty years he spent in exile, mostly in Vermont. Robert Penn Warren, who stuck to English even when living in Italy, once explained, "I like to write in foreign countries, where the language is not your own, and you are forced into yourself in a special way" (5). Therefore, when they are forced into themselves, which means into their own primary languages, is the result any different from what occurs when a writer moves out into another language? Since those very sophisticated writers did know other languages and were alert to the different registers of their primary tongues, even they cannot function as a useful contrast to overtly translingual writers. In fact, since most writers are multilingual or at least vary the registers of their primary language, it is probably more precise to refer to them not as monolingual but rather as isolingual. An isolingual writer is one who writes in a language identical with his or her L1. Johann Wolfgang von Goethe, who studied Latin, Greek, French, Italian, English, and Hebrew, was multilingual, but, because he wrote exclusively in his native German, Goethe must be considered isolingual.

So we are left with this question: Are there any specific markers that signal the translingual origins of a text? When not altered by scrupulous book editors, the existence of calques—examples of locutions transposed from one language directly into another in which they are at best awkward—would certainly be evidence of a prior language. According to his wife, Jessie, Joseph Conrad (né Józef Teodor Konrad Nalécz Korzeniowski) spoke English with a thick Polish accent. And his English prose is a palimpsest of English superimposed over his L2, French, over his L1, Polish. In *The Secret Agent* (1907), when Conrad states that Adolf Verloc "pulled up violently the venetian blind" (84) and that, gazing at Winnie Verloc, Ossipon "was excessively terrified at her" (254), the word order and choice betray the fact that the author is not a native speaker of English. Arguing that Conrad's prose is haunted by French ("l'anglais de Joseph Conrad est littéralement hanté par le français"), Claude Maisonnat has documented a large quantity of gallicisms spread throughout his fiction (par. 29). Nevertheless, a reader in search of something distinctive about translingual writing ought not to be reduced to hunting for calques. Is there not something more significant that distinguishes translingual writing?

Mikhail Bakhtin's theory of "the dialogic imagination" owes much to assumptions about multilingualism. Bakhtin argued that echoes of other languages accounted for the heteroglossia of classical Latin literature. "Roman literary consciousness," he wrote, "was bilingual.... From start to finish, the creative literary consciousness of the Romans functioned against the background of the Greek language and Greek forms. From its very first steps, the Latin literary world viewed itself in light of the Greek word, through the eyes of the Greek word" (61). Bakhtin goes on to note that both Aramaic and Oscan were also part of the linguistic mix of the Roman Empire and to contend that multilingualism alone enables us to step outside any particular language and realize that what we take for granted as "natural" is in fact a function of that specific language. However, Bakhtin's claim that all genuine novels are dialogic would include works by isolingual authors and recognize that the ability to switch voices is not unique to translinguals.

Nevertheless, most of us who have ventured at all beyond L1 become Whorfians to the extent that we sense that each language offers its own template through which to process space, time, number, self, and other fundamental categories of experience. All things being equal (though they often are not), translingual authors are better equipped than isolinguals to step outside the prison-house of language—or at least of L1—and to make us aware of the factitiousness of verbal constructions. Translingual texts are often metalingual in their self-consciousness about their own linguistic medium, the way they make language itself strange, subjecting it to what Viktor Shklovsky called *ostranenie*—defamiliarization (Shklovsky). Nabokov's love of puns, anagrams, and palinodes foregrounds his linguistic medium. In *Pale Fire*, when he makes translation from the fictional language Zemblan a crucial element of the story, a reader is obliged to think about the nature of language itself. *La Leçon* (1951) by Eugène Ionesco, who wrote in French, not his native Romanian, dramatizes the absurdity of primers for learning English. Andreï Makine's novel *Le Testament français* (1995; *Dreams of My Russian Summers* [1997]) is in effect a paean to the Russian-born author's first love: his second language, French. In *An Unnecessary Woman* (2014), Rabih Alameddine, who writes in English rather than his native Arabic, foregrounds language by telling the story of an elderly woman whose meager life revolves around secondary translation—rendering into Arabic novels that have already been translated into English or French. Autobiographies by many translingual authors—among them Ariel Dorfman, Eva Hoffman, Hugo Hamilton, and Luc Sante—are in effect self-begetting linguistic memoirs, the story of how the author achieved enough fluency in a second language to use it to write the book we are reading.

Yet not all translingual texts are reflexive, and not all call attention to language. Writing thirty-one novels, including popular successes such as *Captain Blood* (1922), *Scaramouche* (1921), and *The Sea Hawk* (1915), in his sixth language, English, Rafael Sabatini aimed for a transparent style that does not call attention to itself but instead invites readers to lose themselves in the colorful adventures of his characters. Writing in English rather than her native Russian, Ayn Rand was more interested in pushing her polemics about what she called "ethical egoism" than in reflecting on the medium of those polemics. Nor do translinguals possess a monopoly on reflexive fictions, as evidenced by *The Tempest, Don Quixote, A la recherche du temps perdu,* and *Se una notte d'inverno un viaggiatore*—all written by isolinguals.

In her book *Alien Tongues: Bilingual Russian Writers of the "First" Emigration,* Elizabeth Klosty Beaujour finds "cognitive flexibility," "tolerance for ambiguity," and "greater awareness of the relativity of things" to be characteristic of the Russian translinguals she studies (102). It is tempting to apply those terms to all translingual writers, since all evince a willingness to readjust such categories as time, space, quantity, color, and gender through which language helps them apprehend the world. However, some distinctions ought to be made. Ambilingual translinguals—those who, like Fernando Pessoa (Portuguese and English), Mendele Mocher Sforim (Yiddish and Hebrew), Premchand (Hindi and Urdu), Ngũgĩ wa Thiong'o (English and Gikuyu), and André Brink (Afrikaans and English) write in more than one language—probably demonstrate greater cognitive flexibility than writers such as Julia Alvarez, Aharon Appelfeld, Edwidge Danticat, Assia Djebar, and Irène Némirovsky who choose a language other than their L1 and stubbornly stick with it as their sole medium of literary expression.

Aneta Pavlenko argues that the age at which a second language is acquired is a crucial factor in differentiating among bilinguals. Age of acquisition would probably also be useful in making distinctions among translingual authors and their texts; the fact that Nathalie Sarraute began learning French as a little girl when she moved to Paris from Russia marks her as a different kind of translingual from Jerzy Kosinski, who began learning English in his twenties when he emigrated to the United States from Poland. Pavlenko also distinguishes among coordinate bilinguals ("who learned their languages in distinct environments and have two conceptual systems associated with their two lexicons"), compound bilinguals (who "learned their languages in a single environment and, consequently, have a single underlying and undifferentiated conceptual system linked to the two lexicons"), and subordinate bilinguals ("typically classroom learned who learned the second language via the means of the first, have a single system where the second-language lexicon is linked to conceptual representations through first-language words") (*The Bilingual Mind* 18).

In speciesist English, "to parrot" is to repeat something mindlessly. Yet birds clearly do have minds, albeit nonhuman, of their own. In 2014, when a parrot named Nigel was returned to his British human companion, Darren Chick, four years after disappearing, Nigel spoke Spanish rather than the clipped English that Chick had taught him ("Missing Parrot Turns Up"). "¿Que pasó?" is the way he greeted his old companion at their reunion. If Nigel could be called an avian translingual, he would also have to be classified as a coordinate translingual. Other examples of coordinate translinguals might be Gary Shteyngart, who grew up speaking Russian in Leningrad but switched to English after moving to the United States at age seven, and Aharon Appelfeld, who, a native speaker of German, did not begin learning Hebrew, the only language he wrote in, until he left Bukovina for Palestine at age fourteen. Examples of compound translinguals might be Breyten Breytenbach, who grew up speaking both Afrikaans and English, and Anita Desai, who grew up speaking German, Bengali, and English. Examples of subordinate translinguals are Samuel Beckett, who grew up speaking English but studied French at school, and René Descartes, who grew up speaking French but studied Latin at school.

All things are rarely equal, but when they are, compound translinguals would seem most gifted with cognitive flexibility. The compound translingual's ability from an early age to balance two or more separate linguistic systems simultaneously probably demands a greater awareness of the relativity of things than the sequential initiation into another linguistic template involved with both coordinate and subordinate translinguals. However, most translingual writers would seem more attuned to ambiguity than most isolingual writers. Translingualism would seem to incline writers toward metalingual awareness, manifested in ostentatious verbal play and in reflexive constructions that lay bare the devices of their art. Nevertheless, some translingual writers are largely indifferent to the linguistic medium they happen to be using. And, conversely, work by some isolingual writers is acutely self-aware. William Shakespeare's plays-within-plays and the metafictional architecture of Marcel Proust's *A la recherche du temps perdu* were not produced by switching languages. Moreover, even the most dedicated scholar of translingual literature could not contend that it is somehow superior to isolingual literature. To do so would be to deprecate the achievements of Cervantes, Goethe, Li Po, Pushkin, Shakespeare, Sophocles, and Virgil in favor of Agnon, Beckett, Conrad, Dante, Nabokov, Pessoa, and Rilke.

Therefore, if it is hard to isolate anything unique to translingual literature, and if translingual literature is not necessarily superior to any other, should we be making a fuss over it? Every translingual is translingual in his or her own way, and their lives are of considerable anecdotal interest. The texts they have produced are marvels of adaptation and invention. The poems, plays, novels, short stories, and essays by writers who have switched languages offer rich material for understanding language, the imagination, and the experience of what it is to be human, or even a parrot.

Writer Speaks with Forked Tongue: Interlingual Predicaments

The literary achievements of Samuel Beckett, Joseph Conrad, and Vladimir Nabokov inspire such awe that the history of translingual literature often seems like a narrative of artistic triumph over linguistic handicap. For some writers, switching languages appears seamless, painless, and complete. Petrarch managed to write enduring poetry in both Latin and Italian, Mirza Ghalib in both Urdu and Persian, and Uri Zvi Greenberg in both Yiddish and Hebrew. Rafael Sabatini wrote more than thirty novels in English, his sixth language (after Italian, Portuguese, French, German, and Spanish). Ha Jin arrived in the United States from China with barely a rudimentary knowledge of English, yet it took him only eleven years to win both the National Book Award and the PEN/Faulkner Award for his first novel, *Waiting* (1999). Many of the most celebrated contemporary novelists, poets, and playwrights write in an adopted tongue.

And translingual memoirs are a thriving—and reflexive—genre (Besemeres and Kaplan "On Language Memoir"). Because they tend to foreground and problematize the author's transition from one language to another, they are of particular interest to a study of interlingual predicaments. The implicit concluding sentence of translingual memoirs is often "And so I arrived at the point at which I was able to write these pages, impeccably, in this rich adopted language that you are reading."

For Edward W. Bok, who arrived in New York from the Netherlands without any English, learning the local language required little effort. Writing in English in the third person, he recalls that ". . . the national linguistic gift inherent in the Dutch race came to the boy's rescue, and as the roots of the Anglo-Saxon lie in the Frisian tongue, and thus in the language of his native country, Edward soon found that with a change of vowel here and there the English language was not so difficult of conquest" (4). It is the language that he mastered well enough to compose that memoir.

Nevertheless, for many others, tongue-switching is agony, an excruciating ordeal that is never completely mastered. Indeed, the translingual project is sometimes a failure or even a pathology. Inability or refusal to accept the language of exile may not have caused the suicides of Klaus Mann, Ernst Toller, and Stefan Zweig—writers who, driven into exile by Nazism, could not count on a wide readership when continuing to write in their native German—any more than it drove Paul Celan, Romain Gary, Arthur Koestler, Jerzy Kosinski, and Piotr Rawicz—each of whom wrote well in an adopted language—to kill themselves. But linguistic disorientation does contribute to despondency. In her own travails going from Russian to French to English, Natasha Lvovich recalls ". . . an emotional dysbalance, a psychic discomfort, similar to nostalgia, a 'language sickness'" (71). Elsa Triolet, writing in French rather than her native Russian, bemoans the bilingual malaise that has afflicted her: "On dirait une maladie: je suis atteinte de bilinguisme" 'One could call it a disease: I am afflicted with bilingualism' (54). Among translingual Russian émigrés in general, Elizabeth Klosty Beaujour diagnoses a tendency to "experience the pangs of infidelity and guilt, as well as a sense of self-mutilation" (42). Few writers demonstrate as severe and dramatic a case of *taedium lingua* as Louis Wolfson, who was institutionalized with schizophrenia. His 1970 book *Le Schizo et les langues* documents how Wolfson's revulsion toward his maternal language, English, the language of his terrifying mother, propelled him toward several other languages—including French, Hebrew, Russian, and German—that he did not entirely inhabit. At the very least, linguistic displacement creates a fracture in personal identity that is impossible to restore. At best, a coherent new self is created.

The Phases of Transition Between Languages

The ordeal resembles rites of passage as analyzed by British anthropologist Victor Turner. Studying the Ndembu of Zambia, Turner found three phases defining their initiation rituals: "separation, margin (or *limen*), and aggregation" (94). After a neophyte is isolated from the community, a period of disorientation and ambiguity ensues. During this marginal interim, initiates experience self-abasement, a conviction that they are worthless and unclean. In a successful *rite de passage*, such feelings eventually dissolve, and the outcast—during what Turner calls "aggregation"—is reintegrated into the community. Employing some of the same terminology in what she calls "a psychoanalytic reading" of second-language learning, Colette A. Granger diagnoses the plight of the "liminal self, living unsteadily in two languages and therefore living fully in neither." Using a familiar spatial metaphor, she finds the second-language learner "positioned on the blurred border-line between first and second languages, unable either to turn back and regain the old self or to move forward, unencumbered, into a new one" (62).

For much of her memoir, Eva Hoffman is just such a liminal self. Relocated at thirteen from Cracow to Vancouver, Hoffman is, for many years, what she calls "lost in translation." Her native Polish, now useless, slips away, and her command of English is embryonic and clumsy. However, Hoffman's *Lost in Translation*, written thirty years later in dexterous and sophisticated English, testifies to the successful conclusion of the liminal phase. Nevertheless, a writer as accomplished as Hoffman must be regarded as an anomaly. Millions of people have attempted to start their lives anew in a different culture with a different language, and very few have become as articulate as Hoffman. Of the hundreds of thousands of human beings who began new lives after surviving the devastation of the Third Reich, few managed to be as expressive in an adopted language as Aharon Appelfeld, Louis Begley, Paul Celan, and Elie Wiesel. Translingual literature is the creation of extraordinary nomads who succeed in passing through all three of Turner's phases. There are, according to the United Nations High Commissioner for Refugees, more than 19.5 million refugees in the world today ("Facts and Figures"). Aggregation is a phase of translingualism never attained by most, who remain stranded in a liminal linguistic purgatory.

Except in linguistic atlases, language is not defined by latitude and longitude. Language is a process, a performance, a system of communication—not a place. Yet spatial metaphors are frequently invoked to explain the translingual situation or even culture in general. In *The Location of Culture*, Homi K. Bhabha repeatedly employs spatial tropes when he invokes "'in-between' spaces" (2), "the site of cultural difference" (46), and "that Third Space of enunciations which I have made the precondition for the articulation of cultural difference" (56). Much analysis of second-language acquisition accepts this notion of "third space" or "third place," that, as Claire J. Kramsch puts it, ". . . the major task of language learners is to define for themselves what this 'third place' that they have engaged in seeking will look like, whether they are conscious of it or not" (257). The equation of locution with location becomes even more explicit in a formulation by Daisy Cocco De Filippis, a native of the Dominican Republic who came to the United States when she was thirteen: "El lenguaje ha sido el espacio habitado por aquellos a quienes se le ha negado un lugar" 'Language has been the space inhabited by those who have been denied a place' (149). Assia Djebar writes in a French that, though enriched with resonances of Arabic and Berber from her native Algeria, she calls "mon seul véritable territoire" 'my only true territory' (*Ces Voix* 44). After all of her dislocations, from Russia to Italy to the United States, Lvovich makes a similar claim about the memoir she wrote in English, *The Multilingual Self*: "This book is my home" (xv). And when Eva Hoffman concludes her memoir by stating "I am here now" (280), she, too, is positioning herself within both the English language and the book that she has written in it—as if languages and books possessed cartographic coordinates and every speaker could be located through a linguistic GPS. A writer who travels between languages is what George Steiner, who moves among English, French, and German, calls "extraterritorial" (*Extraterritorial*). Thus can Anton Shammās, an Israeli Arab, worry that he has strayed into hostile territory by writing in Hebrew, and committing "a sort of cultural trespassing and I might one day be punished for it" (Hever 72).

Language as Home

Of course, languages and texts do not occupy physical space, except symbolically, but that symbolism is commonplace in discussions of translingual experience. And, since there is no place like home, many translinguals refer to their language of choice as home. Though he was born in Lithuania, Czesław Miłosz spent almost half of his life in the United States but insisted on writing in Polish, declaring at a poetry reading at the 1998 Modern Language Association Convention, "Language is the only homeland" (qtd. in Umpierre 135). Despite extensive immersion in both Japanese and Chinese, Gary Snyder writes exclusively in English, about which his poem "It" declares, "My language is home" (42). Asked whether he still had a homeland, Albert Camus, torn between his restive native Algeria and the metropole of the French empire, replied, "Oui, j'ai une patrie, la langue française" 'Yes, I have a homeland; the French language' (337). He was echoing what Louis Martin Chauffier wrote a decade earlier in defiance of the German occupation of France: "Ma Patrie, c'est la langue française" 'My homeland is the French language' (62). Chauffier added that the French language is "une patrie sans frontière" 'a homeland without borders' (62). Céline Dion, the French Canadian pop singer who tours widely and records in both French and English, makes a similar claim: "Le français c'est ma maison, mes racines" 'French is my home, my roots' (Coudé-Lord). Though he lives in Spain, Swiss novelist Martin Suter considers the German language his home: "Heimat ist für mich meine Sprache" (Scholz). Noting that many fellow Chicanos are dispersed throughout the Midwest and the Northeast, Gloria Anzaldúa, too, insists that what you speak is where you are: "For some of us, language is a homeland closer than the Southwest" (55).

During the age of nation-states that confounds language and nationality, that considers facility in Polish requisite for Polish identity, in Norwegian for Norwegian identity, those who abandon one language but are not yet secure in another can feel as if they have vacated one apartment but not yet moved all of their belongings into another. Many translinguals suffer from a permanent sense of homelessness. J. M. Coetzee, who grew up speaking Afrikaans and English, mastered the latter well enough to have earned the Nobel Prize in Literature by writing in it. Nevertheless, he told an audience in India that the language he writes in, English, is not his home: "As a child in South Africa, I was sent to an English medium school because my parents thought it was a way to the future. I then studied in English at the university level. Yet I can't say that I can feel at home in English. I feel I am writing in someone else's language" (qtd. in Jalali). Edward Said, who grew up speaking both English and Arabic, confesses, "I have never known which was my first language, and have felt fully at home in neither, although I dream in both. Every time I speak an English sentence, I find myself echoing it in Arabic, and vice versa" (557).

According to Gustavo Pérez Firmat, Ricky Ricardo, the television persona of Cuban émigré Desi Arnaz, embodies the pathos of translingual muddle. On the long-running *I Love Lucy* show, while Ricky's Spanish, corrupted by anglicisms and enfeebled by a diminishing vocabulary, deteriorated, his heavily accented English never improved. "He is homeless in two languages," concludes Pérez Firmat (*Life on the Hyphen* 43). Ricky, and the actor who played him, are examples of the "nilingüe, which Pérez Firmat defines as "someone who doesn't speak either: 'ni español ni inglés'" (43). The metaphor of homelessness posits language as a matter of realty, if not reality. Martin Heidegger contended that language is the House of Being ("Die Sprache is das Haus des Seins. In ihrer Behausung wohnt der Mensch" 'Language is the House of Being. In its habitation resides man' [5]). If so, then those who are not housed securely in a specific language suffer from an ontological deficiency.

Or else they revel in a deconstructionist decentering. Jacques Derrida spatializes language when, in *Le Monolinguisme de l'autre—ou la prothèse de l'origine* (*The Monolingualism of the Other—or the Prosthesis of Origin*), he recounts how he, a Jew growing up in Muslim Algeria, resided "au bord du français, uniquement, ni en lui, ni hors de lui, sur la ligne introuvable de sa côte" 'in a liminal position neither inside nor outside the French language but at its very edge' (14). He poses the paradox of being monolingual in a language that was not his own, to the extent that "depuis toujours, à demeure, je me demande si on peut aimer, jouir, prier, crever de douleur ou crever tout court dans une autre langue ou sans rien en dire à personne, sans parler même" 'he has always wondered whether it is possible to love, enjoy, pray, die of pain or die at all in another language or without saying anything to anyone, without even speaking' (14). Banished to the margins of a destabilized French, Derrida is able to employ it with reflexive sophistication.

It is the language of the metropolis that governed the colonized Algiers of his childhood that he did not leave until he went off to Paris to attend the École Normale Supérieure at age nineteen. Although Derrida was not an observant Jew and did not particularly embrace his ethnic heritage, he was directly affected by the Crémieux Decree of October 1870, which bestowed French citizenship on Maghrebi Jews, as well as by the revocation of that citizenship by the Vichy regime in October 1940 (his altered legal status resulted in expulsion from his *lycée*), and, again, by its restoration following World War II. The vagaries of national identity complicated Derrida's relationship to the nation whose language he spoke as his primary one. He could thus pronounce the typically Derridean paradox that "oui, je n'ai qu'une langue, or ce n'est pas la mienne" 'yes, I have only one language, but it is not mine' (*Le Monolinguisme* 15). Though he was fluent enough in English to teach in it at the University of California, Irvine, Derrida contends that he is condemned to "ce solipsisme intarissable" 'this inexhaustible solipsism' (14) of monolingualism and that it is a universal as well as personal condition. "On ne parle jamais qu'une seule langue" 'One never speaks anything but one language,' he insists but, recognizing that all language is hybrid and interpersonal, immediately follows that with the declaration that "on ne parle jamais une seule langue" 'one never speaks only one language' (21). Situating himself both inside and outside French, Derrida presents his ambivalent thoughts about language by conceiving of language as a place, "un milieu absolu" 'an absolute milieu' (13). It is an imaginary place whose peripheries he inhabits.

Betwixt and Between

Langue of course manifests itself as *parole*, as performance, a succession of symbols in time. Conceiving of language spatially reifies it, reduces it to a static entity that can be located with coordinates of latitude and longitude. Literature offers the same conceptual temptation. Its representation on a printed page leads many readers to regard it as a commodity, to confuse the leaves of Whitman's published book with *Leaves of Grass*. As Stanley Fish, endorsing Gotthold Ephraim Lessing's assignment of poetry to the category of temporal—not spatial—art, insists, a poem is not a well-wrought urn but rather "*the developing responses of the reader in relation to the words as they succeed one another in time*" (126–27). Johann Wolfgang von Goethe's conception of *Weltliteratur*, like discussions of Eurocentrism and Afrocentrism, invites us to think of literature as congruent with the world, hence, like language, occupying positions on a map. Ascribing coordinates of latitude and longitude to them insidiously reinforces nationality. Thinking of languages as spaces implies territoriality, conflating Dutch, Japanese, and Persian with the geopolitical constructs in which they are spoken.

If languages occupy space and the space they occupy is a mental homeland, the preposition *between* (*entre*, *zwischen*, *mellan*, *inter*, *между*, בין) becomes indispensable to any discussion of translingualism. "Betwixt and Between" is the way Turner characterizes initiates in the liminal phase (97), and Marie Arana uses the same phrase to describe her own divided loyalties to the United States and Peru, English and Spanish. "I live on bridges," she reports, using a familiar spatial metaphor. "I've earned my place on them, stand comfortably when I'm on one, content with betwixt and between" (301). Describing Samuel Beckett's relationship to English and French, Brian T. Fitch contends, "Beckett is the Man-between and each of his books is a Work-between" (156). Djebar diagnoses her bilingual dilemma as a condition she calls "entre-deux-langues" 'between-two-languages' (*Ces Voix* 33). Translinguals tend to conceive of themselves as being situated between—or among—languages. A Canadian living in Paris, Nancy Huston imagines herself suspended at an exact midpoint between the two languages in which she writes, French and English. She describes: "Cette sensation de flottement entre l'anglais et le français, sans véritable ancrage dans l'un ou l'autre—de sorte que, au bout de dix années à l'étranger, loin d'être devenue 'parfaitement bilingue,' je me sens doublement mi-lingue" 'This feeling of floating between English and French, without real anchoring in one or the other—so that, after ten years abroad, far from becoming "fully bilingual," I feel doubly mid-lingual' (Huston and Sebbar 77). Ariel Dorfman projects a similar consciousness of being located between two languages, in his case Spanish and English. Geography is destiny for Dorfman, who has written about half of his books in English and the other half in Spanish and calls himself "a bigamist of language" (*Heading South* 270). The very title of his memoir, *Heading South, Looking North*, imagines the author poised somewhere above Central America equidistant from the two poles of his existence, Chile and the United States. However, his vantage point is *utopian* in the root sense: it is a *no place* that is impossible to inhabit since each language keeps jockeying for primacy; at various times, Dorfman even determines to speak one language to the total exclusion of the other.

Thus, because translingual writers often feel closer to one language than another, when they locate themselves *between* languages, the figure described is not necessarily an equilateral triangle—or, in the case of trilinguals such as Vladimir Nabokov, George Steiner, and Edwidge Danticat, a square. Pérez Firmat titles his study of Cuban American culture *Life on the Hyphen*, but his position between English and Spanish is a precarious perch. "Hyphens hurt," he admits (ix). In the topological geometry of language, he, like many other Latinos in the United States, does not calibrate himself exactly "mi-lingue" but tilts more toward North America than Latin America, toward English than Spanish. Brought from his native Havana to Miami as a child, Pérez Firmat identifies himself as a cohort of the "1.5" American immigrant generation—one that, though more assimilated than his parents, still suffers from "a spiritual bilocation, the sense of being in two places at once, or of living in one residing in another" (xi). Spatiality is again invoked to evoke the feeling of dis*place*ment.

Kathleen Saint-Onge, too, employs the metaphor of hyphen, but her language memoir, *Bilingual Being: My Life as a Hyphen*, asserts not that she is situated on a hyphen but that her life *is* a hyphen. And, in contrast to Pérez Firmat, for whom hyphens hurt, in Saint-Onge's case hyphens heal. A Canadian who associates the trauma of childhood sexual abuse with her native French, she uses a spatial metaphor to express the relief she felt after drifting from French to English, a language that, she explains, "created an alternative social space where I made a new life for myself, one so different from that inscribed by my hereditary French setting" (325). However, if switching languages can be liberating, remaining suspended in the space between languages can be exceedingly uncomfortable. Even writers who make a successful transition into another language often feel the residual pain of separation.

Julia Alvarez grew up in the Dominican Republic, but after several decades in Vermont she explains, "I lost the capacity to really express myself in my native tongue. It remains a childhood language" (qtd. in Birnbaum), but one that still exerts a gravitational pull. In a poem whose title, "Leaving English," reinforces the spatial metaphor, as if language were a point of embarkation, Alvarez emphasizes the disparate distances between her and her two languages: "Even if Spanish made me who I was, / it's English now that tells me who I am" (111). Hannah Arendt also adopted English as her medium of written expression, but, in contrast to Alvarez, she continued to feel a gap between it and her that she did not feel with her native German. She observed, in German, "Ich schreibe in Englisch, aber ich habe die Distanz nie verloren" 'I write in English, but I have never lost a sense of distance from it' (qtd. in Gaus 24). Distance is debilitating, but it can also nourish. In Jean Buridan's famous philosophical paradox, a donkey standing equidistant between two bales of hay starves to death because unable to choose. And someone poised on the precise midpoint of Pérez Firmat's hyphen would be rendered what he calls "nilingüe." It is the tongue-tied condition in which Celaya, the "bilingual" protagonist of Sandra Cisneros's *Caramelo*, finds herself. "I don't have the words for what I want," she laments. "Not in English. Not in Spanish" (60).

No Man's Land

When the rhetoric about translingualism combines the connotations of peril and place, it often ends up invoking the image of no man's land, the term applied in World War I to the area between the trenches of opposing armies that was not safe for anyone. Thus, faulting Robert Browning's translation of Aeschylus's *Agamemnon* for being "interlingua, . . . a centaur-idiom" that imposes the vocabulary, syntax, and phonology of ancient Greek on his own Victorian English, George Steiner (the trilingual critic who pointedly titled a 1971 volume of essays on language and literature *Extraterritorial*) pronounced it "a no-man's-land in psychological and linguistic space" (*After Babel* 332)—hence a text treacherous for both Hellenophones and Anglophones because it occupies a space outside either language. In a similar vein, Ilan Stavans, describing how his identity was split between Spanish-speaking and English-speaking selves, recalls, "Every so often I would have a *tête-à-tête* with my *doppelgänger*, which resulted in a moment of intense confusion and despair, making me feel as the personification of a no-man's-land" (*On Borrowed Words* ix).

The metaphor takes even more dramatic form in the polyglot pun that Lise Gauvin employs to describe the dangerous zone that Francophone writers of Quebec, trying to assert themselves within the French literary world as well as against the Anglophone Canadian majority, inhabit. She contends that their struggle ". . . peut conduire à l'aphasie, au silence littéraire ou au no man's langue" 'can lead to aphasia, to literary silence, or to no man's langue' (9).

The phrase "no man's langue" was probably coined by Ghérasim Luca, a Romanian Surrealist who wrote in French but advanced a program of alienation from all languages, native and adopted. An online literary magazine based in Berlin called *No Man's Land: New German Literature in English Translation* serves to make contemporary German-language poetry and fiction accessible to readers of English. As the website explains, "ours is a virtual no man's land between languages and cultures—one which, like the former no man's land of the Berlin Wall, is now open for exploration." But it was not until after childhood's end that the linguistic space favored by Hugo Hamilton became habitable and safe. Hamilton wrote his memoir, *The Speckled People*, in English, but he recalls his Dublin childhood as a "language war" (278) in which his mother spoke German and his nationalist father, who insisted on speaking Irish, prohibited the use of English at home, trying to enforce the rule with his fists.

A demilitarized zone is *terra nemo* that, while remaining contested territory, has been declared off-limits to combat. Across the thirty-eighth parallel, hostile armies of North and South Korea face off against each other, and the UN buffer zone in Cyprus separates Greek and Turkish adversaries. From Quebec to Catalonia to Capetown and beyond, confrontations between languages have generated fighting words. Anton Shammās likens his own situation as a Palestinian writing in Hebrew to a kind of demilitarized zone, a battlefield from which a truce has forced antagonists to withdraw, at least temporarily. Shammās titles his 1979 volume of poetry שטח הפקר (*No Man's Land*) and concludes it with a poem called, with obvious homage to Wallace Stevens, "י"ג דרכים להסתכל בזה" ("Thirteen Ways of Looking at This"). In the final lines of that poem, he declares, "אני לא יודע / שפה מעבר מזה / ושפה מעבר מזה / ואני הוזה בשטח ההפקר" 'How could I know, if you don't mind— / one language ahead, / another behind. / And here I am, / imagining things in my no man's land' (Shammās [Shetakh Hefker] 46; "Three Poems"). But of course in his poetry Shammās stands in treacherous space, daydreaming—perhaps hallucinating—in Hebrew, one of his two adversarial languages.

The Texas-Mexico border has become a dangerously militarized zone, but for Gloria Anzaldúa it is a symbolic space of linguistic freedom. In *Borderlands/La Frontera*, a book whose bilingual title in itself heralds hybridity, she catalogs the eight languages that she inhabits to one degree or another: "1. Standard English / 2. Working-class and slang English / 3. Standard Spanish / 4. Standard Mexican-Spanish / 5. North Mexican Spanish dialect / 6. Chicano Spanish (Texas, New Mexico, Arizona and California have regional variations) / 7. Tex-Mex / 8. *Pachuco* (called *caló*)" (55). This heteroglossia is a product of her residence in the borderlands of south Texas, a contested space between the United States and Mexico in which her people, Chicanos, were conquered and oppressed. But Anzaldúa also uses "borderlands" figuratively, to apply to a state of mind. "La frontera" is the liminal condition, betwixt and between, that causes acute anxiety and cognitive dissonance in other translinguals. However, for Anzaldúa, who declares, "I am my language" (55), the motley nature of that language is the source of strength, not, as with Wolfson, of malaise. Translingualism becomes transcendence, not transgression.

Walter D. Mignolo uses Anzaldúa as a reference point in his own spatializing polemic on behalf of hybridity. Studying the tensions between imperial cultures and languages and indigenous ones that he locates in "the border or line that divides and unites modernity/coloniality" (xvi), Mignolo calls for what he terms "border thinking"—"an epistemology, an ethic and politics that emerge from the experiences of people taking their destiny in their own hands and not waiting for saviors" (xxii). It is, he explains, "tantamount to engaging decoloniality; that is, in thinking and doing decolonially" (xvi). In a revolutionary project that must also transcend the territoriality of scholarly disciplines, what he also calls "border gnosis" (309) includes "languaging," which he defines as "thinking and writing between languages" (226). Instead of the endangered no-man's-land that others describe as the space between languages, Mignolo conceives of it as a privileged vantage point from which to launch a successful foray against hegemonic thinking. "I have to be at war, constantly," he declares, "against competitive ideologies, as well as with decolonial ideologies that do not intend to compete but to delink" (xvii). For Mignolo, as for Hamilton and Stavans, the space between languages is a locus for hostility, though he is confident of worthy purpose and ultimate victory.

Hybrid Pollution and Invigoration

Tatyana Tolstaya was considerably more ambivalent in writing about the Russian French translingual Andreï Makine. In fact, her two reviews of the same novel, Makine's *Le Testament français*, are a striking illustration of the relation between language and thought. Writing in English in the *New York Review of Books*, Tolstaya praised Makine's novel for its ability to express quintessentially Russian attitudes in evocative adopted French (Tolstaya). However, writing in Russian and defending the honor of her own native language, Tatyana Tolstaya denounced Makine, who abandoned their shared L1 to write in French, as "a philological mongrel, a cultural hybrid, a linguistic chimera, a literary basilisk, who, if you believe the old books, was a combination of a rooster and snake, something that flies and crawls at the same time" (qtd. in Wanner 27). Tolstaya's pungent attack on Makine's translingualism draws on a long tradition of disparaging as traitors those who move between languages. When national identity is embodied in language, forsaking or abusing it becomes as reprehensible as burning the flag. Only a vowel and a t separate the Italian word for translators, *traduttori*, from the word for traitors, *traditori*.

Analyzing strategies for translating *Die Emigranten*, a neglected German-language play published anonymously in St. Louis in 1882, Lawrence Rosenwald identifies a topos he calls "the language traitor" common to American immigrant-language fiction. In such works, the dominant language is German, Chinese, Italian, Yiddish, or some other foreign import, but characters occasionally attempt to speak in English. According to Rosenwald, the language traitor is an unsympathetic newcomer who uses his imperfect command of American English to belittle more recent arrivals and advance his own narrow mercenary interests. Rather than evidence of his linguistic dexterity and emotional resiliency, the language traitor's code-switching demonstrates the flaws in his personality (Rosenwald). Implicit in literature written in the United States primarily in a language other than English might be a loyalty to that language that is betrayed whenever characters attempt to express themselves in English, even—or especially—when fractured.

Linguistic patriotism is the motive behind the various authoritative institutions, including the Académie Française, the Latvian State Language Center, and the Institute of the Czech Language, that attempt to enforce verbal conformity and governments from Malaysia to Poland to Quebec that impose fines on those who pollute the official language, especially by adulterating it with words from another tongue. It is the source of establishment disdain for Franglais, Spanglish, Deutschrussisch, Chinglish, and other macaronic tongues. It was what motivated Noah Webster's pioneering lexicographical labors in cataloging a distinctly American English and led him to champion orthographical independence from Britain and unity within the United States. In the preface to his *American Spelling Book*, Webster proclaims that "to diffuse an uniformity and purity of language in America, to destroy the provincial prejudices that originate in the trifling differences of dialect and produce reciprocal ridicule, to promote the interest of literature and the harmony of the United States, is the most earnest wish of the author, and it is his highest ambition to deserve the approbation and encouragement of his countrymen" (4). Proper use of the national language is associated with notions not only of loyalty but also of what Deborah Cameron calls "verbal hygiene" (Cameron). A spurious belief in "linguistic purity" leads many to regard those who mix tongues as unclean. They are polluting the "spaces" that languages occupy. Tolstaya's image of "something that flies and crawls at the same time" suggests that translingualism is unnatural and loathsome.

In racial terms, mixing languages is tantamount to miscegenation, and xenophobic projects of ethnic cleansing have often been accompanied by demonization of those who sully the national tongue. (According to Judges 12, the Gideonites identified Ephraimites by their inability to pronounce *shibboleth* and then killed them; and in 1937, during the "Parsley Massacre," Dominican authorities slaughtered approximately twenty thousand people when their inability to trill the "r" in *perejil* exposed them as Haitians.) Moreover, if many languages encourage us to regard

L1 as the mother tongue (*maternam locutionem, Muttersprache, langue maternelle, madrelingua, idioma materno,* 語, *modersmål, anyanyelvük,* שפת האם, *Язык матери,* מאמע-לשון, اللغة الام), abandoning it for another constitutes a kind of psychic matricide.

Nevertheless, hybridization of crops—heterosis—yields more robust corn and rice than the conventional kind, lending genetic support to Anzaldúa's defense of heteroglossia and to the code-switching practiced by her and other Chicano writers. Anzaldúa's work is congruent with the contemporary postcolonial multicultural moment, in which alterity is valorized and *métissage* and *Mischling* become virtues, not vices. Notions of cultural and linguistic purity such as Tolstaya's are condemned as what Albert Memmi calls "heterophobia," fear of difference (115). Thus does translingual (French, Creole, English) Françoise Lionnet, employing a spatial metaphor and emphasizing language as a crucial element in global mixing, extol "all those who must survive (and write) in the interval between different cultures and languages" (1). Likewise, in addition to race, religion, and culture, language is crucial to the syncretism that Antillean writers Jean Bernabé, Patrick Chamoiseau, and Raphaël Confiant call for in their 1989 manifesto for "creolization," *Eloge de la Créolité.* "La Créolité," they proclaim, "est une annihilation de la fausse universalité, du monolinguisme et de la pureté" 'Creolization is an annihilation of false universality, monolingualism, and purity' (28).

Such exaltation of heterogeneity recalls the mysticism of José Vasconcelos, who in 1925 heralded what he called "la raza cósmica," the glorious cosmic race of the future that will be a synthesis of all the disparate elements—racial, cultural, and linguistic—found in Latin America. Looking forward to a supreme *mestizaje*, he prophesied that out of the human mix will emerge "la raza definitiva, la raza síntesis o raza integral, hecha con el genio y con la sangre de todos los pueblos y, por lo mismo, más capaz de verdadera fraternidad y de visíon realmente universal" 'the definitive race, the synthetical race, the integral race, made up of the genius and the blood of all peoples and, for that reason, more capable of true brotherhood and of a truly universal vision' (60). Even more grandiose was Walt Whitman's conception of English as the supreme syncretic language: "View'd freely, the English language is the accretion and growth of every dialect, race, and range of time, and is both the free and compacted composite of all. From this point of view, it stands for Language in the largest sense, and is really the greatest of studies. It involves so much; is indeed a sort of universal absorber, combiner, and conqueror" (572).

Whitman's conception of English as "universal absorber, combiner, and conqueror" anticipates Léopold Sédar Senghor's glorification of French as the universal language of civilized humanity. A translingual, from Serer to French, Senghor hailed the Francophone movement for spreading an egalitarian humanism: "La francophonie, c'est l'humanisme intégral qui se tisse autour de la terre, cette symbiose des énergies dormantes de toutes les races, de toutes les consciences et qui se réveillent à leur chaleur complémentaire" 'Francophonie is that integral humanism that is woven into the earth: that symbiosis of dormant energies of all races, all forms of consciousnessness awakening to their complementary ardor' (363). The exalted claims by Whitman and Senghor echo the historical ambitions of imperial languages such as Latin, Farsi, and Han Chinese that presumed to subsume scattered vernaculars within a single language that embodies the highest values of the human race. Though postcolonial discourse, by contrast, rejects the hegemony of any particular language, it, too, yearns to transcend local languages that are partial and divisive.

Panlingual Aspirations

The translingual project is ultimately and implicitly panlingual. The urge to accumulate languages culminates in a *reductio ad infinitum*, the dream of transcending all languages to arrive at a space of universal truth. It would shatter the "monolingual paradigm" that, according to Yasemin Yildiz, developed in the eighteenth century with the rise of the monolingual nation-state. Though most people speak more than one language, hegemonic nation-states could define and police their borders by insisting on the congruence of one nation and one language. By contrast, the panlingual space of universal truth is currently symbolized by the seventeen acres in the Turtle Bay neighborhood of Manhattan that are occupied by the United Nations. The property of no nation, the UN Headquarters, where 6 languages are deemed official and another 514 languages are recognized as equally valid for articulating the "Universal Declaration of Human Rights," is legally extraterritorial ("About the Universal Declaration"). It is simultaneously no-man's-land and everyman's (and every person's) land. The UN is a site of global pathology, for focusing the conflicts of the world and, occasionally, resolving them. However, as an embodiment of humanity's highest aspirations for peace and justice, but also as a place that is no place, it is translingual utopia.

Promiscuous Tongues:
Erotics of Translingualism
and Translation

The tongue is a sexual organ, and use of the word *tongue* (*langue, Zunge, lengua, lingua,* لسان, язык, γλώσσα, *dil, nyelv,* etc.) as metonomy for *language* underscores the widespread link between *logos* and *eros*. In Hebrew, not only does לשון double as tongue and language, but language can also be signified by the word שפה, which refers as well to another erogenous zone, the lip. Circle II of Dante's *Inferno* is reserved for the lascivious, and the first sinner whom the poet encounters there is Semiramis, the ruler of Assyria who was so overcome "a vizio di lussuria" 'by the vice of lechery' that she had incestuous relations with her own son. However, conflating language and lust, the first thing that Dante notes about Semiramis is that "fu imperadrice di molte favelle" 'she was empress over many tongues' (84).

If, as Roland Barthes contends, "le langage est une peau" 'language is a skin,' then contact between languages ought to induce sensual excitement. "Je frotte mon langage contre l'autre" 'I rub my language against the other,' Barthes writes. "C'est comme si j'avais des mots en guise de doigts, ou des doigts au bout des mots. Mon langage tremble de désir. . . . j'enroule l'autre dans mes mots, je le caresse, je le frôle, j'entretiens ce frôlage" 'It is as if I had words in the form of fingers, or fingers at the tips of my words. My language trembles with desire. . . . I wrap the other in my words, I caress him, I brush against him, I continue this rubbing of skin' (*Fragments* 87). George Steiner, too, celebrates the sensuality of interlingual links. "Eros and language mesh at every point," he contends. "Intercourse and discourse, copula and copulation, are subclasses of the dominant fact of communication" (*After Babel* 39–40). Like adultery, translation is, then, a transgressive form of copulation, illicit to those who insist on absolute fidelity to a text's original words. Giacomo Casanova, the most famous philanderer in European history, the man whose very name is an eponym for womanizer, ended up writing his memoirs, *Histoire de ma vie*, not in his native Venetian dialect but in French. Because Steiner moves at ease among English, French, and German, he is more familiar than most others with the ecstasy of discourse. But he is also acutely aware of the anxiety of babel when he declares, "I have every reason to believe that there is a 'Don Juanism' of the polyglot, an eros of the multilingual. I believe that an individual man or woman fluent in several tongues seduces, possesses, remembers differently according to his or her use of the relevant language. That the love and lechery of the polyglot differs from that of the monoglot, faithful to one language, as the suggestive phrase has it" (*Unwritten* 72). Yet damnation is the traditional price of adultery, the sin that is proscribed by the seventh of the Ten Commandments. For all the thrill of his sexual escapades, Don Juan, Shaw reminds us, goes to hell.

Writers who switch tongues—either by translating a text into a different language or by composing original work in a language other than their primary one—are the libertines of the literary world. Translators and translinguals include some of the most distinguished men and women of letters, but, because of their transgressions against monolingual orthodoxy, the letters they bear are scarlet. Thus, Richard Philcox, discussing his own renderings of Maryse Condé's French fiction into English, refers to translation as "legalized infidelity or adultery" (30). And August Wilhelm von Schlegel confesses that he is driven to translate out of lust for another's text, resulting in a kind of compulsive philandering: ". . . leider kann ich meines Nächsten Poesie nicht ansehen, ohne ihrer zu begehren in meinem Herzen, und bin also in einem beständigen poetischen Ehrenbruche begriffen" 'I cannot look at my neighbor's poetry without immediately coveting it with all my heart, so that I am caught in a continuous poetical adultery' (107). Tahar Ben Jelloun, a native of

Morocco who became the first Maghrebian to be awarded France's prestigious Prix Goncourt, employs a similar metaphor of extramarital sex to describe his adoption of French as literary medium, declaring, "My wife is Arabic, and my mistress is French, and I maintain a relationship of betrayal with both of them" (qtd. in Markham A7). Moreover, when the Russian-born Vladimir Nabokov amended a critic's description of *Lolita* as "the record of my love affair with the romantic novel," by insisting that "the substitution 'English language' for 'romantic novel' would make this elegant formula more correct" ("On a Book" 316), he, too, was confessing to linguistic adultery.

Comparisons between translation and matrimony abound. Philcox, for one, insists on ". . . the importance of the bond between author and translator as wife and husband. It is a permanent interaction between two people living in harmony, traveling and living together" (31). But, of course, not all marriages are particularly harmonious, or faithful. In fact, Barbara Johnson contends that it is the responsibility of the translator to violate the conjugal vows: ". . . the translator ought, despite his or her oath of fidelity, to be considered not as a duteous spouse but as a faithful bigamist, with loyalties split between a native language and a foreign tongue. Each must accommodate the requirements of the other without their ever having the opportunity to meet. The bigamist is thus necessarily doubly unfaithful, but in such a way that he or she must push to its utmost limit the very capacity for faithfulness" (142–43). Extending the metaphor beyond mere bigamy to polygamy, Robert Wechsler argues that the translator couples with multiple partners: "Polygamy goes beyond bigamous marriage to two languages; it includes obligations to the original work as well as other obligations, for instance to the translator's literary culture" (107). According to the tired Italian adage *traduttori, traditori*, the mere act of translation constitutes betrayal, and the noun *traditori* carries connotations of sexual perfidy. Its nominal form, *il tradimento*, is Italian for adultery. Johann Sebastian Bach's three-movement secular cantata *Amore Traditore* (BWV 203) is a reflection on love betrayed.

Paid modest fees for services on demand, translators are the streetwalkers of literary culture, used and abused by poets, novelists, and critics. They provide guilty pleasure to serious readers too proud to admit they ride a pony to get through Petronius or Genesis. Demeaning sexual metaphors are often employed to describe the inglorious toil of the translator. One of the hoariest (and whoriest) likens a translation to a nubile woman, who is incapable of being both beautiful and faithful. "Une traduction est comme une femme," according to the familiar phallogocentric French maxim. "Si elle est belle, elle n'est pas fidèle. Et si elle est fidèle, elle n'est pas belle." 'A translation is like a woman. If she is beautiful, she is not faithful. And if she is faithful, she is not beautiful.' South African poet Roy Campbell gave it an even more cynical and misogynistic twist when he quipped, "Translations, like wives, are seldom faithful if they are in the least attractive" (337). Impressed by Nicolas Perrot d'Ablancourt's loose rendering of Lucian into French, Gilles Ménage declared that he, for one, preferred such wayward beauties—"belles infidèles." An entire school of neoclassical translation theory—unfaithful beauty—was thus founded on Ménage's erotic tastes. Praising Perrot d'Ablancourt's transpositions from Latin, he explained, "Pour moi je l'appelai la belle infidelle, qui étoit le nom que j'avois donné étant jeune à une de mes maîtresses" 'As for me, I called it the unfaithful beauty, which was the name I gave when young to one of my mistresses' (186). Four centuries later, Kevin West described translation as "an art in need of an erotics," but writers have never been furtive about asserting art's analogies with sexuality (25).

    Fidelity is a commonly invoked standard for judging translations as well as marriages, and parallels between the two are often implicit and even explicit in discourse about translation. Milan Kundera uses violent sexual imagery to express his rage over reworked texts. The Czech French author felt betrayed by English translations of his fiction, and, in an essay collected in *L'Art du roman* (1986), he responds. Against those who abused his Czech prose, Kundera invokes the curse uttered by Jacques the Fatalist's master, as Kundera interpreted it in *Jacques et son maître: hommage à Denis Diderot en trois actes*. His own 1981 theatrical adaptation (i.e., translation) of the Diderot novel declares, "Que périssent tous ceux qui se permettent de réécrire ce qui a été écrit! Qu'il soient empalés et brûlés à petit feu! Qu'ils soient châtrés et qu'on leur coupe les oreilles!" (177). Enraged over the damage that he believes translators have done to his own books, Kundera seeks appropriately sexual revenge: "Death to all who dare rewrite what has been written! Impale them and roast them over a slow fire! Castrate them and cut off their ears!" Jacques

Derrida is much more permissive than Kundera about the freedom of the translator, but he, too, suggests sexual transgression when he states that "... une 'bonne' traduction doit toujours abuser" 'a good translation must always abuse' ("The Retrait of Metaphor" 22). In French as in English, *abuser*—to abuse—often carries sexual connotations; *l'abus sexuel sur mineur* (sexual abuse of a child) violates a fundamental social taboo. Expanding on Derrida's parenthetical comment, Philip E. Lewis elaborated an entire program for what—in an essay that he wrote in French as "Vers la traduction abusive" and later himself translated as "The Measure of Translation Effects"—he calls "abusive translation." Recommending the oxymoronic strategy of "abusive fidelity," Lewis prefers "... the strong, forceful translation that values experimentation, tampers with usage, seeks to match the polyvalencies or pluralivocities or expressive stresses of the original by producing its own" (261). Thus is translation conceived of as rough, adulterous sex.

The dictionary is an essential tool of the translator, and nowhere is the sexuality of transposing words made more overt and physical than in the colonial institution of the "sleeping dictionary," sometimes also called a "pillow dictionary." Tracing the slang term back to 1928, the *Oxford English Dictionary* defines *sleeping dictionary* as "a foreign woman with whom a man has a sexual relationship and from whom he learns her language" ("Sleeping dictionary"). Civil servants sent from Britain or France to the outposts of their empires would often recruit a native woman to serve as both concubine and language instructor for the term of their assignments. In *The Sleeping Dictionary*, a 2003 film written and directed by Guy Jenkin, young John Truscott (Hugh Dancy) is sent to serve His Majesty's Government in Sarawak, then—in 1936—part of the British protectorate of Borneo. A beautiful local woman named Selima (Jessica Alba) is assigned to teach him Iban by sharing his bed. Though John and Selima unexpectedly and inappropriately fall in love, their union is extramarital and temporary. For all the allure of Selima and Iban, John reluctantly capitulates to the conjugal conventions of British culture and, abandoning Selima, weds Cecilia Bullard (Emily Mortimer), a respectable white Anglophone. However, for the duration of John's relationship with Selima, his sleeping dictionary provides carnal demonstration that language is not only a body of knowledge but also knowledge of a body. Analyzing the development of the *sleeping dictionary* during the European imperium in Africa, David Spurr unpacks the implications of the term: "The metaphor suggests an entire series of unstated connections between the sexual and lexical. It suggests, for example, that the African woman is a text to be opened and closed at will, and whose contents allow entry into the mysteries of African language; that the language, and by extension African culture, is itself contained within and revealed by the female body; that sexual knowledge of her body is knowledge of Africa itself" (171). Though Samuel Johnson characterized it as harmless drudgery, lexicography as practiced by agents of European empire became colonialist lechery.

However, even more than translation, translingualism is imagined through metaphors of sexual transgression, as if the act of taking up with a foreign tongue is tantamount to degrading one's mother or spouse. On the assumption that our first lessons in language usually come from our mothers, the term *mother tongue* is commonly used to signify a person's first language, what linguists call L1. A mother's tongue is of course not necessarily the child's primary language, as is apparent in the case of tennis champion Roger Federer, who grew up in Switzerland with Swiss German as his primary language, though the native language of his mother, born in South Africa, was English. Nevertheless, calling L1 the mother tongue—*Muttersprache, langue maternelle, madrelingua,* 母語, *modersmål, anyanyelvük,* שפת האם, *Язык матери,* اللغة الأم—suggests a kind of oedipal betrayal when it is abandoned for another tongue. (Emily Apter invokes Freud's account of the tragic king of Thebes when she asserts that "translation is an oedipal assault on the mother tongue" [xi]).

Henry James conceived of L1 as the mother and the language that an author chooses to write in as the wife. Although fluent in French, James wrote all his fiction in English and thus never left his mother's linguistic embrace. However, advising a French writer, Urbain Mengin, who was contemplating a career in English, James wrote, "One's own language is one's mother but the language one adopts as a career, as a study, is one's wife, and it is with one's wife that one se met en ménage." Setting up a household with a wife who does not get along with one's mother might create problems, but the point of James's metaphor is not to warn against friction between mother and wife but rather against extramarital relations: "English is a very faithful and well-conducted person, but she will expect you not to commit infidelities" (187). James's friend Joseph Conrad committed linguistic infidelities when, neglecting L1 (Polish) and L2 (French), he cast his fate with the English novel.

An émigrée to France, Elsa Triolet was conscious of committing infidelities against her native Russian. She likened her career of writing in both Russian and French to the actions of an unfaithful spouse: "Être bilingue, c'est un peu comme d'être bigame" 'Being bilingual is a bit like being a bigamist' (84). Translinguals, writers who, like Nabokov—called by one scholar "a linguistically promiscuous logophile" (McMillin 418)—move between languages would thus be the prototype of the artist as adulterer. Though Assia Djebar, a native of Algeria, agonizes over her shift from Berber and Arabic to French as "double betrayal" ("Writing" 26), Kundera seems free of guilt over jilting his native Czech for French. "J'ai préféré ma liberté à mes racines" 'I preferred my freedom to my roots,' he declares, reveling in his power to choose a new tongue. "La langue tchèque m'appelle: reviens à la maison, voyou! Mais je n'obéis plus. Je veux rester avec la langue dont je suis éperdument amoureux" 'The Czech language calls me: come back home, you scoundrel! But I no longer obey. I want to stay with the language I have fallen in love with' (qtd. in Clavel 4). In James's terms, Kundera chose his lover over his mother.

Translingualism is also overtly sexual in what, in the subtitle to a book called *Tongue Ties*, Gustavo Pérez Firmat calls the "logo-eroticism" of Latin American writers seduced by English. Ariel Dorfman, who presents Chile and the United States as the two poles of his existence, writes in both English and Spanish, translates his own texts from one to the other, and, calling himself "an adulterer of language," deploys the metaphor of bigamy when he describes himself as "married to two tongues, inhabited by both English and Spanish in equal measures, in love with them both now that they called off war for my throat" ("Wandering Bigamists" 33). Love affairs are not marriages; they threaten them. Sexual/linguistic metaphors pervade *Heading South, Looking North*, Dorfman's 1998 memoir of his prolonged ambivalence toward each of his two languages, as they do a later essay in which he presents his own situation as an "in flagrante case of linguistic adultery" ("Footnotes" 207).

One of the most dramatic instances of translingualism conceived as adultery occurs in the memoirs of Elias Canetti, who wrote in German, his mother's tongue, though he spoke Ladino, Bulgarian, English, and French first. Canetti claims that his father's sudden, fatal heart attack was a direct result of his mother's linguistic adultery. The family was living in England, but, during a summer rest cure at the spa of Bad Reichenhall, his mother flirted with a handsome physician. It was an innocent encounter, except for the language in which it was conducted. Canetti explains that ". . . ihre Untreue lag eben darin, daß sie die intime Sprache zwischen sich und dem Vater, Deutsch, mit einem Mann gebraucht hatte, der um ihre Liebe warb. Alle wichtigen Ereignisse ihrer Verlobung, ihrer Ehe, ihrer Befreiung von der Tyrannei des Großvaters hatten sich auf deutsch abgespielt. Vielleicht war ihr das nicht mehr so bewußt, seit der Vater in Manchester sich um die Erlernung des Englischen solche Mühe gab. Aber er empfand sehr wohl, daß sie sich mit Leidenschaft wieder dem Deutschen zugewandt hatte und meinte vor Augen zu haben, wozu es geführt haben müsse" 'her infidelity had consisted in speaking German, the intimate language between her and my father, with a man who was courting her. All the important events of their love life, their engagement, their marriage, their liberation from my grandfather's tyranny, had taken place in German. Possibly she had lost sight of this because in Manchester her husband had taken so much trouble to learn English. But he was well aware that she had reverted passionately to German, and he had no doubt of what this must have led to' (Canetti, *Augenspiel* 272; Canetti, *Play* 755–56). Canetti believes that the shock of realizing that his wife had switched back to German to converse with a sexual rival is what killed his father.

The trope that switching tongues is adulterous is pervasive, found at least as early as the second century, when Aulus Gellius, deploring the importation of foreign vocabulary into Latin, termed it *verba adulterina*—adulterous words. He reports that his friend Favorinus called ten words imported from Greek not only barbarous but adulterous: "Quae mihi decem verba ediderit Favorinus, quae usurpentur quidem a Graecis, sed sint adulterina et barbara" 'Although used by the Greeks, the ten words pointed out to me by Favorinus are adulterous and barbarous' (142).

Likening linguistic transgression to errant sexuality is a special form of the larger claim—expressed by figures as diverse as Plato, Whitman, and Freud—that verbal expression in general is erotic. Rainer Maria Rilke, whose infidelity to his native German produced some remarkable poetry in French in addition to his major work in L1, insisted, in a letter to the aspiring young poet Franz Xaver Kappus, that sexual and artistic passions are interchangeable: "Und tatsächlich liegt ja künsterisches Erleben so unglaublich nahe am geschlechlichen, an seinem Weh und an seiner Lust, dass die beiden Erscheinungen eigentlich nur verschiedene Formen einer und derselben Sehnsucht und Seligkeit sind" 'And as a matter of fact, artistic experience lies so unbelievably close to the sexual, to its torment and its bliss, that the two phenomena are truly but different forms of an identical yearning and delight' (*Briefe an einen jungen Dichter* 20). Steiner, too, insists on the congruence of eros and logos: "Sex is a profoundly semantic act. Like language, it is subject to the shaping force of social convention, rules of proceeding, and accumulated precedent. To speak and to make love is to enact a distinctive twofold universality: both forms of communication are universals of human physiology as well as of social evolution. It is likely that human sexuality and speech developed in close reciprocity" (*After Babel* 40).

It might indeed be true that, as Theseus puts it in *A Midsummer Night's Dream*, "The lunatic, the lover and the poet / Are of imagination all compact" (V 1 7–8). But lunacy, love, and poetry are all defined and inspired by the protocols of particular times and places. Just as marriage is a social convention—One man one woman? One man many women? One woman many men? Two men? Two women? Transgender permutations? Till death? Till divorce?—the meaning of conjugal infidelity varies with the specific society in which it occurs. Though the abduction of another man's wife was the *casus belli* of the Trojan War, Homer does not censure Odysseus's erotic adventures during the ten years it takes him to return to faithful Penelope. The Greeks were in general tolerant of the sexual escapades of their married gods, and satyriasis in a satyr was not considered a pathology. Nevertheless, though adultery is no longer illegal in most Western countries, it was a felony in traditional English common law, and it remains a justification for "honor killings" in many parts of the world.

Medieval courtly love was illicit but ennobling; Tristan's transcendent passion for the married Iseult is, though doomed, exquisite. But Emma Bovary's extramarital liaisons are merely tawdry.

So the significance of "an unfaithful translation" or of "linguistic promiscuity" is not the same in Japan or Nigeria as it is in Brazil or Norway. Are polyglot readers such as John Milton and Erich Auerbach who are faithful to nothing but the dream of universal enlightenment promiscuous monsters or panlingual masters? Some cultures stone adulterers; others romanticize them. For taking the sacred words of holy writ and transposing them into the vulgar English tongue, William Tyndale was strangled and burned at the stake. Yet the Septuagint, the identical Greek translation of the Hebrew Bible produced, according to legend, by seventy-two scholars working independently, was received as a miracle of divine inspiration. And the King James Version was welcomed into the canon of English literature.

Extolling the mother tongue as the glory of the German *Volk*, Nazi propaganda denounced Jews as wanton triflers with the languages of the world. In Christopher M. Hutton's analysis, "the Jews were a special case and a unique threat, since their capacity for racial survival was superior to that of the Germans, since they had no need of territory and no need of mother-tongue" (5). Hutton sees Nazi anti-Semitism as the product of revulsion over the "linguistic promiscuity" of rootless Jews (305). Nevertheless, at other times and in other places, the linguistic migrations of Jewish authors S. Y. Agnon (from Yiddish to Hebrew), Saul Bellow (from Yiddish to English), Joseph Brodsky (from Russian to English), and Elias Canetti (from Ladino to German) were honored with the Nobel Prize. Another Nobel laureate, Isaac Bashevis Singer, remained stubbornly faithful to Yiddish, though genocide and assimilation had eliminated most readers of that language and he knew that he wrote to be read in translation. Singer, who collaborated in transposing his own work into English, described the act of translation as a kind of sexual wantonness, in which the translator "undresses the literary work, shows it in its true nakedness" (Delisle and Wordsworth v).

Adultery is betrayal on a personal level. Betrayal of the nation constitutes treason. "If I had to choose between betraying my country and betraying my friend," proclaimed E. M. Forster, "I hope I should have the guts to betray my country" (78). But much metaphorical thinking about those who move between languages, *traduttori*, implies both forms of *traditori*. *Le plaidoyer d'un fou*, the 1893 novel that August Strindberg wrote in French (and that has been translated into English as *A Madman's Manifesto*), has been described—in metaphors of both adultery and sedition—as "a document of infidelity, of treason toward Sweden and Swedish literary history" (Stenport 53). And it is probably no mere coincidence that, while the father of modern Swedish literature was offending his native land through his choice of an alien tongue, he was composing a work whose deranged narrator is tormented by his wife's adultery. Similarly, in a letter to Edmond de Goncourt dated 17 December 1891, Oscar Wilde claimed that he wrote *Salomé* in French as a hostile act against English colonialism: "Français de sympathie, je suis Irlandais de race, et les Anglais m'ont condamné à parler le langage de Shakespeare" 'French by sympathy, I am Irish by race, and the English have condemned me to speak the language of Shakespeare' (qtd. in Ellmann 351). Premiered while the author was in prison, Wilde's erotically charged play dramatized not in L1 English but in exotic French Herod's illicit lust for his own wife's daughter. In the case of Ha Jin, who switched from Mandarin to English, the brutal repression of demonstrators at Tiananmen Square in 1989 convinced him that it was his country that had abandoned him. "I feel I have been betrayed by China, which has suppressed its people and made artistic freedom unavailable," he offered as the justification for his abandonment of his mother tongue. "To preserve the integrity of my work, I had no choice but to write in English" (Jin).

The verb *to translate*—to carry over—is similar in etymology and meaning to *tradire*, which means to hand over and was supposedly first used to describe the treachery of Judas Iscariot in handing Jesus over to the Romans. Peter, too, betrayed Jesus, by denying him three times. However, on the third occasion, according to Matthew, Mark, and Luke, Peter himself was betrayed by his own language—a Galilean accent that marked him as a suspicious outsider in Jerusalem. The word *traditor* shows up repeatedly in Cantos XXXI–XXXIV of the *Inferno* to refer to figures such as Archbishop Ruggieri degli Ubaldini, whose skull is gnawed at for eternity by Count Ugolino della Gherardesca in punishment for Ruggieri's treachery against Pisa. Dante calls Bocca degli Abati "malvagio traditor" 'vile traitor' (Canto XXXII l. 110) for betraying the Guelphs to the Ghibellines. But one of the most memorable cases of *traditore* in the *Inferno* involves a master of languages, Brunetto Latini, Dante's mentor. While never ceasing to revere the older scholar, Dante places him in Circle VII of the *Inferno*, ostensibly for the sin of sodomy. However, in his *Convivio* and *De Vulgari Eloquentia*—and, by example, in the language in which he chose to compose his *Commedia*—Dante argues eloquently for literary use of *parlar materno* so that the Italian poet might also have wanted to condemn Brunetto for having written his masterpiece, *Li livres dou trésor*, not in the Florentine mother tongue but in French. In that case, Brunetto would have earned a place in the ninth, and last, circle—the icy realm reserved for *traitors* such as Ugolino, Ruggieri, and Bocca.

Hyperpolyglots, people who speak at least six languages fluently, might seem to represent the ultimate case of speech as adultery. Like Lord Byron, who claimed to have had sex with two hundred women during the year he spent in Venice, where the principal language was not his native English (Marchand 285–86), hyperpolyglots are people who conjugate and then move on. Could Emil Krebs (1867–1930), a German diplomat who is said to have mastered sixty-eight languages and studied almost twice that number, have been trusted to honor his nation's secrets or his wedding vows? Cardinal Giuseppe Mezzofanti (1774–1849), reputed to have spoken seventy-two languages, might seem a poor risk to remain faithful to the Church or his vows of chastity. If language is culture, hyperpolyglots—linguistic lotharios—refuse to be true to any one version of it. Emphasizing the point, a report on a sixteen-year-old New Yorker, Timothy Doner, who knows more than twenty languages, described him and others who share his rare talent and passion as possessing "a restless linguistic promiscuity" (Leland).

So a book-length study of hyperpolyglotism might be expected to indulge repeatedly in metaphors of adultery. Yet what is remarkable about Michael Erard's *Babel No More* (2012), which surveys four hundred hyperpolyglots through personal interviews and historical documents, is that it is devoid of sexual metaphors. Though Erard recognizes a common perception that people who learn dozens of languages "are doing something deviant," he immediately demurs, noting, "But the hyperpolyglots

I met are no more shy or more reclusive than any other gifted, eccentric person—or any shy person, for that matter" (210). Instead of adultery, Erard employs neurology as a way of understanding manic movement among languages, noting that the structure of the brain is different for those who perform frequent linguistic shifts. What is characteristic of hyperpolyglots, according to Erard, is not that they are linguistic cads but that they possess what he calls "the will to plasticity." He explains that "the will to plasticity is the 'incessant augmentation of circuits in the brain—among them language'" (86). Thus is the long *tradition* (a word etymologically related to both translation and betrayal) of imagining language-switching through the metaphor of marital infidelity reduced to the catchword of *The Graduate*, a classic film about adultery: "Plastics."

Writing South and North: Ariel Dorfman's Linguistic Ambidexterity

At the tender age of nine, Ariel Dorfman met Thomas Mann. In the memoir that he published forty-seven years later, Dorfman recalls being introduced to the German novelist aboard the ship that was carrying the Dorfman family on a visit to Europe. The precocious child observes the awe with which fellow passengers view an illustrious Nobel laureate and, envious, resolves that he, too, will pursue a literary vocation. However, the novelist's "thick, strange accent in English" (*Heading South* 86) piques young Dorfman's curiosity, and he asks his father what language Mann writes his books in. The answer, German, will be a counterpoint to Dorfman's own career. Unlike Mann, he will grow up to become what he calls "a bigamist of language" (*Heading South* 270) / "un bígamo del lenguaje" (*Rumbo* 366).

Despite relocation to an alien linguistic ambience, some writers cling to the language of their mothers' lullabies. Mann wrote *Doktor Faustus* (1947), *Der Erwählte* (*The Holy Sinner*) (1951), and other works in German—"that authentic and inalienable country which I had carried with me into exile and from which no potentate could banish me" (qtd. in Hokenson and Munson 163) during more than a dozen years spent in exile in Anglophonic Southern California. All the books that Aleksandr Solzhenitsyn produced during nearly two decades in Vermont were in Russian, and, long after the annihilation of most other Yiddish speakers,

Isaac Bashevis Singer insisted on using his *mame loshn* as the medium for all his fiction. Though she left Chile as a child, Marjorie Agosín writes her poetry exclusively, and prolifically, in Spanish.

However, in contrast to those writers' stubborn fidelity to their beloved first tongue is the linguistic "bigamy" of authors such as Samuel Beckett (English and French), André Brink (Afrikaans and English), Mirza Ghalib (Urdu and Persian), Kaka Kalelkar (Hindi and Gujarati), Mendele Mokher Sforim (Yiddish and Hebrew), Fernando Pessoa (Portuguese and English), Petrarch (Italian and Latin), and Kateb Yacine (French and Arabic). Dorfman, who has published more than forty books, about half in Spanish and half in English, is another such translingual, an author who writes in more than one language or a language other than his or her primary one. *Heading South, Looking North* (1998) is a translingual memoir in the sense that in it Dorfman, who describes himself as "this hybrid mongrel of language" (269), examines his life as shaped by his languages. Moreover, the book itself is a translingual performance, since it exists in two versions, each written by an author who pines for a unitary self but is forced to embrace the rich and vexing condition of being double.

Both *Heading South, Looking North* and its Spanish-language doppelgänger *Rumbo al Sur, deseando el Norte* (1998) recount multiple displacements—geographical, cultural, and linguistic. Emphasizing the discontinuities in his life, Dorfman does not proceed in linear fashion. Beginning with September 11, 1973, when a coup against the socialist government of Salvador Allende forces Dorfman, an aide to the Chilean president's chief of staff, into hiding and then exile, the text jumps backward and forward in time. Dorfman was born in Buenos Aires to Eastern European Jews who spoke Russian and Yiddish, respectively, but bonded through the Spanish each adopted after migrating to Argentina. However, the family moved to New York when Adolfo, his father, accepted a position with the fledgling United Nations. In his earliest memory, Dorfman, not yet three years old, is stricken with pneumonia shortly after arriving in the United States. When his parents check him into a hospital in New York, the child speaks only Spanish; but when they check him out three weeks later, and for the next ten years, he refuses to speak anything but English.

In 1954, harassed for their leftist views during the McCarthy red scare, the family leaves the United States and settles in Chile. Enrolled in a school in Santiago, young Dorfman is at first handicapped because his command of Spanish has atrophied to the point that he can barely formulate a coherent sentence. But he vows to win the school prize for excellence *en español*, and, by the time he graduates, he does. Initially distraught over the loss of the North American culture he adored, Dorfman eventually becomes infatuated with Chile—its people, its language, and, especially, its embodiment in Angélica, the Chilena who becomes his wife and to whom he dedicates his memoir. In 1968 he travels to Berkeley for graduate work at the University of California, but instead of reaffirming his ties to the United States and the English language, Dorfman becomes so appalled by Yankee domination and exploitation of Latin America that, in a reversal of his childhood determination not to speak Spanish, he now vows to abandon English. And the first book that he publishes, in collaboration with Armand Mattelart, is in Spanish. Titled *Para leer al Pato Donald* (1971), it is a scathing indictment of American cultural imperialism as exemplified by the popular Disney cartoon character Donald Duck. At a demonstration outside the American embassy in Santiago, Dorfman relishes the irony that he is able to articulate his grievances against the United States in flawless, idiomatic English.

Eager to support and identify with the workers of Chile, he becomes active in the socialist movement that leads to Allende's election as president. But, after General Augusto Pinochet seizes power and initiates a reign of terror, Dorfman is forced into hiding. He ends up taking refuge in the Argentine embassy, where his knowledge of English ingratiates him with the American wife of the Argentine ambassador and facilitates his departure from Chile. He eventually makes his way to the United States, where his fluency in both English and Spanish enables him to function as a bridge between cultures. In 2001, teaching at Duke University, he would describe himself to an interviewer in North Carolina as "almost cursedly bilingual" ("Dorfman Explores"). In a 2003 essay he concludes, ". . . what I finally arrived at was not the victory of one tongue over the other one but rather a cohabitation, my two languages reaching a truce in order to help the body they were lodged in to survive" ("Wandering Bigamists" 36).

Because of his father's admiration for Lenin, the leader of the Russian Revolution, Dorfman is originally named Vladimiro and nicknamed Vlady. However, intent on passing as a typical English boy, he begins calling himself Edward. In *Heading South, Looking North*, he explains that he chose Edward because that is the name of the prince in his "favorite story" (79), Mark Twain's *The Prince and the Pauper*. Torn between the internal doppelgängers of a Spanish self and an English self, Dorfman notes the appropriateness of "twins, doubles, duality, duplicity, there at the start of my life" (80). Later, as an adult, he in turn rejects Edward and decides to be known by his middle name, Ariel. By doing so, he associates himself with the greatest of English writers, William Shakespeare, who assigned the name Ariel to the sprite in *The Tempest*. But he is also aligning himself with José Enrique Rodó, the Uruguayan essayist who, in a 1900 book titled *Ariel*, identifies Latin America with Shakespeare's ethereal creature and implores it to resist the crass materialism of the North American Caliban. Thus, in settling on Ariel, both a figure out of English literature and a totem of Latin America, Dorfman exhibits the same ambivalence embodied in the title of his memoir, in its English version, *Heading South, Looking North*, as well as its Spanish rendition, *Rumbo al Sur, deseando el Norte*. Each iteration of the book is composed of two parts—"North and South" and "South and North" in the former, and "Norte y Sur" and "Sur y Norte" in the latter—as if the author remains unable to resolve the binary opposition that has defined his life.

The Promised Land (1912), Mary Antin's classic immigration memoir, concludes triumphantly, with its author confident that she has shed her European, Yiddish-speaking identity and become an Anglophonic American, eager and able to speak only English, which she praises unequivocally in euphoric English (164). It is not so for Dorfman, who can never abandon what he elsewhere calls "my own personal seesaw romance with two languages" ("Wandering Bigamists" 34) and who, at the end of his memoir, quite literally leaves himself and the reader up in the air. He concludes his story at the moment that, having escaped from the Chile in which he has become persona non grata, he is flying back to the United States. He notes that, though one circle has closed, another has opened. But he fails to impose closure in his final words: "I do not know then as I do not know now if that circle will ever close" (*Heading South* 277).

The copyright page in *Rumbo al Sur, deseando el Norte* indicates that its *"título original"* is *Heading South, Looking North*, and the record for the book in the electronic WorldCat reads "traducido del inglés por el autor." In the preface of each edition, Dorfman states, "I forced myself to write and rewrite it, first in one language and then in the other" / "Me forcé a escribir una y otra vez esta vida, primero en un idioma y luego en el otro" (*Heading South* Preface; *Rumbo* 7). If primacy is simply a matter of chronology, the English version would have to be considered authoritative; though the author himself created both the English and Spanish texts, *Heading South, Facing North* was published in April 1998, six months before the publication of *Rumbo al sur, deseando el Norte*. And the second sentence of the Spanish edition adds a reference to Dorfman as "este hombre que en Carolina del Norte traduce al castellano palabras originalmente imaginadas en inglés" 'this man who in North Carolina translated into Spanish words originally imagined in English' (*Rumbo* 11). If the terms retain any meaning in the age of digital reproduction and global, perpetual recycling, the English text must be the original, the Spanish text a copy.

However, Dorfman's movement between English and Spanish is an act of self-translation/*autotraducción*, in which the author/translator not only revises his material with a freedom that no outsider would dare assume, but his memoir, in either incarnation, refuses to endorse a single definitive linguistic form. Just as Dorfman himself remains suspended between English and Spanish, his text itself exists in the space between the English and Spanish versions he created. It is a bilingual inscription, seesawing between what he tells Angélica are "the two languages that raged for my throat during years and that now share me, the English and the Spanish that I have finally come to love almost as much as I love you" (*Heading South* Preface) / "las dos lenguas que se disputaron mi garganta durante años y que ahora me comparten: el inglés y el castellano, que finalmente he llegado a querer casi tanto como te quiero a ti" (*Rumbo* 11). Just as the English title, *Heading South, Looking North*, positions Dorfman equidistant between competing linguistic identities, so, too, does he place the English and Spanish texts in fruitful equilibrium.

Translations into other languages, including Portuguese (1998), Dutch (1999), German (1999), Italian (1999), and Danish (2001), were not done by Dorfman and must all be considered derivative of what he himself wrote. However, they all privilege the English text. *Kurs nach Süden, Blick nach Norden: Leben zwischen zwei Welten,* for example, states that it was translated into German by Gabriele Gockel, Barbara Reitz, and Maria Zybank, "aus dem Amerikan." And *Heading South, Looking North* is listed as the source for each of the others. Moreover, the title of Dorfman's Spanish text, *Rumbo al Sur, deseando el Norte,* appears to give the North priority over the South. *Rumbo,* meaning "bearing" or "direction," is neutral, but *deseando* ("wishing," "longing for") indicates that the compass of the author's heart points north. Yet that seems to contradict what Dorfman told an interviewer for the Mexican newspaper *Reforma*. He notes that, since he experienced the most traumatic events in his life in Spanish, putting them into English enabled him to distance and free himself from them ("al escribir el libro en inglés pude tomar distancia y mirarme desde fuera," [Bertran]). He goes on to state that, though writing each version was an arduous ordeal, writing in Spanish was more painful because his identity is more profoundly invested in that language than English: "Hacerlo en el idioma de los Estados Unis me costó trabajo, mi dio dolor de cabeza, pero cuando empecé a traducir el texto al español me dio dolor de estomago y me puse a trembler porque creo el castellano está mas profundamente metido dentro de mi yo que el inglés" (*Rumbo* 2). It is quite possible that, speaking in Spanish to an interviewer from Mexico, Dorfman might naturally favor the language of El Sur. But in doing so, he contradicts his own principle of balanced bilingualism, the "linguistic ambidexterity that," as he explained in the *New York Times,* "I will be the first to admit is not all typical" ("If Only").

In a later essay, Dorfman describes the composition of his memoir as a veritable linguistic psychomachia, a struggle between his two languages for command of his soul ("Footnotes"). He claims that, torn between the competing claims of English and Spanish, he agonized for nine months before committing himself to framing his first sentence. Desperate, he even toyed with resorting to a neutral language, French. Ultimately, the words came out in English, but not without traces of Spanish nor without a subsequent Spanish edition that makes significant departures from the English. Dorfman reiterates his belief that English provided insulation from the traumas he experienced as a Spanish-speaker: ". . . [English served as] a sort of oblique mirror that allowed me to see the events in a different (or at least tolerable) light, work through this confession, show myself, perhaps reveal myself, use the distance, treat myself as an almost fictional object." When writing about the same events in Spanish, "I would find myself sick and trembling, faint with anxiety" ("Footnotes" 212).

In the English version of his memoir, Dorfman writes of his British school in Chile as "rememorating an old empire that no longer existed" (*Heading South* 113). Seizing on this unusual locution, Fiona J. Doloughan contends that "the neologism 'rememorating' is not simply a (mis)translation of the Spanish 'rememorar' but consciously combines the English notions of commemoration and remembrance in a term freshly coined for the occasion and available to Dorfman because of his bilingualism" (151). A passage in Vladimir Nabokov's *Pnin* (1957) belies Doloughan's claim of Dorfman's linguistic priority: "In the rememoration of old relationships, later impressions often tend to be dimmer than earlier ones" (138). However, whether or not Dorfman is rememorating Nabokov's use of *rememorating*, it is true that his bilingualism, like Nabokov's, provides him with a verbal ambidexterity and a binocular vision lacking in monolingual authors.

Self-conscious about the proliferation of passive forms, the rich system of verbs, the fluid use of time, and the complexities of the subjunctive in Spanish ("Footnotes to a Double Life" 214–15), Dorfman foregrounds the act—and impossibility—of translation in each of his two texts. At the moment in which he finally feels communion with ordinary Chileans, he states, "I had ceased to be a stranger and had finally become a *compañero*" (*Heading South* 137). He uses the Spanish word in the English text but goes on to explain, in both the English and Spanish texts, that it is "a word for which there is no adequate English equivalent, because soul mate, buddy, friend, comrade, even companion, do not contain, like an echo, the Spanish word for bread—*pan*. . . ." (137). In the Spanish version, he reiterates the frustration he had felt in trying to come up with an equivalent for *compañero*: "Cuando yo escribí estas memorias en inglés, me di cuenta de que no existe en ese idioma ninguna palabra equivalente" (*Rumbo* 191). A bilingual life cannot be recounted with the vocabulary of a single language.

Dorfman scatters phrases in Spanish throughout his English text and phrases in English throughout his Spanish text. The preface to *Heading South, Looking North* concludes with a bilingual dedication to his wife, Angélica: "*Sin ti, no hubiera sobrevivido*. Without you, I wouldn't have survived."

The preface to *Rumbo al Sur, deseando el Norte* concludes with the same two sentences, except that the order is reversed, English first, then Spanish. In the English version, when Dorfman explains to Taty Allende how the Chilean police have coerced him into not marching in support of her father's presidential campaign, she exclaims, "*Hijos de puta!*" (*Heading South* 169). No translation is needed, and none is provided. *Rumbo al Sur* in turn recounts an incident at the breakfast table when five-year-old Dorfman is asked by his parents whether he would like "un arroz con leche." Willfully monolingual, he pretends not to understand, while admitting to the reader that he in fact understood perfectly, as his English reply to the Spanish makes clear: ". . . entiendo perfectamente, puesto que a los pocos minutes en forma sumamente pertinente irrumpo en inglés en medio del intercambio de mis padres en castellano, me refiero a lo que antes mencionaron, '*I'd really love some of that rice with milk*'" (*Rumbo* 89).

Like the discussion of *compañero*, this translingual exchange, not found in *Heading South*, where it would not have had the same dramatic impact, dispels what Lawrence Venuti calls "the translator's invisibility" (*Translator's Invisibility*). Like similar code-switching in the English version, it produces what Bertolt Brecht, in his 1949 "Kleines Organon für das Theater" (A Short Organum for the Theater), termed *Verfremdungseffekt* (alienation effect) (192), and Friedrich Schleiermacher, in his 1813 lecture "Ueber die verschiedenen Methoden des Uebersetzens" ("On the Different Methods of Translating"), termed *verfremdende Übersetzung* (foreignizing translation) (Schleiermacher). It makes the reader conscious of the verbal medium and of the truth that languages are not fungible. If, as Venuti suggests, foreignizing translation "can be a form of resistance against ethnocentrism and racism, cultural narcissism and imperialism, in the interests of democratic geopolitical relations" (*Translator's Invisibility* 20), Dorfman uses it to overcome both Yankee hegemony and Latin American isolation. He uses it to exit from *El laberinto de la soledad* (the labyrinth of solitude) in which Octavio Paz found Mexico, at least, trapped (Paz). Dorfman himself explains his method as an attempt to simulate his own linguistic confusion: "Introduce Spanish directly into the text (or English if the text is in Spanish), often without explaining or translating, no help to the reader, you're on your own, as I was, shipwrecked in a sea of words we don't understand. A tiny taste of what it means to be adrift in someone else's language" ("Footnotes" 210–11). A sense of the opacity and arbitrariness of words reinforces the memoir's self-conscious awareness of its own facticity, a pervasive sense that the author is engaged in what he calls "the biggest con game ever invented by humanity: literature" '[el] juego más grande de engaños que ha inventado la humanidad: la literatura' (*Heading South* 81; *Rumbo* 117). Occasional insertions of avowedly false memories—for example, a scene in which Angélica is spirited away by the secret police or Taty Allende's faulty claim to have seen Dorfman at La Moneda during the attack on the presidential palace—add to a pervasive sense of the instability and treachery of verbal representation.

Both *Heading South, Looking North* and *Rumbo al Sur, deseando el Norte* begin with the September 11, 1973, deadly assault on La Moneda and Dorfman's realization that it was only a set of contingencies that kept him away from his office there that day. If a series of circumstances had not led him to swap shifts with another member of the staff, Claudio Jimeno, he would have been on duty, and he, not Jimeno, would have been killed in the coup. Dorfman ponders the improbability of his own survival, and he resolves to put it to good purpose. Without ever dispelling "the fear that life is blind and hazardous and that we stumble in the tender darkness and try to fool ourselves into believing there is a pattern to all this" (*Heading South* 39), Dorfman accepts the premise that the reason that he lived was to tell the story of what happened to Chile. He survives, he explains, "haunted by the certainty that I have been keeping a promise to the dead" (40). His memoir will be the instrument of that mission, but he will tell the story differently to different readers. An eyewitness *testimonio* to the emergence of a military dictatorship in Chile, the book will also fulfill "the possibility of living in two languages, using each one for a different community" (269). It will need to be oriented differently when heading south than when looking north. The difference in implied reader is apparent in the variations between the English and Spanish versions of Dorfman's memoir.

Although the author might have had little to do with it, the covers of the original paperback editions each clearly target a distinct reader. Promising a real-life bildungsroman, a photograph of schoolboy Dorfman in dress shirt and tie stares out at the reader of *Heading South, Looking North*. By contrast, the cover of *Rumbo al Sur, deseando el Norte* shows General Augusto Pinochet, clothed in a cape and ceremonial uniform, accompanied by his military staff. A Spanish reader would surely recognize Pinochet and care more about his role in Chilean history than would a Yankee reader, more likely to associate September 11 with the World Trade Center than La Moneda. The cover of the Spanish edition also promises "un testimonio intenso y angustiante sobre el derrocamiento de Salvador Allende." An intense and agonizing account of the overthrow of Salvador Allende would be hard to market to North Americans, who might at best recall Allende as one of many fallen foreign leaders. The English-language edition is packaged as the story of a boy. Perhaps because the culture that produced *Huckleberry Finn* and *Moby-Dick* conceives of life as a journey and the culture that nourished Violeta Parra and Victor Jara casts it as a ballad, the English edition is subtitled *A Bilingual Journey*, the Spanish *Un romance bilingüe*.

Dorfman's ambilingual attention to two different communities is apparent in the separate ways he handles cultural references in the English and Spanish editions. Early in the book, noting the multiple migrations that his parents, his own children, and he have undertaken, he refers to a tendency "to change countries the way others, perhaps most of those who read these words, change brands of cereal" (*Heading South* 41). Those who read the words in English might likely breakfast on cereal, purchased in a supermarket with a vast selection of the packaged grains, but because Chileans might change shoes more frequently than corn flakes, he alters the Spanish to read ". . . cambiar de país como otros cambian los zapatos" (*Rumbo* 61). Dorfman characterizes his embarrassingly feeble performance in Spanish after moving from New York to Santiago as "my massacre of the language of Cervantes" (*Heading South* 103). However, he renders the same moment in Spanish as "mi asesinato de la lengua de

Quevedo" (*Rumbo* 148). An Anglophone might be expected to be familiar with the author of *Don Quixote* but not with Francisco de Quevedo, one of the leading poets of the Spanish Baroque. Elsewhere, Dorfman describes how, immediately after arriving in Buenos Aires, his Yiddish-speaking grandfather immediately begins peddling blankets door-to-door among the gentiles: "En poco tiempo ya se atrévia a golpear las puertas de los goyim que hablaban la lengua del *Martín Fierro*" (*Rumbo* 27–28). *Martín Fierro* is the title of a nineteenth-century epic by José Hernández about a quintessentially Argentine gaucho, and a South American reader might be expected to recognize that "the language of *Martín Fierro*" is a synonym for Spanish. However, unable to assume any acquaintance with Argentine literature, the English text states merely that the grandfather "was soon knocking at the doors of Spanish-speaking goyim as well" (*Heading South* 16).

Recounting how political repression in the United States forces his family to abandon the culture he loves, Dorfman, playing on a phonological symmetry, describes it as "Joe McCarthy parting me from Charlie McCarthy" (*Heading South* 74). However, even a Chilean familiar with the anti-Communist demagogue from Wisconsin would be unlikely to know that Charlie McCarthy was the wooden dummy who served as a partner to the popular American ventriloquist Edgar Bergen. So instead he writes in Spanish that McCarthy pushed him into the arms of Cantínflas: "Que Joe McCarthy me mandara a los brazos de Cantínflas" (*Rumbo* 106). The most beloved figure in Mexican cinema, Cantínflas would be familiar to Spanish readers but probably be almost as obscure to North Americans as Charlie McCarthy is to Chileans. Because they are too arcane to mean much in Spanish, a paragraph in *Rumbo al Sur* (167) describing how young Dorfman, newly arrived in Santiago, pines for the popular culture of the land he left behind simply omits references made by the English text to *the Saturday Evening Post*, *MAD* magazine, and the Hollywood hack Ed Wood (*Heading South* 118). Elsewhere, when the prose of *Heading South* echoes a familiar English nursery rhyme—"round and round the mulberry bush, the monkey chased the weasel" (*Heading South* 67)—or sentences in an English primer—"Look at Spot. Look at Spot run. Run, Dick, run" (*Heading South* 82)—the Spanish version passes over it (*Rumbo* 97, 119). However, just as the English text can make reference to Yogi Berra (*Heading South* 95) without specifying, as the Spanish text does, that he is "el gran *catcher* norteamericano Yogi Berra" (*Rumbo* 136), *Rumbo al Sur* can, in recounting a street urchin's troubles with the law, mention "*los pacos*" (174) without the parenthetical explanation provided in the English version, "the *pacos* (the Chilean police)" (*Heading South* 123). It can also make elliptical mention of "la Alameda Bernardo O'Higgins" (*Rumbo* 213), whereas, without being able to assume knowledge of O'Higgins as a hero of Chilean independence, the English text refers to "Santiago's main avenue, the Alameda" (*Heading South* 153).

In New York, when their leftist sympathies place the Dorfman family at risk amid a climate of political repression, young Vladimiro, as he was still called, is tempted to inform on his father by telling his teacher that Adolfo Dorfman is a Communist. He ultimately resolves to remain loyal to his family, but the theme of betrayal pervades his memoir, written first in English, the language he adopted after rejecting Spanish, the language of his parents' courtship, and later in Spanish, the language he embraced after turning against the North American culture he loved. Betrayal is there in the abandonment two-and-a-half-year-old Dorfman feels when his parents deposit him in a New York hospital. And it is there when the Chilean army turns against the nation's elected president, as it is there in Dorfman's survivor's guilt that he did not die with his comrades at La Moneda. Connected to a conviction of his own doubleness is an inner reproach over his personal duplicity, and each time he leaves one country for another, he experiences it as an act of disloyalty. Most tellingly, Dorfman regards switching languages as bigamy. In love with both English and Spanish, he feels both languages competing for his affection and is convinced that whenever he chooses one over the other it constitutes "an in flagrante case of linguistic adultery" ("Footnotes" 207). Writing his memoir first in English and then again in Spanish is a strategy designed to appease and reconcile two jealous rival lovers, despite the Italian adage that translation is itself betrayal.

For much of his life, Dorfman provides a case study in the "dialogic imagination" that Mikhail Bakhtin attributes to the genre of the novel. The conversations between his Spanish self and his English self are heated and often hostile. At times, one or the other is ruthlessly silenced. Impatient with the complexities of negotiating between two languages, he often longs for the integrity of monolingualism. "I have myself been a fundamentalist of language," he later wrote, "someone who, for decades, tried to escape the bifurcation of tongue and vocabulary, a back and forth that was determined by exile and repression and geography" ("Wandering Bigamists" 32). Contrasting poetry with the novel, Bakhtin identifies linguistic fundamentalism with the lyric impulse. Monologic where the novelist is dialogic, "the poet," Bakhtin claims, "is a poet insofar as he accepts the idea of unitary and singular language and a unitary, monologically sealed-off utterance" (296). Despite a nostalgia for linguistic purity and occasional stints of English-only or Spanish-only, Dorfman eventually rejects a unitary identity. From its genesis to its aftermath in Dorfman's paratextual essays and interviews, the bilingual project of *Heading South, Looking North/Rumbo al Sur, deseando el Norte* recapitulates two centuries of linguistic theory—from the monadism of the Romantics, for whom the local *Volksgeist* was unique and immutable, to a postmodern globalism of porous borders and mingling, morphing tongues. Dorfman's imagination has grown from monologic to dialogic. In Bakhtin's terms, he moves from the lyrical to the novelistic.

With his fluency in Spanish and intimate knowledge of Chile, Dorfman comes close to fulfilling an early ambition: "I thought that I could become the first Latin American writer to address the United States and Europe directly in English, without any need of translation" (*Heading South* 196). But with his self-translation into Spanish, he is also one of the few North Americans capable of addressing Latin America directly in Spanish. Facing both North and South but not belonging entirely to either, he positions himself as hemispheric go-between. After decades of struggling with bifurcated identities, Dorfman writes as an evangelist of *métissage*, "this hybrid mongrel of language" (*Heading South* 269). Who touches these two books—in English and Spanish—and the spaces between them touches a man, "this man who is shared by two equal languages and who has come to believe that to tolerate differences and indeed embody them personally and collectively might be our only salvation as a species" (*Heading South* 42).

Alien Autographs: How Translators Make Their Marks

Acts of treason can provoke a sovereign state into either concealment or exposure. The option of concealment is illustrated by the Roger Hollis case, in which, despite duplicity in the highest circles of government, an official British cover-up attempted to preserve the illusion of impregnable national security. In *Spycatcher*, a book that was banned in England when published in 1987, Peter Wright contends that Hollis, director-general of Britain's MI5 from 1956 to 1965, was a mole who used his position to protect Soviet spies and convey crucial intelligence to the Kremlin (Wright). Although Hollis's treachery was eventually detected, Prime Minister Margaret Thatcher, anxious to maintain the illusion of trustworthiness, lied to Parliament and the public about his misdeeds. In the United States, by contrast, after Julius Rosenberg was caught passing secrets about the Manhattan Project to his Soviet handlers in 1950, he was publicly tried, convicted, and executed. The sorry spectacle of the Rosenberg case not only presumably deterred future spies, but it was also an instance of what a Russian Formalist—if not Communist—would call laying bare the devices of Cold War espionage.

If *traduttori, traditori* (translators are traitors), publishers can respond to the treason of translation with a choice of strategies analogous to those confronting a counterintelligence agency. The act of treachery can be camouflaged, even effaced, or it can be flaunted, even celebrated.

Although translators are often ignored, William Tyndale, for one, was, like Julius Rosenberg, executed for his treason—rendering the Bible into English; making Scripture available to those unlearned in Latin challenged the Church's authority. Much earlier, the Septuagint, one of the most influential of all translations, was said to have been created when seventy-two Jewish scholars were summoned to Alexandria to create a Greek version of the Hebrew Bible. Although a letter that someone calling himself Aristeas addressed to a Philocrates in the second century BCE specifies that the collective task was completed in seventy-two days, neither it nor the Septuagint itself identifies any of the translators. Like a myriad of other literary texts created throughout history by unsung, underpaid interpreters, the Greek version of the Pentateuch erases its origins. For the devout, the sacred Scripture *is* the Septuagint, or the Vulgate, or the King James Version, or the Luther Bible, or the Russian Synod Bible, or its rendition in one of hundreds of other languages. The ubiquitous Gideon Bible omits the names of its translators. The invisibility of biblical translation is demonstrated by literalists who insist on adhering to the exact letter of the Holy Book—as it is available to them in their tongue. According to apocryphal anecdote, Miriam "Ma" Ferguson, opposing foreign language requirements for public school students, once observed, "If English was good enough for Jesus Christ, it's good enough for the children of Texas." If so, the Texas governor was serenely unaware of translation. In Kurt Vonnegut's *Timequake* (1997), the narrator proclaims, "Yes, and I am here to suggest that the greatest writer in the English language so far was Lancelot Andrewes (1555–1625), and not the Bard of Avon" (131). The piquancy of the remark comes from the fact that the Bible, composed in Hebrew and Greek, is read as English literature, and few know the name of its most influential translator.

Like the history of espionage, the history of translation is an argument between advocates of disclosure and advocates of concealment. Distinguishing between "illusionist" and "anti-illusionist" methods of translation, Czech theorist Jiří Levý explains that "the illusionist translator hides behind the original which he presents to the reader, as it were, without a mediator, in order to evoke in him an illusion by translation: that is to say, the illusion of reading the original text." By contrast, "*anti-illusionist* methods trifle boldly with the fact that it is only an imitation of reality which they are offering to the public," according to Levý, who places himself firmly in the camp of illusionism (339). So, too, does Anthea Bell, a prolific translator from French, German, Danish, and Polish into English, who describes herself as "an unrepentant, unreconstructed adherent of the school of invisibility" (59). Bell insists on hiding her own presence in the published text: ". . . all my professional life, I have felt that translators are in the business of spinning an illusion. The illusion is that the reader is reading not a translation but the real thing" (59).

The assassination of Hitoshi Igarashi, who translated Salman Rushdie's *The Satanic Verses* (1988) into Japanese, and the stabbing of its Italian translator, Ettore Capriolo, suggest not just theoretical but practical reasons for a translator to remain out of sight. William Nygaard, who published the Norwegian version of the novel, was shot three times, and Azis Nessin, who translated it into Turkish, barely escaped death at the hands of an angry mob. However, radical Islamists were even more intent on eliminating the blasphemer who created *The Satanic Verses*. They were set on fulfilling Roland Barthes's prophecy for *La Mort de l'auteur* ("The Death of the Author"). Amid the obsequies, translators, too, would disappear. In any case, the fate of Etienne Dolet (1509–1546), who was, according to André Lefevere, "burnt at the stake because his translation of Plato contained some errors" (27), might concentrate the minds of translators on making themselves invisible.

Nevertheless, some translators and translations are intent on exposing and emphasizing the illusion that Bell and others try to spin. In *The Translator's Invisibility: A History of Translation*, Lawrence Venuti defines a spectrum that ranges between "fluent" or "domesticating translations"—versions in which the fact of translation seems to have been erased—and "foreignizing translations"—texts that in one way or another call attention to the fact that they have been altered linguistically (21). Venuti's conception of the options for translation is similar to Levý's illusionist/anti-illusionist binary. Much translation theory situates itself along an axis of visibility, between texts that lull readers into thinking they are encountering the author's original words and those intent on calling attention to the fact that they have been transposed into another language. A French consumer encountering an ad touting Coca-Cola as "la vraie chose" is probably unaware that the phrase is an invisible calque on an

American slogan. However, the reader of *Reft and Light: Poems by Ernst Jandl with Multiple Versions by American Poets* (Waldrop) cannot avoid thinking about translation. By offering texts by Jandl, a linguistically innovative contemporary Austrian, each followed by numerous renditions by more than a dozen Americans, the volume questions whether any version, even the German "original," is definitive.

The opposition between domesticating and foreignizing, illusionist and anti-illusionist, visible and invisible translations is another version of the eternal argument over whether self-consciousness is an asset or an encumbrance. Does it herald the existential autonomy of the Cartesian *cogito* or the paralysis of Hamlet, "sicklied o'er with the pale cast of thought"? The ambivalence recalls the tensions between proscenium-arch naturalism and *Verfremdungseffekt* in theater and between transparency and metafiction in the novel. "In a sense," writes Julie Rose in the Preface to her translation of Victor Hugo's *Les Misérables*, "all translation is a performance, a piece of theater" (xxiv). However, some performances sabotage the fourth-wall illusion that others take elaborate pains to sustain. Stylistic idiosyncrasies make visible the mechanisms of language and, for Vladimir Nabokov at least, are not defects in translation: "In the first place," he insists, in the foreword to his 1958 translation of Mikhail Lermontov's *A Hero of Our Time*, "we must dismiss, once and for all the conventional notion that a translation 'should read smoothly' and 'should not sound like a translation' (to quote the would-be compliments, addressed to vague versions, by genteel reviewers who have and never will read the original texts). In point of fact, any translation that does *not* sound like a translation is bound to be inexact upon inspection . . ." ("Translator's Foreword" viii). By contrast, Robert Lowell tried to make his audaciously unservile *Imitations* (1961), poems adapted from French, German, Greek, Italian, and Russian, *not* read like translations. "I have tried to write alive English and to do what my authors might have done if they were writing their poems now and in America," he explains (xi). Whereas a successfully fluent translation will by definition erase its tracks, covering up any evidence of its origins in another language, a foreignizing translation displays, even flaunts, telltale signs of linguistic treason. A variety of paratexts can serve as accessories to the crime.

Within the ecology of literary culture, translators tend to be ignored by reviewers and other readers. They typically receive modest recompense for what they produce as "work for hire," without royalties or control over use of their text, and they are sometimes not even credited on the cover or title page of the volume they have translated. In 1656, when Sir John Denham Englished the *Aeneid*, he did sign his name to the finished product. However, he domesticated the Latin epic, generating a work that for his contemporary compatriots would not betray its origins in an ancient language: "If Virgil must needs speak English," Denham wrote in a preface, "it were fit he should speak not onely as a man of this Nation, but as a man of this age" (qtd. in Venuti, "Lawrence Venuti" 549). However, the earliest texts were often acts of overt espionage, in which concealing translation was not an important objective. At the outset of the Akkadian text (c. 1200 BCE) of *Gilgamesh*, a Babylonian priest named Sin-liqe-unninni identifies himself as responsible for compiling the epic from its sources in Sumerian (2150–2000 BCE). And the very first page of the first book printed in English, by the printer William Caxton, Raoul Lefèvre's *Recuyell of the Historyes of Troye* (1474), announces that it is "translated and drawen out of frenshe in to englisshe by Willyam Caxton mercer of ye cyte of London" (707). Embedding the name of the translator within the text itself is one way to signal that the words in the book are not exactly those of the credited author. Stylistic idiosyncrasies can also expose the illusion of translation. Other ways are provided by a variety of paratexts.

The degree zero of translational invisibility occurs in utilitarian prose that is designed simply to convey information. The owner's manual to a Toyota Prius or a Toshiba laptop does not identify the persons responsible for transposing its turgid Japanese into turgid English, Arabic, or Portuguese, and a reader is not expected to attend to the transparently opaque text's elegance of expression. The "Universal Declaration of Human Rights" is, according to *Guinness World Records*, the most widely translated document ("Most Translated Document"). The United Nation's Office of the High Commissioner for Human Rights recognizes 520 versions of the Declaration, though its website states that "OHCHR bears no responsibility for the quality and accuracy of any translations other than those of the six official UN languages" ("About the Universal Declaration"). However, although those who drafted the document in 1948 (including John Peters Humphrey, Eleanor Roosevelt, René Cassin, Stéphane Hessel, Henri Laugier, Charles Malik, and Jacques Maritain) were largely Anglophonic and Francophonic, no priority or special authority is accorded to any one of those 6 versions. Esperanto, linguist L. L. Zamenhof's attempt to concoct a neutral, global medium of communication, is one of the 519 other languages, but in principle every one of the world's languages should be an impartial vehicle for conveying the identical ideas. The "Universal Declaration of Human Rights" was signed not by its translators but by delegates of the UN member nations, and the rights enshrined in it are meant to be absolute, independent of their embodiment in any particular language and applicable to speakers of any tongue. It is supposed to be irrelevant whether they are read in Abkhaz or Zulu. The postapartheid Constitution of the Republic of South Africa recognizes 11 official languages, and during sessions of the Parliament in Cape Town an army of anonymous, interchangeable linguists sequestered in booths in the rear of the hall translates speeches back and forth among Sepedi, Sesotho, Setswana, siSwati, Tshivenda, Xitsonga, Afrikaans, English, isiNdebele, isiXhosa and isiZulu. The perfect interpreter is heard but not seen.

Because it has the effect of destabilizing beloved texts, making a reader aware that the words are fungible, translation tends to be invisible in children's books. A popular edition of *Pippi Longstocking* (1997), for example, supports the illusion that Astrid Lindgren wrote it not in Swedish but directly in English. Perhaps grownups are trying to shelter tender minds from verbal relativism, from the shock of realizing that the words they cherish are not definitive. Since learning that beloved tales such as "The Boy Who Cried Wolf," "The Fox and the Grapes," and "The Ant and the Grasshopper" were transposed from Greek could be as unsettling as the discovery that there is no Santa Claus, *The Classic Treasury of Aesop's Fables* (1999) omits indication that its contents are translated. Similarly, all traces of its linguistic origins have been expunged from an American edition of *Heidi* (2007), which Johanna Spyri first published in German in 1880. Furthermore, *Bambi: A Life in the Woods* (1956) credits Felix Salten as its author but provides no indication, not even on the copyright page, that some unidentified person translated it from *Bambi, Eine Lebensgeschichte aus dem Walde* (1923). In fact, the standard English translation, first published in 1929, was done by Whittaker Chambers, who would later gain notoriety—and unwanted visibility—for defecting from the American Communist Party and denouncing others who had spied for the Soviet Union.

In *De oratore* (55 BCE), Cicero, using the persona of Lucius Crassus, sanctions "imitation," an inexact translation that is free to diverge from its source. By giving his 1749 poem "The Vanity of Human Wishes" the subtitle "The Tenth Satire of Juvenal Imitated," Samuel Johnson makes visible the process of transposition from Latin to English. But, in "The Knight's Tale," Geoffrey Chaucer acknowledges that he is paraphrasing the Italian of Giovanni Boccaccio's *Teseida delle nozze di Emilia* only in his vague opening line: "Whilom, as olde stories tellen us" (37). Though he titled it "The Rubaiyat of Omar Khayyam," saluting the authority of a twelfth-century Persian poet, Edward Fitzgerald privately called his very creative rendition, which survives as a work of Victorian English poetry, a "transmogrification" (Kerney 55). The most famous example of a transmogrified imitation during the last century, Ezra Pound's "The River Merchant's Wife: A Letter" (1914), is a loose adaptation of a Li Po work. But Pound's poem foregrounds its status as translation and its intertextuality, because its style, departing from the traditions of Western verse, is so manifestly an appropriation of a Chinese model. Pound invites the reader to admire his inventiveness in transforming a classical Tang dynasty text into modern English poetry. By contrast, when William Butler Yeats published "When You Are Old" as part of his 1892 collection *The Countess Kathleen and Various Legends and Lyrics*, he provided no marker that it was a variation on Pierre de Ronsard's "Quand vous serez bien vieille" (1574). A reader in this case of invisible translation is not encouraged to think about how Yeats has reworked Ronsard's Petrarchan sonnet to reflect his own sensibility. Unacknowledged translation shades insidiously into plagiarism, as in the case of Melanie Grobler, a South African poet who was forced to relinquish the 2005 Eugýne Marais literature prize when it was determined that "Stad," a poem in her winning collection *Die Waterbreker*, was an almost verbatim but uncredited rendering into Afrikaans of Canadian poet Anne Michaels's "There Is

No City That Does Not Dream" (Breytenbach). As Thomas De Quincey and later scholars such as Norman Fruman have noted, Samuel Taylor Coleridge inserted into his *Biographia Literaria* extensive passages translated from the German of Friedrich Schelling and Friedrich Schlegel, passing them off as his own (Fruman).

Some editions strive to disguise the fact, but translations are composed by translators. And as soon as attention is called to an intermediary, the illusion of unmediated contact with the original words is shattered. If a book publisher acknowledges the reality of translation at all, it occurs on a title page, usually just below the name of the author. Laetitia Devaux is only partially visible when she credits her 2001 French translation of Michael Cimino's novel *Big Jane* to the pseudonym "Anne Derouet." The presence of a translator becomes even fainter when she signs her translations of works by Dave Eggers, Thomas H. Cook, George Pelecanos, and Ali Smith merely with the initial "L." However, in most other cases, the name of the translator on a title page is authentic. The English edition of *Suite Française* (2006) informs the reader that it is by Irène Némirovsky and "translated by Sandra Smith," of *The Leopard* (2007), that it is by Giuseppe Tomasi di Lampedusa and "translated from the Italian by Archibald Colquhoun," and of *Children of the Alley* (1996) that it is by Naguib Mahfouz and "translated by Peter Theroux."

Less frequently, the name of the translator might also appear on the cover and/or the spine of the book. That is more likely to occur when the translator has achieved a certain level of recognition, at least in literary circles. In 1970, when neither author nor translator was familiar to English-language readers, Gabriel García Márquez's *One Hundred Years of Solitude* identified its translator, Gregory Rabassa, only on the title page. But the success of García Márquez helped transform Rabassa into that rare phenomenon, a celebrity translator, and his name appears on the cover of more recent editions of José Donoso's *Taratuta and Still Life with Pipe: Two Novellas* (1994), José Lezama Lima's *Paradiso* (2000), and António Lobo Antunes's *The Return of the Caravels* (2002). The gifted and prolific Stephen Mitchell is identified as the translator on the cover of the Vintage edition of Rainer Maria Rilke's *Letters to a Young Poet* (1984), but it is not until the title page that Joan M. Burnham, who conducts her operations more covertly, is identified as the translator of the

New World Library edition (2000) of the same work. Jorge Luis Borges, himself a major figure in Latin American letters, is named prominently on the cover of *Las palmeras salvajes* (2007), his translation of William Faulkner's *The Wild Palms*, and poet Seamus Heaney gets prominent billing on the cover of his translation of *Beowulf* (2001), which of course does not name the original poet. Haruki Murakami (村上春樹) is named on the cover of キャッチャー・イン・ザ・ライ, the Japanese novelist's translation of J. D. Salinger's *The Catcher in the Rye* (2003), though Spanish translator Carmen Criado is not identified on the cover of her version, *El guardián entre el centeno* (1997), nor, despite his renown, is Heinrich Böll on the cover of his, *Der Fänger im Roggen* (1954).

It would take a systematic examination of publishing practices throughout the world to determine whether publishers in English-speaking countries are more or less inclined than publishers elsewhere to highlight the fact of translation. However, it is clear that they are less inclined to publish translations. The website threepercent.com derives its name from revulsion over the dismally low portion of books published in the United States that originated in languages other than English—about 3 percent, and if only poetry and literary fiction are considered, the figure is closer to .7 percent ("About Three Percent"). With the exception of a few small presses, such as Arcade, Archipelago, Dalkey Archive, Deep Vellum, Europa, Ibis, Oneworld Classics, Open Books, Restless Books, and Zephyr, dedicated to making literature in other languages available to Anglophones, publishing houses in the United States and Britain tend to be English-only zones. By contrast, the *New York Times*, which puts the quantity of translations produced by American publishers at 2.67 percent, finds that 29 percent of books published in both the Czech Republic and South Korea are translations; the figure for Spain is 25 percent, for Italy 22 percent (J. Hoffman).

The situation in publishing corresponds roughly to trends in film distribution. Audiences in the United States are notoriously disinclined to buy tickets to movies that were made in languages other than English. Cinematic imports in Chinese, French, German, Italian, Japanese, and Spanish are generally consigned to art house ghettoes, and even the most successful almost always fare better at the domestic box office when remade in English. Coline Serreau's *Trois hommes et un couffin* qualified as a foreign hit in the American market when it grossed $2,052,466 in 1985 ("Box Office Business for *Trois hommes*"). However, Leonard Nimoy's 1987 remake, *Three Men and a Baby*, took in $167,780,960 domestically ("Box Office Business for *Three Men*"). Cameron Crowe's *Vanilla Sky* (2001) earned $100,618,344 in the United States ("Box Office Business for *Vanilla Sky*"), far exceeding the $370,720 that the Spanish original, Alejandro Amenábar's *Abre los ojos*, earned during its American release in 1997 ("Box Office Business for *Abre los ojos*").

The United States Census Bureau reported that in 2006 foreign films accounted for 3 percent of all ticket sales in American theaters ("Foreign Films"). The figure, a sharp contrast with South Korea, where 52 percent of respondents in early 2009 reported favoring Hollywood films ("S. Korea Moviegoers") over domestic productions, is remarkably close to the notorious 3 percent of books published in the United States that are translations. In countries in which a "minor" language such as Danish or Thai is dominant, translation is likely to be commonplace and undisguised. Speakers of global languages such as English, Spanish, or Mandarin are more likely to regard their cultural polysystems as complete in themselves and not in need of importations through translation. When encountering translated texts, regardless of whether they possess telltale markers, such speakers might be less attentive to linguistic relativism.

More emphatic than credit on the title page or even on the cover in exposing the reality of translation is an explanatory essay positioned at the beginning of a book. Translator's prefaces go back at least as far as the fourth century CE, when Evagrius of Antioch wrote a prologue to justify his loose transposition from Greek to Latin of the *Life of St. Anthony* by Athanasius of Alexandria. "Word-for-word translation from one language into another clouds the sense, and like uncontrolled weeds, smothers the crop," Evagrius insists, alerting readers to disparities between his text and Athanasius's (Evagrius). In the preface to his tenth-century translation of the Vulgate Genesis into Anglo-Saxon, Ælfric observes that he has had to change the word order, because "always whoever translates or teaches from Latin into English must ever order it so that the English has its own way, otherwise it is very misleading for those to read who do not know the ways of Latin" (41). Ælfric's laying bare of the devices of translation is only partial, since he does not mention that the word order in his Latin model is not identical with the Hebrew version it was in turn derived from. Constance Garnett uses her preface (1914) to *Crime and Punishment* to introduce readers to Fyodor Dostoevsky and explain how he came to write the 1866 novel that she was bringing into English for the first time. Charles Jarvis begins the preface to his 1819 translation of *Don Quixote* by trying to justify his project—by pointing out weaknesses in the three existing English versions of Cervantes's novel. "As much as I dislike the usual practice of translators, who think to recommend their own by censuring the former translations of their author," writes Jarvis, "that, had I not thought those of *Don Quixote* very defective, I had never given myself or him the trouble of this undertaking" (7). Other translators use prefaces to explain the strategies they employed to deal with the fact that no two languages have exact equivalents with each other. Noting that "Greek is swift, much swifter than English," Paul Roche describes how, in translating Sophocles's plays, he resorted to what he calls "Freewheeling Iambic" (xvi) to approximate the playwright's iambic trimeter, "a twelve-syllable line set out in two sets of three with a caesura" (xv).

Nabokov begins the introduction to his 1964 translation of Aleksandr Pushkin's *Eugene Onegin* by faulting Walter W. Arndt's 1963 rendition for sacrificing sense to rhythm and melody. His own version of the Russian poem (Pushkin) is blatantly "foreignizing," in that, eschewing smoothness, it deliberately attempts to simulate in English the experience of reading in a Slavic language. Moreover, Nabokov provides not only a preface but also an epilogue and "Notes on Prosody," as well as elaborate commentary, in an edition that fills four volumes and in which Nabokov's word count far exceeds Pushkin's. If Nabokov's novel *Pale Fire* (1962)—in which the words of critic and translator Charles Kinbote occlude those of the poet John Shade—is metafiction, fiction that questions its own fictionality, the Nabokov *Onegin* is metatranslation. It is one of the most overt if not brazen reminders that the text at hand is a translation. The facsimile of the 1837 Russian edition appended to the final volume further subverts any illusion of a pure, primal text.

Marjorie Rawlings begins the foreword to her translation of *Phèdre* by conceding, "I know that it is impossible to translate the incomparable verse of Jean Racine" (9). And she emphasizes that impossibility by printing Racine's verse on facing pages beside her English approximations. Other dual-language editions similarly have the effect of keeping the reader acutely aware of the reality of translation. Rawlings puts the French original on the left-hand pages, and in the Loeb Classical Library, it is either Greek or Latin on the left, facing an English trot on the right. The Collection Budé also presents Greek or Latin on the left, but a French version on the right. And the Clay Sanskrit Library offers classic Sanskrit texts on the left, English translations on the right. No one picking up a dual-language edition can retain the illusion that language is unitary and the text definitive.

Entries in the flourishing subgenre of translators' memoirs and personal testaments also serve as paratexts that, as addenda to their authors' translations, insist on making visible the commerce between languages. Some of the more noteworthy examples of the species include Edith Grossman's *Why Translation Matters*; Michael Hamburger's *String of Beginnings: Intermittent Memoirs 1924–1954*; Edmund Keeley's *Borderlines: A Memoir*; Donald Keene's *Chronicles of My Life: An American in the Heart of Japan*; Suzanne Jill Levine's *The Subversive Scribe: Translating Latin American Fiction*; Gregory Rabassa's *If This Be Treason: Translation and Its Dyscontents*; and Jean Starr Untermeyer's *Private Collection*. Umberto Eco's *Experiences in Translation* (2001) lays bare the work of transferring words between languages, but its own translator, Alastair McEwen, remains invisible. It is not the translator, but rather the chairman of the university department that commissioned the lectures that form the substance of the book, who got to write the brief preface.

Second-degree translations—translations of translations—can both display and conceal the derivative nature of the final text. When *Ferdydurke* (1937), Witold Gombrowicz's landmark of Polish modernism, was published in English by Harcourt, Brace and World in 1961, the title page indicated that it was translated by Eric Mosbacher but did not reveal that Mosbacher based his translation on Georges Lisowski's French translation of the Polish original. Small type on the copyright page does indicate that Carol Brown Janeway's 2001 translation of Márai Sándor's *Embers* was in turn based on *Die Glut*, Christina Viragh's translation of the original Hungarian, *A gyertyák csonkig égnek*. Overtly and covertly, second-degree translation proliferates to a surprising—and disturbing—degree. Publishing *Ang Munting Prinsipe* (1969) in Tagalog, translator Lilia F. Antonio relied on *The Little Prince* and not *Le Petit Prince*, the words actually written by author Antoine de Saint-Exupéry. And *Gefährlichte Geliebte* (2000), Giovanni Bandini and Ditte Bandini's German rendition of Haruki Murakami's 1992 国境の南、太陽の西 *(South of the Border, West of the Sun)*, was based not on the Japanese text but on J. Philip Gabriel's 1998 English translation.

Although Ismail Kadare is world-renowned as laureate of the Man Booker International Prize and a Prince of Asturias Award, most of the Albanian novelist's work available in English was adapted from French translations. David Bellos, who has translated five of Kadare's books into English, received the 2005 Man Booker International Translation Prize, but he has stated that he does not know Albanian. His versions of *The Pyramid* (1996), *The File on H.* (1998), *Spring Flowers, Spring Frost* (2002), and *Agamemnon's Daughter* (2006) were drawn from French translations by Jusuf Vrioni. A fifth book, *The Successor* (2008), relies on the French translation by Tedi Papavrami. Barbara Bray's English translations of Kadare's *The Concert* (1994) and *The Palace of Dreams* (1996) are likewise based on French translations by Vrioni. A French translation, by Jean-Michel Jasiensko, is also the basis for the English translation, by Joanna Kilmartin and Steve Cox, of Polish novelist Stanislaw Lem's influential *Solaris* (1970).

Second-degree translation is central to the plot of Rabih Alameddine's 2014 novel *An Unnecessary Woman*. It demonstrates how utterly *de trop*, a nonessential speck in the cosmos, is its seventy-two-year-old narrator, Aaliya Saleh. Aaliya, a resident of Beirut, has spent each of the past thirty-seven years translating a different novel into Arabic. Since her fellow Lebanese can read French and English, she concludes that there is no point in translating novels written in French or English. However, since Aaliya's own linguistic repertoire is limited to only Arabic, French, and English, she dedicates her life to translating into Arabic works by such authors as W. G. Sebald, Roberto Bolaño, Italo Calvino, Sadegh Hedayat, Knut Hamsun, Bilge Karasu, Imre Kertész, Danilo Kiš, Cees Nooteboom, José Saramago, Bruno Schulz, and Leo Tolstoy that have been translated into French or English. Aaliya's completed manuscripts clutter a storage room in her apartment, but, since there is no market for translations of translations, they remain without any prospect of publication. The translator and her life's work are superfluous.

Second-degree translation, along with the kind of elaborate paratextual apparatus that Nabokov himself concocted for his idiosyncratic translation of *Eugene Onegin*, is lampooned in *Pale Fire*. The novel employs inaccurate translation as a plot device and as a means of examining how we are constructed by language and how language is arbitrary. Narrator Charles Kinbote, who fancies himself the exiled king of Zembla, is, in his mind, the nephew of a noted translator of Shakespeare into Zemblan. Much of the meaning of the novel hinges on a passage from *Timon of Athens* (IV iii 439–40) in which Timon proclaims, "The moon's an arrant thief, / And her pale fire she snatches from the sun." The image, suggesting the derivative, parasitic quality of translation and criticism, eludes Kinbote, because the only *Timon of Athens* that he has access to is his uncle Conmal's Zemblan version, in which the lines, boomeranging back into English from the translation into Zemblan, are rendered as "The moon is a thief: / he steals his silvery light from the sun" (Nabokov *Pale Fire* 80). This is a seriously flawed distortion of the Shakespearean text, but since Zemblan is of course a figment of Kinbote's—and Nabokov's—imagination, it is a playful instance in which a fictional back-translation is used to demonstrate the treachery of attempting linguistic equivalences, or of using language at all.

If there are reasons—such as vanity or commerce—to disguise a text's origins in translation, there can also be reasons to claim that a text is a translation when it is not. If a book that appeared in London in 1762 had presented itself simply as a young Scot's literary concoction instead of as *Fingal, an ancient epic poem, in six books: together with several other poems, composed by Ossian the son of Fingal* and "tr, from the Galic language, by James Macpherson," much of the European reading public would not have become enamored of what it thought was authentic medieval Celtic poetry. Though he was himself an active translator, of Shakespeare, Calderón, Dryden, and Pope, among others, Voltaire was skeptical of the entire enterprise. In a 1754 letter to Madame du Deffand, he declared, ". . . les poètes ne se traduisent point. Peut-on traduire de la musique?"' 'poets cannot be translated. Can one translate music?' (*Letter* 119). Yet Voltaire bills *Candide* as "traduit de l'allemand de Mr le Docteur Ralph, avec les additions qu'on a trouvées dans la poche du docteur lorsqu'il mourut" 'translated from the German of Doctor Ralph, with additions found in the doctor's pocket when he died' as a way of mocking his contemporaries' fascination with German philosophy, particularly the philosophical optimism of Gottfried Wilhelm Leibniz. In 1850, after being persuaded by her husband, Robert, to change the title from *Sonnets from the Bosnian*, Elizabeth Barrett Browning published the forty-four love poems she had written in English as *Sonnets from the Portuguese*. The fiction of translation made it easier for the author, who had been hesitant about publishing the sonnets at all, and it enticed English readers with a soupçon of the exotic.

When first published in 1764, the title page of Horace Walpole's popular Gothic novel announced: "The Castle of Otranto, A Gothic Story. Translated by William Marshal, Gent. From the Original Italian of Onuphrio Muralto, Canon of the Church of St. Nicholas at Otranto." And the preface to that first edition explains: "The following work was found in the library of an ancient Catholic family in the north of England. It was printed at Naples, in the black letter, in the year 1529. How much sooner it was written does not appear. The principal incidents are such as were believed in the darkest ages of Christianity; but the language and conduct have nothing that savours of barbarism. The style is the purest Italian" (Walpole, *The Castle* 1764 2). Nevertheless, by 1769, Walpole was ready to confess that the claim that his book was translated from Italian was purest fabrication. In the preface to the third edition, the true author explains his subterfuge: ". . . it is fit that he should ask pardon of his readers for having offered his work to them under the borrowed personage of a translator. As diffidence of his own abilities, and the novelty of the attempt, were his sole inducements to assume that disguise, he flatters himself he shall appear excusable" (Wapole, *The Castle* 1769 xiii). Walpole can surely be excused, but also interrogated. If most translations aspire to invisibility, the disparities between English and Italian are made visible in the first edition of *The Castle of Otranto*. But thoughts about the contingencies of linguistic expression do not entirely disappear when the work is exposed as a faux translation. They are, instead, compounded. If translation is betrayal, realization that what a reader took to be translation is nothing of the kind constitutes double betrayal.

Boris Vian was being playful but also taking advantage of the French vogue for hard-boiled detective novels from the other side of the Atlantic and his compatriots' exoticization of African Americans when he pretended that *J'irai cracher sur vos tombes* (1946) was his translation of a novel by a black American named Vernon Sullivan. The camouflage did not spare the author from scandal when his book was banned as immoral. In 1894, when Pierre Louÿs wrote some boldly erotic poems of love between women, he presented them in a respectable antiquarian package; they were published under the title *Les Chansons de Bilitis* and under the guise of being Louÿs's translations from an ancient Greek poet. Pierre François Godart de Beauchamps's scabrous *Histoire du Prince Apprius* was published in 1728 under the guise of being a translation from Persian, and the steamy passions of the pseudo-translation *Lettres portugaises* (1669) were cloaked in an anonymity so opaque that it was not until the twentieth century that it was definitively determined that the work was written not by a Franciscan nun and her lover in Portuguese but by the Comte de Guilleragues in French.

Modesty is the professional virtue of the translator. For many, the act of translation is an exercise in negative capability, in expunging their own identities in service to the authors whose voices they are transmitting. In the preface to her translation of three Greek plays, Edith Hamilton contends, "There are few efforts more conducive to humility than that of the translator trying to communicate an incommunicable beauty" (16). And Julie Rose, translator of Alexandre Dumas, Jean Racine, Michel Leiris, Pierre Bourdieu, and Marguerite Duras, writes of "channeling" Victor Hugo in the process of giving English habitation to *Les Misérables*: "You try to 'be' the role you're playing, to stay 'in character.' This is one way of expressing how I was taken over by this masterpiece in the process of translating it" (xxiv). Translation would be an exaggerated instance of that "continual self-sacrifice, a continual extinction of personality" that T. S. Eliot, in "Tradition and the Individual Talent," takes to be "the progress of an artist" (40).

For a self-effacing author, the guise of translator can be a revealing camouflage. In the preface he appends to "Rappaccini's Daughter," Nathaniel Hawthorne claims that the story was taken from the writings of a "M. de l'Aubépine," whose other works include *Contes deux fois racontées*, "Le Voyage Céleste à Chemin de Fer," and "L'Artiste du Beau" (186–87). Since *aubépine* is French for hawthorn and the titles are French translations of works by Nathaniel Hawthorne, *Twice-Told Tales*, "The Celestial Railroad," and "The Artist of the Beautiful," respectively, the story's framework of fictional translation is a vehicle for the author to mock his own aspirations toward literary glory. And since "Rappaccini's Daughter" is set "very long ago" (188) in southern Italy, the specious claim that the text is a translation serves to create further distance from a tale that stretches a reader's credulity. Like many other works, it is following in the venerable tradition of *Don Quixote*, a complex metafiction that pretends to be the work of the Moorish historian Cid Hamete Benengeli, translated from Arabic into Spanish.

Major poets in various languages—among them Charles Baudelaire, Jorge Luis Borges, Stefan George, Ben Jonson, Eugenio Montale, Mu Dan, Boris Pasternak, and Shaul Tchernichovsky—have also devoted significant energy to translation. Yet, more than any other assessment of the endeavor, a poet's put-down, Robert Frost's familiar dictum that "poetry is what gets lost in translation" (159) remains for many the first, and last, word on the subject. John Keats thought otherwise. Though fascinated by the god Hyperion, the shepherd Endymion, and a tantalizing Grecian urn, he knew little Latin and less Greek. Without mediation, the *Iliad* and the *Odyssey* were impenetrable to him. When, one evening in October 1816 Keats's friend Charles Crowden Clarke brought over a translation of Homer, the two of them stayed up the entire night reading it aloud. Keats was enthralled by the work and within less than a day composed a response: "On First Looking into Chapman's Homer," an exquisite sonnet that is a poet's tribute to the power of translation. It is a paratext that highlights and celebrates linguistic transformation.

The famous poem begins by likening the speaker's experience as a reader to that of a European explorer. He has traveled extensively (i.e., read widely) but, for all his maritime adventures, knows one island (i.e., Homer) only by reputation. The situation changes dramatically when, introduced to a translation, he "heard Chapman speak out loud and bold" (l. 8). George Chapman published his English version of the *Iliad* and the *Odyssey* exactly two hundred years earlier, in 1616, yet that mediating text is still able to mesmerize the nineteenth-century reader. Keats concludes the sonnet by comparing himself first to an astronomer astonished "when a new planet swims into his ken" (l. 11) and then to the first Europeans to behold the Pacific. Like "stout Cortez" (historical accuracy if not metrical regularity would have demanded substitution of Vasco Núñez de Balboa) and his men before the vast new ocean, the reader of Chapman's Homer is left speechless, "silent, upon a peak in Darien" (l. 14).

Keats might have read any of nine other translations of the *Iliad* or the *Odyssey* or both that were available in 1816—by John Ogilby (1660, 1665), Thomas Hobbes (1676), John Ozell, William Broome, and William Oldisworth (1712), Alexander Pope (1715, 1725), James Macpherson (1773), William Cowper (1791), Joshua Bak (1797), P. Williams (1806), or James Morrice (1809). However, when he specifies George Chapman as his inspiration, he lifts him out of the shadows of history, making his darkness visible and transforming him into one of the most famous of all translators. Between a poet and a translator, it is usually the translator, even an obscure one, who has the last word. But, although Keats composed his words almost two centuries after Chapman, who died in 1634, ceased speaking, the final line of "Of First Looking into Chapman's Homer" is hypostressed. In contrast to the iambic pentameter of the rest of the poem, "Silent, upon a peak in Darien" contains only four stressed syllables, suggesting that, confronted with the force of a magnificent translation, words fail the poet, and the reader. Chapman's text diverges sharply from Homer's, but, if this be treason, Keats has made the most of it.

Translingual Memoirs of the New American Immigration

"Pour un écrivain, changer de langue, c'est écrire une lettre d'amour avec un dictionnaire" 'For a writer, to change languages is to write a love letter with a dictionary,' wrote aphorist E. M. Cioran, who changed languages anyway, from Romanian to French (39). It is difficult enough to put the right words in the right place in one language. "All you do," noted sportswriter Red Smith, "is sit down at a typewriter and open a vein" (qtd. in Reston 94). How vain, then, are those who presume to write compelling literature in a foreign tongue. "No man fully capable of his own language ever masters another," proclaimed George Bernard Shaw (254), who, despite the translingual accomplishments of Kamala Das, Isak Dinesen, Leah Goldberg, Ruth Prawer Jhabvala, Katia Kapovich, Yiyun Li, Bharati Mukherjee, Téa Obreht, Yoko Tawada, Ayelet Tsabari, Marina Tsvetaeva, and others, would probably have extended the pronouncement to women as well.

Though raised in Spanish, George Santayana wrote his poetry in English. Yet he declared that no poets can be great who do not use the language in which their mothers sang them lullabies. Nevertheless, Chaim Nachman Bialik became the greatest Hebrew poet of the twentieth century, though his mother tongue was Yiddish. Though the roster of translingual authors is long, switching languages is not easy. Yiyun Li reports that, during the difficult transition from Chinese to English, she attempted suicide twice. "I disowned my native language," she declares, with a twinge of guilt. The switch was neither smooth nor complete. "It is hard to feel in an adopted language," she recognizes, "yet it is impossible in my native language" (Li).

The tradition of authors who struggled to feel their way through an alien tongue extends for more than two millennia. Latin literature is said to have begun with Livius Andronicus, a Greek slave who wrote a Latin version of the *Odyssey*. The Latin canon was in no small measure the creation of men who adopted the language of Rome even though they were, like Seneca, Quintilian, Martial, and Lucan, from Spain, like Ausonius, from Gaul, or like Apuleius, Terence, and Augustine, from Africa. The thirteenth-century Catalan troubadour Ramon Vidal de Besalú moved freely among Catalan, lemosi (Occitan), and parladura francesa (French). Spanish American literature commences with Garcilaso de la Vega, a native speaker of Quechua, who wrote his masterpiece, *Commentarios reales*, in Spanish. The emergence of written literature in sub-Saharan Africa cannot be understood apart from the role of English, French, and Portuguese as translingual media.

English dominates current global discourse, and contemporary translinguals as diverse as André Aciman, Chimamanda Ngozi Adichie, Rabih Alameddine, Breyten Breytenbach, Edwidge Danticat, Junot Diaz, Cristina García, Xiaolu Guo, Mohsin Hamid, Li-Young Lee, Hisham Matar, Miroslav Penkov, and Charles Simic have chosen it as their medium of expression. If the United States is what, in a short book by that title, John F. Kennedy called "a nation of immigrants," (Kennedy) much of its literature has been the product of linguistic migration. As early as the eighteenth century, Phillis Wheatley wrote her poetry in English, the language of the culture that enslaved her, not in her native Fulani, and Michel-Guillaume-Jean de Crèvecoeur certified that he was an American farmer, not a French one, by publishing *Letters from an American Farmer* in English. (Two years later, in 1784, he reverted to his primary language, publishing an augmented *Lettres d'un cultivateur américain*.) Later authors who switched languages to American English have included literary immigrants as varied as Felipe Alfau, Julia Alvarez, Isaac Asimov, Louis Begley, Irving Berlin, Carlos Bulosan, Abraham Cahan, Marilyn Chin, Ursula Hegi, Aleksandar Hemon, Khaled Hosseini, Henry Kissinger,

Jerzy Kosinski, Shirley Geok-lin Lim, Azar Nafisi, Viet Thanh Nguyen, Ayn Rand, and Louis Zukofsky.

The American Dream promised penniless newcomers that, with pluck and luck, they, too, could, like Scotland native Andrew Carnegie, acquire vast wealth and power. It also promised access to the riches of the English language. Though he arrived in America with just a few English words in his pocket, Andrei Codrescu, variously adept at Romanian, German, Hungarian, and Russian, became a prominent Anglophonic poet. Ha Jin managed to win the National Book Award for a 1999 novel, *Waiting*, that, though set in the author's native China, he wrote in English. Less than twenty years after leaving Leningrad, Joseph Brodsky, who began writing in English while continuing to write in Russian, was named poet laureate of the United States. Recent memoirs of immigration often provide the most explicit accounts of the ordeal of translingualism. The mere publication of a memoir in English constitutes proof that the migrant author has succeeded in forging a new identity.

According to the powerful metaphor of the melting pot, assimilation is both desirable and uncomplicated. Immigrants exchange their old-world customs and beliefs for those of an American identity, and the process is usually depicted as a narrative of triumph. Language, the medium that both facilitates and validates the transformation, is not often called into question. Speakers of Italian, Norwegian, Polish, and Yiddish beget monolingual Anglophones who balk at looking back. Memoirs produced by the massive influx of Europeans to the United States from 1880 to 1920 rarely focus on language, as if writing in English were transparently natural and appropriate. But for later translinguals, particularly those who arrived in the United States during the "new immigration" of the past three decades, language has become opaque and resistant. Rejecting the paradigm of the melting pot in favor of a multicultural model, they no longer accept the exchange of languages as seamless and beneficent. The very title of Cristina García's 1992 novel about a family living in exile in Brooklyn, *Dreaming in Cuban*, suggests that it is language that shapes consciousness and defines self. And switching languages is not such an innocent transaction. Similarly, the titles of many recent memoirs foreground the ordeal of mastering a new language and problematize the medium they employ to tell their story. Eva Hoffman calls her book *Lost in Translation: A Life in a New Language*, Ilan Stavans calls his *On Borrowed Words: A Memoir of Language*, Firoozeh Dumas calls hers *Funny in Farsi: A Memoir of Growing Up Iranian in America*, and Ariel Dorfman calls his *Heading South, Looking North: A Bilingual Journey*. All underscore how language has become a metaphor for personal identity and itself the subject of the story. "There is a violence in the very language, American English, that we have to face, even as we work to make it ours, decolonize it so that it will express the truth of bodies beaten and banned," observes Meena Alexander in her 1993 memoir, *Fault Lines* (199). The English that Alexander, a native of India who has written in French, Hindi, and her mother tongue, Malayalam, employs is no longer transparent. Other translingual immigrant memoirs that could also be termed language memoirs include André Aciman's *Out of Egypt: A Memoir* (1994), Leila Ahmed's *A Border Passage: From Cairo to America* (1999), Galareh Asayesh's *Saffron Sky: A Life Between Iran and America* (1999), Andrei Codrescu's *An Involuntary Genius in America's Shoes (And What Happened Afterwards)* (2002), Gustavo Pérez Firmat's *Next Year in Cuba: A Cubano's Coming-of-Age in America* (1995), and Luc Sante's *The Factory of Facts* (1998). Even as they often culminate and exult in the ability to write in English, recent translingual memoirs interrogate their own medium.

However, for Carlos Bulosan, language is, like Flaubert's ideal author, everywhere present but nowhere visible. Born in the Philippines to a family of struggling farmers, he set off alone for the United States in 1930 while still just seventeen. In his 1946 autobiography, *America Is in the Heart*, Bulosan recounts the bigotry, poverty, and violence he endured while toiling in fields and canneries along the West Coast. Less than halfway through the book, he learns the address of his brother Macario in San Luis Obispo, California, and begins to write him a letter. Bulosan has had very little formal schooling and disembarked at the port of Seattle speaking almost none of the local language. Yet now, after a few years in America, he is writing Macario in English. It is a dramatic moment, one that confirms the nascent writer in his literary vocation: "Then it came to me, like a revelation, that I could actually write understandable English. I was seized with happiness. I wrote slowly and coldly, drinking the wine when I stopped, laughing silently and crying. When the long letter was finished, a letter which was actually a story of my life, I jumped to my feet and shouted through my tears: 'They can't silence me any more! I'll tell the world what they have done to me!'" (180). Nowhere in his memoir does Bulosan mention even the name of his native tongue, Tagalog, which has simply been expunged from the record. Despite passing reference to difficulties in understanding and speaking English after he arrives in the United States, *America Is in the Heart* testifies to the author's success in finding a local voice to articulate his experiences in the United States. The impassioned letter that Bulosan writes to his brother is an early draft of the entire book that he will write in English, one whose emphasis is on the hardships of labor, not language.

Romanian immigrant M. E. Ravage titled his 1917 memoir *An American in the Making*, and mastery of English was crucial to Ravage's success at making himself not only into an American but also into a professional writer. However, the memoir makes but a single, oblique reference to the language its author spoke before acquiring English. During his first few days in New York, Ravage is hawking chocolates to Christmas shoppers along Fourteenth Street when another peddler suddenly addresses him "in my native tongue." Ravage asks the stranger "how he had recognized me for a Rumanian" (69), and the reader is left to infer that the author's native tongue is Romanian. Five chapters later, however, he refers to Yiddish, which he knows well enough to teach his friend Esther, as "the humble mother tongue" (117). Whatever their order of priority, though, it seems that both Romanian and Yiddish preceded Ravage's command of English, which he acquires by attending lectures and classes in the evenings, after shifts at the shirt factory. He recounts being stumped by John Milton's poetry, but, in less than six years, Ravage is fluent enough to offer himself as a tutor in English, at twenty-five cents an hour.

A more recent memoirist might have reflected on the peculiar qualities of Romanian, Yiddish, and English, how they are mutually untranslatable, how English enables specific thoughts and creates a different identity than is possible in either Romanian or Yiddish. Yet for Ravage, language seems to be a neutral tool. Picking up one, he discards another, without waxing sentimental over the music and meanings that are unique to Romanian, Yiddish, and English, respectively. With the same resolve he brought to finding work and housing, he applies himself to overcoming the obstacle of language. He takes a class in elocution at the University of Missouri, recites long passages from Mark Twain, and jots down unfamiliar words he overhears in conversations. For Ravage, English is a simple test of fortitude, not the intricate instrument for recalibrating identity—among Russian, French, and English—that it is in Vladimir Nabokov's memoir, *Speak, Memory* (1951, 1966). But the publication and warm reception of *An American in the Making* proved that he passed that test.

The classic assimilationist memoir, Mary Antin's *The Promised Land*, recounts how an anxious girl from a shtetl in the Russian Pale became an ostensibly sanguine American woman. That transformation is conceived largely through language, the novice Anglophone author's proudly won ability to "think in English without an accent" (282). Antin's autobiography is in effect a linguistic palimpsest, an elaboration and reconception of an extensive letter that a precocious fourteen-year-old wrote in Yiddish to her maternal uncle, Moshe Hayyim Weltman, across the Atlantic, then translated into English and published, as *From Plotzk to Boston* (1899), when she was eighteen. However, the final English version, published as *The Promised Land* in 1912, obscures its author's ordeal of translingualism, the fearful process of acquiring and articulating a new self through a new language.

The Promised Land both embodies and celebrates Yiddish-speaking Mashinke's metamorphosis into Mary, the young woman who conquers Boston through English, "this beautiful language in which I think" (164). It is the tongue she praises without a trace of treason, of guilt over abandoning her *mame loshn*. Extolling the medium in which she has chosen to write, Antin says of English, ". . . in any other language happiness is not so sweet, logic is not so clear" (164). Suppressing any doubts about the virtues of the melting pot, Antin tells her sweet story of success in clear and happy English. Borrowing a term more often used to describe racial camouflage, Hana Wirth-Nesher calls Antin's strategy "linguistic passing, where erasure of Hebrew and Yiddish would be her submission to the nativist pressures and linguistic policies of her day" (57). By contrast, Anzia Yezierska, who left the Russian Empire for New York at almost the same time and almost the same age as Antin left for Boston, explicitly dramatizes the ordeal of switching from Yiddish to English. In her 1920 story collection *Hungry Hearts*, the Jewish immigrant Shenah Pessah demonstrates the same exhilaration as Antin's but not yet her linguistic command. "I got yet a lot of luck," Shenah Pessah declares. "I learned myself English from a Jewish English reader, and one of the boarders left me a grand book. When I only begin to read, I forget I'm on this world. It lifts me on wings with high thoughts" (Yezierska 8).

In 1959, sixty-five years after Antin left Polotzk, Eva Hoffman, too, sailed across the Atlantic to a new life, first in Canada and later the United States. Like Antin, Hoffman was thirteen years old when she left Europe. As Hoffman tells her story, in English, she still feels nostalgia for what she left behind, not least a language. And she employs the Polish term *tęsknota* to identify this sad longing, and to indicate that her English lexicon is still not entirely adequate to encompass her emotions.

The implied reader of Antin's *The Promised Land* is exclusively Anglophonic, and the book comes equipped with a glossary to assist in pronouncing and understanding the relatively few foreign terms, in Yiddish, Hebrew, Russian, and German, that Antin employs. The fact that such common words as *icon, ruble, Purim, vodka, Torah,* and *pogrom* are thought to require translation suggests how hermetically monolingual is the culture in which Antin would now position herself. She reveals none of the anguish or regret that later translinguals would express. When she enrolls in a Chelsea public school, Antin cannot even name the days of the week in English, yet she dismisses the enormous linguistic challenge she has to take on with the pronouncement "I was Jew enough to have an aptitude for language in general, and to bend my mind earnestly to my task" (*Promised Land* 163). Of the Jewish language that she abjures, Yiddish, Antin says nothing.

Hoffman, by contrast, accentuates the ordeal of switching languages. On the ship from Gdynia to Montreal, she resists the English lessons that another passenger offers. And when the family settles in Vancouver, she is distraught over how imperfectly the local language fits her universe: "... the problem is that the signifier has become severed from the signified," she explains in the academic English she later mastered. "The words I learn now don't stand for things in the same way they did in my native tongue" (106).

Instead of the seamless transition from one language to another that Antin claims to have enjoyed, Hoffman finds herself suspended, inarticulately, between Polish and English: "Polish, in a short time, has atrophied, shriveled from sheer uselessness. Its words don't apply to my new experiences; they're not coeval with any of the objects, or faces, or the very air I breathe in the daytime. In English, words have not penetrated to those layers of my psyche from which a private conversation could proceed" (107). Whereas Antin's accomplished autobiography is testimony to her mastery of English, Hoffman's dwells on the tribulations and imperfections of translingualism. "Shuddup," reports Hoffman (104), is the first word she understands in English, a forbidding tongue that leaves the newcomer temporarily mute, and permanently at a loss.

From its title to the final paragraph, in which Hoffman recites the recondite names of flora in a Massachusetts garden, *Lost in Translation: A Life in a New Language* problematizes its own medium and uses language as a metaphor for talking about the first four decades of a woman's life. "Like everybody," concludes Hoffman, "I am the sum of my languages" (273). It is the problematic transition from Polish to English that constitutes the great drama of Hoffman's life and the central theme of her published life.

Hoffman adduces the distinctive Polish *polot*—"a word that combines the meanings of dash, inspiration, and flying" (71)—and the peculiarities of the English *friend* (148) to argue that linguistic systems are not interchangeable. In effect endorsing the Sapir-Whorf thesis, the doctrine of linguistic determinism by which each language is unique in the way that it governs a speaker's apprehension of experience, Hoffman is aware that Polish enables certain thoughts and emotions she can never have in any other language and that English imposes perceptions and conceptions she might otherwise resist. When, as a present for her fifteenth birthday, Hoffman is given a diary, her decision to construct a daily textual self in English rather than Polish is as momentous as the first letter that Bulosan writes to his brother in English. However, proceeding "as if the totality of the world and mind were coeval with the totality of language" (217), Hoffman lacks the linguistic innocence of either Bulosan or Antin. For Antin, achieving her dream of becoming an American means setting her agile mind to memorizing English vocabulary and then expunging Yiddish. But for Hoffman, translingualism leaves untidy traces. Polish obtrudes through her English, with a reminder that languages are never exactly commensurate, that each always processes experience in its own unique way. Antin would have her readers believe that language is merely instrumental, a tool that can be adapted or discarded not only without trauma but also without distorting thought. But for Hoffman language is so fundamental and problematic that it serves as a metaphor for many of the other anxieties that she experiences. *Lost in Translation* is suffused with the melancholy awareness that no single tongue suffices to digest the universe. Her English, unlike Antin's, is inflected with a mournful sense of its own inadequacy.

Like Hoffman, Padma Hejmadi resisted English. According to her 1999 memoir, *Room to Fly*, Hejmadi, who was born in southern India, refused to attend school at age five because, a native speaker of Konkani, a mother tongue without a script, she rejected being forced into literacy in English. Growing up in a polyglot household in which four languages (Hindi, Tamil, English, and Konkani) were spoken on an average day, she diagnoses herself as "afflicted with a lifelong interior astigmatism" (21). The highly literate English in which she eventually articulates her memories is haunted by the haphazardness and inadequacy of her chosen language as well as by "the infinite vocabularies of silence" (93).

Ariel Dorfman begins his memoir when a last-minute change in plans kept him from his job in Chile's presidential palace, at the moment that a military junta stormed the building and killed its occupants. *Heading South, Looking North* crosscuts between chapters that scan its author's fifty-six years and those that recount in detail the violent fall of Salvador Allende, leader of Latin America's first popularly elected socialist government. The book basks in quickened memories of "the best years of my life" (246), a fervent time when Dorfman—alienated in crucial ways from each of the three countries he has called home, Argentina, Chile, and the United States—felt connected to others in an ardent effort at social transformation. In his memoir and in everything he has written since 1973, insists Dorfman, he bears witness to the wrenching experience of idealism betrayed.

Yet betrayal of a more fundamental sort is the true theme of *Heading South, Looking North*. If indeed *traduttori, traditori*, translators are traitors, Dorfman's life—faithful to two languages and three nationalities—has been a sustained act of treachery. Beyond its value as a document of the Allende debacle, Dorfman's book, begun in Spanish but completed and published in English, is an exploration of duplicity—"the anxiety, the richness, the madness of being double" (42). It is the fluent testimony of a man whom circumstances and stubborn ambition have made into "a bigamist of language" (270). *Heading South, Looking North*—a schismatic title that would have been as meaningful in reverse, as *Heading North, Looking South*—is another work that that not only traces but, in its very mastery of the verbal medium, demonstrates the identity of an author who lives between languages.

He remains an outsider, a "wanderer in love with the transitory" (6). In the United States, Dorfman is Chilean, in Chile *norteamericano*; to the general population of each society, he is an unassimilable anomaly, a relatively affluent, cosmopolitan, Jewish intellectual. The United States that entices Dorfman is a society publicly dedicated to personal reinvention, to jettisoning prior memories and languages, and the young man's repudiation of part of his past is most apparent not only in his abandonment of Spanish but also in his temptation to betray his own father. During the McCarthy hysteria over Soviet subversion, he comes close to informing his devoutly patriotic teacher that Adolfo Dorfman is a Communist. Eventually, though, Yankee xenophobia becomes too intense for the family to remain in New York, and they relocate again, to Chile, where Dorfman's dormant Spanish awakens. One of the most striking passages in the book describes how Castilian syntax and lexicon infiltrate Dorfman's being, transforming him into a Chilean, while an Anglophonic self maintains its discrete identity: "I was not aware of what was happening to my mind: it was a subtle, cunning, camouflaged process, the vocabulary and the grammatical code seeping into my consciousness slowly, turning me into a person who, without acknowledging it, began to function in either language" (115). In Spanish, he writes a scathing, best-selling indictment of Yankee imperialism, and he vows ". . . to renounce English along with the America of the North and its empire and its culture, renounce and denounce and try to suppress henceforth the man inside me who had spent his life identifying through that language, speaking and writing himself into personhood in that language" (101). *Heading South, Looking North* demonstrates the failure of that resolution, that neither the English Dorfman nor the Spanish Dorfman can be permanently suppressed. Written in lucid English prose (a Spanish version followed), it is an affirmation of its author's bilingual identity, of a life suspended between North and South and English and Spanish.

Born in Mexico City, Ilan Stavans became a citizen of the United States in 1994. But, though he wrote his 2001 memoir, *On Borrowed Words*, in English, he calls Yiddish his mother tongue and Spanish his father tongue. The book follows its author's restless rambles in Europe, Israel, and Cuba and through infatuations with Marxism, Judaism, and several women. However, as its subtitle stresses, *On Borrowed Words* is *A Memoir of Language*, and it is in and through words that its author finds himself, lost. "I was a wandering soul, inhabiting other people's tongues" (224) declares Stavans, brilliantly fluent but never at home in Yiddish, Spanish, or English.

The immediate effect of the liberalizing Hart-Celler Act of 1965 was a massive increase in immigration to the United States. A long-term consequence was the flowering of translingual memoirs decades later. Too numerous to encompass in a single chapter, the new newcomers are more wary than their predecessors about the project of acculturation and, specifically, about switching languages. Born in Belgium in 1954, Luc Sante was five years old when his parents moved to New Jersey and forced him to set aside his native tongue for the language of an alien environment. Sante became a professional writer in English, though his 1998 memoir, *The Factory of Facts*, says of his two languages, French and English, "one is a wound and the other is a prosthesis" (269).

"The fact that I / am writing to you / in English," writes poet Gustavo Pérez Firmat, in English, "already falsifies what I / wanted to tell you" (*Next Year* 126). A native of Cuba relocated to Miami then Ann Arbor and Durham (he moved to New York after publication of his memoir), Pérez Firmat published two autobiographies, one in English and one in Spanish. So did Esmeralda Santiago, who was born in Puerto Rico in 1948 and moved to New York when she was thirteen. For her 1993 memoir, *When I Was Puerto Rican*, Santiago found herself unable to render into English such distinctive Puerto Rican concepts as *dignidad* and *jíbaro* and instead kept them in Spanish, with a glossary in the back for the benefit of monolingual Anglophones (*When I Was*). For the Spanish version of *When I Was Puerto Rican*, published the following year, as *Cuando era puertorriqueña*, Santiago added a special preface that discusses her linguistic predicament: how she is torn between two tongues, Spanish and English, and can express certain feelings only in her native Spanish (*Cuando*).

Thirty years after abandoning Iran for California at the age of seven, Firoozeh Dumas can mock her mother's malapropisms and recall how her father "had two left tongues" (9). Writing confidently in American English, she can afford to call her flippant memoir *Funny in Farsi*, but for many others the ordeal of being wrenched from one language and thrust into another is no laughing matter. Growing up in Malacca amid a polyglot mélange of Malay, Chinese, and Hindi, Shirley Geok-lin Lim is reminded by her British teachers that "English was only on loan, a borrowed tongue which we could only garble" (121). The English with which she wrote her 1996 memoir, *Among the White Moon Faces*, is not garbled, though it is cast into the anxious role of subject as well as medium.

Skepticism about the very possibility of genuine translingualism is perhaps most vividly embodied in Marjorie Agosín, a literary transplant who was in her late teens in 1974 when her family moved from Chile to the state of Georgia. However, despite residence in the United States of more than forty years, she cannot bring herself to write in English. Agosín's memoir, *The Alphabet in My Hands: A Writing Life*, was published in English translation before the Spanish original, but by the time she came to write it, in 2000, she had come to accept her identity as "a Jewish writer who writes in Spanish and lives in America" (155). Recognizing that she will never be at home in English, she writes, "The English language never took on the texture of my soul, the feel of my skin" (151). Though she is, for practical purposes, bilingual, Agosín declares, "For me, life between two cultures was no life at all" (152). Nevertheless, for most of the other translinguals who have employed English to record and reflect on their experiences of dislocation, life exists within, between, and beyond their languages.

INCUBUS AND THE ESPERANTO MOVIE INDUSTRY

Hollywood has long been a laboratory of translingualism, inducing some of the world's major filmmakers—including Michelangelo Antonioni, Ingmar Bergman, Bernardo Bertolucci, Alfonso Cuarón, Michael Curtiz, Miloš Forman, Werner Herzog, Alejandro González Iñárritu, Fritz Lang, Ang Lee, Ernst Lubitsch, Roman Polanski, Jean Renoir, Josef von Sternberg, Billy Wilder, and William Wyler—to make at least one film in English. But American monolingualism is nowhere more insistent than at the movies. In Ridley Scott's medieval epic *Kingdom of Heaven* (2005), Saladin, played by Ghassan Massoud, negotiates with a hostile French Crusader in halting modern English. In Stanley Kubrick's *Spartacus* (1960), it is not Latin in which Tony Curtis, playing Roman slave Antoninus, delivers his lines, inflected by the Bronx. It is "I am Spartacus"—not "Ego Spartacus"—that thousands of captured Roman slaves proclaim out of loyalty to their rebel leader. Like Marlene Dietrich, Catherine the Great grew up speaking German, but, despite all her accomplishments, the Russian monarch, who wrote her memoirs in French, never spoke English, as Dietrich does portraying her in Josef von Sternberg's *The Scarlet Empress* (1934).

The conventions of the Hollywood Western compel Native American characters to stammer their thoughts in pidgin English, even when conversing among themselves. Indian speak with forked tongue, when that tongue is tied by the studio chiefs. But Kevin Costner's *Dances with Wolves* (1990) stands out from the pack by conducting much of its dialogue in Lakota Sioux, with subtitles for the benefit of viewers who cannot comprehend the words of the Great Plains tribe. More typical is Delmer Davies's *Broken Arrow* (1950), whose narrator, Tom Jeffords (James Stewart), announces at the outset, "I was involved in the story and what I have to tell happened exactly as you see it—the only change will be that when the Apaches speak, they will speak in our language." Putting the words of an alien tongue into the mouths of characters not fluent in it seems like a minor concession to audience deficiency, until one tries to imagine *The Bridge on the River Kwai* (1957) if the script had obliged its British and American prisoners of war to communicate among themselves in Japanese. In *Waterloo* (1970), Rod Steiger's Napoleon speaks only the language of his Anglo-Saxon adversary.

At the beginning of the 1983 remake of *To Be or Not to Be*, the dark comedy of a Polish theater troupe trapped in wartime Warsaw, actors Mel Brooks and Anne Bancroft exchange angry words, and the medium of their altercation is, appropriately, Polish. However, several minutes into the proceedings, a disembodied, Olympian voice announces, "Ladies and gentlemen, in the interests of sanity and clarity, the rest of this movie will *not* be in Polish." And Brooks and Bancroft immediately resume their squabble, in English. *To Be or Not to Be* thereby mocks the movie convention that demands suspension of linguistic disbelief; even as the actors use only English, we are asked to assume that their characters are really speaking something else. Although Hollywood was created largely by immigrants from Eastern Europe, the founding moguls made their movies talk almost exclusively in the language of their adopted country. As far as the studios have been concerned, if English was good enough for Jesus Christ, as it was in *The Robe* (1953), *The Last Temptation of Christ* (1988), and other biblical dramas (but notably not *The Passion of the Christ* [2004]), it was good enough for Moses, Alexander the Great, Christopher Columbus, Michelangelo, Wolfgang Amadeus Mozart, Marie Curie, Joseph Stalin, Oskar Schindler, Eva Perón, Bugs Bunny, Darth Vader, and Black Panther.

It was good enough for James Fenimore Cooper, Herman Melville, Emily Dickinson, Mark Twain, William Faulkner, and Toni Morrison, but the literature of the United States has also been written in many languages other than English. Texts in Arabic, Chinese, French, German, Hawaiian, Italian, Navajo, Norwegian, Polish, Russian, Spanish, Swedish, Vietnamese, Welsh, and Yiddish, among many others, also deserve a place in the American literary canon and have attracted scholarly attention (Øverland; Shell and Sollors; Shell, *American Babel*; and Sollors). However, the enormous costs of creating and marketing commercial feature films discourage linguistic variety. It is a safer investment to produce a script in English than in Czech, Nahuatl, or Zulu—in fact than in any alternative to the world's most popular second language.

Nevertheless, a small body of American feature films in languages other than English does exist. During the 1930s, the first decade of talking movies, more than sixty features, including *Der Yiddishe Koenig Lear* (1935), *Yidl Mitn Fidl* (1936), and *Mirele Efros* (1939), were produced in the United States in Yiddish. Spanish-language productions included *El presidio* (1930), *El tenorio del harem* (1931), *¿Cuándo te suicidas?* (1931), *Contra la corriente* (1935), *Alas sobre el Chaco* (1935), *El día que me quieras* (1936), and *La vida bohemia* (1937). A smaller group, including *La donna bianca* (1930), *La vacanza del diavolo* (1931), and *Amore e morte* (1932), was made in Italian. More recently, Wayne Wang made *Chan Is Missing* (1982) in Cantonese and English, *Eat a Bowl of Tea* (1989) in Mandarin and English, and *The Joy Luck Club* (1993) in Cantonese, Mandarin, and English. Tony Bui filmed *Three Seasons* (1999) and Ham Tran filmed *The Anniversary* (2003) in Vietnamese. *El Super* (1979), *El Norte* (1983), *La Ciudad (The City)* (1998), and *Maria Full of Grace* (2004) were each made mostly in Spanish, as was *Hombres armados* (*Men with Guns* [1998]), whose writer-director, John Sayles, taught himself the language and determined to create dialogue appropriate to his screenplay's setting, an unnamed Latin American country. Like *Dances with Wolves*, *The Godfather Part II* (1975) also makes use of English subtitles, during the extended flashback to Vito Corleone's childhood in Sicily, when he, quite naturally, speaks Italian. And not the least unusual feature of *The Passion of the Christ* is the fact that, in order to underscore the biblical story's authenticity, director Mel Gibson had his characters speak Latin and Aramaic throughout (though most would have been speaking Greek instead). In Gibson's 2006 *Apocalypto*, set in the Yucatan in the early sixteenth century, the characters speak the Yucatec Maya language.

Derived from Greek, the term *hapax legomenon* refers to a word or phrase that occurs only once in the recorded history of a language. And within the extensive archives of American film production the singular work that remains a cinematic *hapax legomenon* is a seventy-six-minute allegorical horror fantasy called *Incubus*. Written and directed by Leslie Stevens in 1965, it is said to be the only feature film ever made in Esperanto: "*Incubus* estas la unusola filmo usona iam farita tute en Esperanto," declares the website marketing its DVD (*Incubus, Movie Fanatic*). Thirty years after its release, *Incubus* was lost to American audiences, because of negligence at a Los Angeles laboratory that was storing what its producer, Anthony Taylor, believed were all the existing prints. However, in 1996 he discovered one surviving copy at the Cinémathèque Française in Paris, where weekly midnight screenings had become a cult ritual. Following protracted negotiations to make a copy and take it out of France, Taylor restored the dilapidated print, superimposed English subtitles over the French ones, and put the work back into circulation in the United States in 1999. A DVD was marketed in 2001, and the film was aired on the Sci Fi Channel in 2002. Still the only feature film ever made in Esperanto, the artificial language introduced by its inventor, Warsaw oculist Ludwig L. Zamenhof, in 1887, *Incubus* has acquired a devoted American following its unexpected rediscovery. Though one reviewer, writing for fantasticadaily.com under the byline Mervius, dismissed the work as "dated, melodramatic, and silly," Keith Bailey at badmovieplanet.com called it "a visual feast" and "a weirdly compelling movie," and *TV Guide* described it as "a mind-boggling curiosity" (*TV Guide*). At Daily-Reviews.com, Rick Luehr, assigning it four out of five stars, called *Incubus* "one of the most original films in American cinema history." Though *Entertainment Weekly* and Salon.com both reported on the return of *Incubus*, other prominent publications continued to ignore the film.

Because of its rationalized grammar, simplified phonology, phonetic orthography, and a familiar lexicon drawn from several natural languages, a working knowledge of Esperanto can be acquired with relative ease and speed. Zamenhof designed his linguistic system to facilitate universal adoption, in the hope that a world language would encourage global peace and justice; in Esperanto, the name of the language itself means "I hope." And the hope is that adoption of a common tongue would eliminate many of the causes of misunderstanding and oppression. "Ni estas movado por la homa emancipiĝo" 'We are a movement for human emancipation,' concludes the "Prague Manifesto" issued by the Eighty-First World Esperanto Congress in 1996 ("Manifesto de Prago").

The Universal Esperanto Association estimates that 10 to 15 million people speak the language, though other calculations place the figure as low as 100,000. Since Esperanto complements but does not replace the native languages of its dévotés and since it is L1 (the native language) for virtually no one, use of Zamenhof's artificial language constitutes an act of translingualism. Scattered throughout the world, with concentrations in parts of Asia and Europe, the Esperanto population is relatively sparse in North America, hardly enough in one location to keep a movie theater filled for a week. Despite 30 million Spanish speakers within the United States, attendance at Spanish-language films is anemic. At theaters in the United States, the gross for *Y tu mamá también*, at that point the most commercially successful of any film not produced in English, was $13,839,658 ("Box Office Business for *Y tu mamá también*"), a figure easily outdone during the year of its release, 2001, by the lavish blockbuster manqué *Pearl Harbor*, whose take, at $198,542,554, was considered disappointing ("Box Office Business for *Pearl Harbor*"). At least for the purposes of capitalizing on the North American market, releasing a film in Esperanto was even more perverse than releasing one in Spanish, however appropriate the invented language might be to the themes of the *Incubus* screenplay.

Except for Stevens, who initiated and drove the project, the limited population of Esperantists did not include anyone in the cast or crew of *Incubus*. Stevens had created and produced *The Outer Limits* and recruited several associates, including young William Shatner, for a movie that promised to be as strange as anything on that science fiction television series. Before production began, everyone was sent to "Esperanto Camp," a ten-day session of instruction by tutors in the language. Once shooting began, Stevens insisted that only Esperanto be spoken on the set, a restriction that one actor later claimed resulted in the dazed look visible on the faces of characters. Closer in style to Japanese Noh performance, the symbolist theater of Maurice Maeterlinck or William Butler Yeats, and German expressionist cinema than classic Hollywood naturalism, the film's hieratic acting, like Esperanto itself, strives to embody universal verities.

Set in the fictional village of Nomen Tuum (Latin for Thy Name, an invocation of the Lord's Prayer that immediately alerts the viewer to the presence of religious themes), the film dramatizes a fierce struggle by the forces of darkness to vanquish a human exemplar of virtue. In the opening sequence, Kia (Allyson Ames), a beautiful young succubus, entices a vain and lecherous man into death and damnation. It is her third conquest of the day, but Kia is not content. "I am weary of luring ugly souls into the pit," she complains to Amael (Eloise Hardt), an older succubus. "I want to find a saint and cut him down." The opportunity soon presents itself when she observes Marc (played by Shatner, a year before becoming Captain James T. Kirk in *Star Trek*) walking out of church. Accompanied by his virtuous sister and soul mate, Arndis (Ann Atmar), Marc is a military hero still recovering from wounds incurred during courageous defense of his comrades. Amael warns Kia that Marc is a genuinely good man and not to underestimate the power of love to thwart her evil designs. "Then he has a soul worth fighting for!" insists Kia, eager to take on the challenge (*Incubus*, Written).

The rest of the film follows Kia's efforts to seduce and destroy Marc. Marc is indeed smitten by the ravishing stranger, but he resists her entreaties to follow her to the sea. Instead, Marc draws Kia, who falls helplessly in love with her prey, back inland, toward the church. Indignant that an unsuspecting succubus has been contaminated by goodness, Amael summons up the Incubus (Milos Milos) from subterranean depths. Along with a band of succubi, the Incubus sets out to retrieve Kia and wreak vengeance on Marc. Revenge takes the form of demonic rape of Marc's sister, but the effort to deliver Kia leads to a climactic confrontation on the threshold of the church. Appropriating the form of a monstrous snarling goat, the Incubus engages in mortal—and immortal—combat with Marc, a human agent of divine love. And loses.

Preposterous as realistic drama, *Incubus* must be read as psychomachia, an allegory of the struggle between the forces of light and the forces of darkness for possession of the soul. Aside from the language of its dialogue, the most remarkable feature of the film is its expressive black-and-white lighting and cinematography. Early in a career that would earn him three Academy Awards, for *Butch Cassidy and the Sundance Kid*, *American Beauty*, and *The Road to Perdition*, cinematographer Conrad Hall deliberately overexposed footage in the first half of the film, set in luminous daylight before the arrival of the Incubus. However, moments after Kia, pretending to be a lost traveler, arrives at the cottage that Marc shares with Arndis, an unexpected lunar eclipse darkens the frame, temporarily blinding Marc's sister. The rest of the film belongs to the night, to the powers of darkness that, like the succubi dressed in dark cassocks when they perform their black mass, set about to extinguish the radiance emanating from Arndis and Marc.

Examined in the light of day, *Incubus* is silly stuff, the kind of hokey dross that thrives on midnight screenings, when reason and discernment are asleep and the rowdy spirit of a youthful crowd proclaims collective carnival. To relish fully the film's campy bravura, it might help to experience it stoned, the condition of cast and crew, Hall claims in an interview on the DVD, throughout the ten days in May 1965 that it took to finish shooting. While they dominate contemporary geopolitics, Manichean oppositions of absolute evil and absolute good disappeared from serious art when chiaroscuro entered painting. Filmed in part at the Mission San Antonio in Monterey, California, *Incubus* is a postmodern invocation of pre-Reformation Christian motifs. On the DVD, Taylor, the producer, recounts how, in order to obtain permission to use the old Spanish Catholic mission, as well as the state park at Big Sur, he disguised the project, submitting a stealth script as an alternative to what they were in fact shooting. However, its title, *Religious Legends of Old Monterey*, might do as well for the finished work.

A pioneer of independent American cinema at a time when big studios still controlled production, distribution, and exhibition, *Incubus* was the last film released by Daystar, a company created by Taylor. Its budget was approximately $100,000, according to Taylor, who recalls how, after he was unable to get his film screened in commercial theaters in the United States, Daystar soon went bankrupt. One of the practical reasons for the peculiar choice of language for *Incubus* had been the belief that the art house market, accustomed to presenting subtitled films from overseas, would be receptive. However, any expectation that Esperanto, the language of hope, might be good for business proved unfounded. Aside from a few festivals as well as in France where, without being canonized along with Jerry Lewis, it was hailed in *Paris Match* by novelist Julien Green as "le meilleur film fantastique depuis Nosferatu" 'the greatest fantasy film since *Nosferatu*' (Wagner), *Incubus* remained unseen for more than thirty years.

Hall's innovative camera work, with contributions from William Fraker (who later served as director of photography for more than forty productions, including, not surprisingly, *Rosemary's Baby*), is still worth viewing. When the succubus Kia, finding herself in a church, panics at the sight of Christian effigies, the camera rotates vertically 180 degrees as she dashes past, back out into the night. Another shot frames her in the distance, through the window of an abandoned house. The effect, in that as in other long shots and in the use of low angles, is to aestheticize the proceedings, reinforcing the use of black and white and Esperanto to lift the story into myth.

Translated into English, much of the dialogue is as wooden as the burning stick Marc uses to defeat the Incubus. "He has defiled you with love," Amael, disgusted by Marc's pious hold on Kia, declares. "Revenge, sister, revenge!" Figures in an allegory, the characters declaim instead of speaking. But, heard in Esperanto, an artificial language alien to movie soundtracks, the hackneyed, sententious lines are defamiliarized, their speakers deautomatized. What most distinguishes *Incubus* from the black mass of formulaic horror flicks is its use of Zamenhof's linguistic invention to make strange the bizarre clichés of demonic possession. In *What's Up, Tiger Lily?* (1966), Woody Allen dubbed incongruous English lines over the dialogue of a Japanese gangster movie, thereby defamiliarizing tediously familiar content. The unusual choice of language in *Incubus* likewise produces an alienation effect, though one that was not at least intended to be comic. Esperanto, which appears to be dubbed over Ames's voice and pronounced by Shatner with the French accent of his native Montreal, helps stylize what might have seemed the record of a self-indulgent troupe of actors camped at Big Sur. Anglophone viewers are even able to experience another layer of abstraction. In addition to the American version (with English subtitles blocked in over the French that Taylor was not able to remove), the DVD offers the variant that was a hit at the Cinémathèque Française—and an opportunity to experience *Incubus* through the distancing scrims of both an Esperanto soundtrack and French subtitles.

Nomen Tuum could be located in any wooded temperate region that possesses a seacoast. The war that Marc has just returned from is never specified, nor is the army for which he fought. The year, too, is indeterminate; guileless siblings Marc and Arndis share a timeless fairy-tale cottage in a world in which the most advanced technological device is a church bell. Similarly, the use of Esperanto enables the story to elude the coordinates of space and time. Like the Incubus, it is otherworldly. Natural languages, by contrast, anchor their speakers in a particular culture and era. The modern English in which Stevens wrote his screenplay, before it was translated into Esperanto, would have undercut his aspirations to transcend the familiar. And the international cast he assembled, including narrator Paolo Cossa from Italy, Milos from Yugoslavia, Shatner from Canada, and others from various regions of the United States, would have emitted a distracting array of accents in English. However, Esperanto, like mathematics, is universal, and it is an appropriate medium in which to reenact the eternal clash of good and evil.

Viewing *Incubus* in the twenty-first century as a lost cinematic curiosity, a newly opened time capsule from the 1960s, adds yet another layer of abstraction to the experience. Furthermore, the production that disguised itself as *Religious Legends of Old Monterey* has itself become legendary not only for its use of Esperanto and its disappearance from circulation for three decades. The infamous "curse of *Incubus*" now shadows the film, like one of the screenplay's own malevolent succubi. According to Shatner, who on the DVD seems to relish spinning supernatural tales about a supernatural movie (he also alleges that Gene Roddenberry intended to make *Star Trek* in Esperanto), an unknown hippie who wandered near the set in Big Sur was treated rudely by the cast and crew. In response, he pronounced a malediction on them all. The consequence—or at least, the aftermath—was not only the commercial failure of *Incubus* and the bankruptcy of Daystar. A few weeks after the film wrapped, Atmar committed suicide, and within the year, after appearing in *The Russians Are Coming, The Russians Are Coming*, Milos killed

Barbara Ann Thompson, the estranged fifth wife of Mickey Rooney, and then himself. Later, Hardt's daughter was kidnapped and murdered. And Dominic Frontiere, who composed the eerie music for the film, spent nine months in prison on a charge of evading taxes for tickets to the 1980 Super Bowl he had scalped. Shatner and Hall thrived, but Stevens, whose marriage to Ames ended in divorce not long after completion of *Incubus*, died suddenly of a blood clot in 1998.

The cover of its DVD advertises *Incubus* as "the only film shot entirely in the artificial language of Esperanto." The claim is belied by *Angoroj*, a crime drama set in Paris that was completed in 1964, a year before *Incubus*. Despondent over his failure to find a distributor for *Angoroj* (Esperanto for *Agonies*) and to recoup his substantial financial investment in it, filmmaker Jacques-Louis Mahé reportedly destroyed most of the prints. The film is not readily available but, at only sixty-one minutes, would not qualify in any case as the first feature-length film in Esperanto. *La eta knabino* (1997) is only six minutes and *Senmova* (2010) only fourteen.

A few more widely known movies have offered bit parts to Zamenhof's artificial language. In *The Great Dictator* (1940), Charles Chaplin, mocking the anti-Semitism of his Hitler proxy, Adenoid Hynkel, flaunts Zamenhof's Jewish background by printing the signs in shops windows of the Tomania ghetto in Esperanto. (In *Mein Kampf*, Hitler denounced Esperanto as part of a global Jewish conspiracy, and his Nazi regime singled Esperantists out for elimination, killing all three of Zamenhof's children.) In *Gattaca* (1997), a dystopian drama about a totalitarian society in which genetic engineering eliminates individual freedom, the fact that the public address system issues official announcements in Esperanto, a medium created through linguistic engineering, intensifies the dread of sacrificing our humanity to technocracy. Poetry and fiction have been published in Esperanto, which is said to have thus far produced a library of thirty thousand volumes. But it was mere whimsy when Elvis Costello issued the liner notes to his 1986 album *Blood and Chocolate* in Esperanto and Michael Jackson used Esperanto in his 1995 music video *Redeeming Eastern Europe*. (Recurring charges of pedophilia against the singer make even more bizarre its inclusion of children crying, "Mi amas vin, Michael Jackson"—I love you, Michael Jackson.) And it seems unlikely that, at least in the United States, an Esperanto movie industry will arise from the impetus of *Incubus*. Motion pictures are a popular and populist art that affirms the messy specificities of culture and thrives on the vernacular. When Marlon Brando murmurs, "I could have been a contender," and Mae West suggests, "Let's get out of these wet clothes and into a dry Martini," the distinctive English words convey details about who and where they are that a neutral language designed to be devoid of personal idiosyncrasies cannot provide. A vibrant Esperanto movie culture will not be possible until there is a critical mass of native speakers using variants of the language that reflect region, class, and historical moment. For them alone, *Incubus* would not be a translingual experience.

Like the artificial smoke made to billow above the ground where demons menace Marc and Arndis, Esperanto in *Incubus* suggests something spooky; we experience otherworldly happenings to the accompaniment of the putative world language. Goran Markovic intensifies the horror in his 1987 film *Vec Vidjeno* by inserting some Esperanto in addition to the Serbo-Croatian expected in its Belgrade setting. However, it is unlikely that many other horror or science fiction screenwriters will follow the example of *Incubus* and put all their dialogue into Esperanto, if only because Stevens has already tried it. Devices for *ostranenie*—making strange—are productive only as long as they have not themselves become familiar, and anyone familiar with the alienating effects of Esperanto in *Incubus* would surely begin to take the language for granted in other films. "Been there, done that" is the American idiom, whose closest equivalent in Esperanto might be the very title of Markovic's cinematic latecomer: *vec vidjeno* (Esperanto for *déjà vu*). Unless Esperanto becomes a living language, *Incubus* is destined to remain what those who still speak Latin call *sui generis*.

An Italian in English: The Translingual Case of Francesca Marciano

From its very inception, Italian as a vernacular literature was the creation of translingual authors—that is, authors who write in more than one language or an adopted language. The three most illustrious pioneers of Italian poetry and prose—Dante, Petrarch, and Boccaccio—also wrote eloquently in Latin. In the eighteenth century, Giacomo Casanova and Carlo Goldoni each composed his memoir in French, not his native Italian. In the twentieth century, Italo Svevo came to Italian, the medium of all his fiction, most notably the novel *La Coscienza di Zeno* (1923) as his third language, after his native Triestine dialect and German. However, the contemporary Italian novelist Francesca Marciano, who has published all four of her books to date in English, represents a remarkable case of translingualism. A study of her Anglophone fiction, in which language itself is often an explicit theme, bears witness to extraordinary, self-conscious linguistic transformation.

Immigration and imperialism are the most common motives for literary translingualism. When Ha Jin moved from China to the United States, he began to write in English, rather than his native Chinese, and when Aharon Appelfeld moved from Bukovina to what became Israel, he began to learn Hebrew, the language in which, instead of the German he learned as a child, he wrote all of his fiction. Senegalese poet Léopold Sédar Senghor wrote in French, the language of the European colonial power, rather than his native Serer, and Nikolai Gogol wrote most of his work in the language of the Russian empire, rather than his native Ukrainian.

However, Marciano is an anomaly among authors who choose to write in an adopted language. Born in Rome in 1955, she naturally grew up speaking Italian. However, she has thus far published three novels and one volume of short stories in English, a language she began to learn only when she was fourteen. Moreover, Marciano's fiction reflects her own extensive travels, so that her work not only crosses linguistic borders but also challenges national categories. Her settings include Italy, Kenya, the United States, Britain, Greece, Afghanistan, Tanzania, and India, making her oeuvre international, if not transnational or even post-national, and Marciano impossible to pigeonhole as an Italian writer or an American one. It is true that the only scholarly study of her work to date, an analysis of memory and forgetting in her second novel, *Casa Rossa*, uses Marciano's own translation of the book into Italian, and links it to the work of other Italian writers such as Elsa Morante and Alberta Moravia (Rorato). However, Marciano has less in common with Elena Ferrante, Paolo Giordano, and Dacia Maraini, or with Louise Erdrich, Jonathan Franzen, and Barbara Kingsolver, than she does with Inez Baranay, Brian Castro, J. M. Coetzee, Pico Iyer, Alberto Manguel, Ngũgĩ wa Thiong'o, Tim Parks, and Ilija Trojanow—literary nomads who are creating a global literature that transcends the boundaries of nation and language. Arianna Dagnino dubs them "transcultural writers"—"that is imaginative writers who, by choice or because of life circumstances, experience cultural dislocation, follow transnational life patterns, cultivate bilingual or plurilingual proficiency, physically immerse themselves in multiple cultures, geographies, or territories, expose themselves to diversity, and nurture plural, flexible identities" (1). Marciano defies national and linguistic categories.

Her command of English became more secure during her first major cultural dislocation, the seven years she spent in New York, to which she moved at age twenty-one in order to study film. Nevertheless, despite prolonged residences in Kenya and India as well, Marciano still considers Rome her base of operations. Indeed, in Italy and Italian, she is a prolific, successful screenwriter, nominated for five David di Donatello Awards (Italy's equivalent of the Oscar) and winner of one. She is credited with more than twenty scripts for Italian film and television, including *Io non ho paura* (*I'm Not Scared*) (2003), *La bestia nel cuore* (*Don't Tell*) (2005), *Io e te* (*Me and You*) (2012), *Miele* (*Honey*) (2013), *Viaggio sola* (*A Five Star Life*) (2013), and *Euforia* (2018). "It's almost as if by now I have two brains that are running parallel to one another," Marciano explained to an interviewer on NPR. "One brain writes in Italian and the other brain seems to be writing in English" (Martin). By contrast, there was nothing categorical about the way André Brink composed his novels, now in Afrikaans, now in English. "Sometimes, it just depends on the mood I'm in on that particular day," he explained (qtd. in Kraft). However, Marciano's ability to compartmentalize her verbal expression, so that all of her screenwriting is done in her native Italian and all of her prose fiction is written in English, might recall the case of Kamala Das, the South Indian author who wrote her poetry in English and her fiction—under the pen name Madhavikutty—in Malayalam. "I speak three languages, write in / Two, dream in one," Das wrote in English, in a poem called "Introduction" (5). It is as if each language embodies a different sensibility, even personality.

Like many of the most notable translingual authors, including Samuel Beckett, Isak Dinesen, and Vladimir Nabokov, Marciano has translated her own work, relishing the control and freedom in finding Italian substitutes for her English prose: "I have translated my own novels in the past, thinking that it would allow me to have total control on my own voice," she has recalled. "The idea being that I'd know exactly how nuanced the irony would come off; how much to be blunt, and how lyrical, or how direct a phrase I'd want to capture a given moment. And, of course, being my own translator gave me endless freedom to revise, to change, to cut, even to elaborate." However, after translating her first three books into Italian herself, she conceded to an interviewer that she might prefer the services of a professional translator: "But I have to admit that now, four books later, I'm no longer so sure I'm my own best translator. Being fluent in a language doesn't automatically make you a good translator. And I'm also beginning to see that having all that freedom to change things around doesn't necessarily do the best service to my writing, and I'm eager to see how my work will sound in the hands of another person who can regard it with more transparency, while still remaining (I hope) loyal to the voice, accurate in preserving a story's and a character's essential nature" (Mair). (Marciano translated her first novel, *Rules of the Wild*, as *Cielo scoperto*. Her second novel maintained the same title, *Casa Rossa*. She rendered her third novel, *The End of Manners*, as *La fine delle buone maniere*.)

After living in Nairobi for several years, Marciano began writing her first novel, *Rules of the Wild* (1998), in Italian. Although its narrator and protagonist, Esmé, is from Rome, the novel focuses on expatriates, naturalists, journalists, and the offspring of Europeans living in East Africa. It is, as Esmé explains, "a story about white people in Africa," (Marciano, *Rules* 60), and their lingua franca is English. As Marciano explained to an interviewer, writing the novel in Italian, a language alien to the environment, seemed stilted to her: "The story was set in Kenya, and the characters were English and spoke English. And I remember that I first started writing the first few pages of the book in Italian. And it just sounded so inauthentic. And I stopped. And then a very good friend said try to write in English and see how it goes. And I remember how the minute I started writing in English, I felt I was on this, like, highway that would take me somewhere" (Martin). That highway has so far taken Marciano through a remarkable body of fiction written in supple English and in which language itself is often an explicit theme.

Brought by a lover to Kenya on a vacation, Esmé soon abandons the lover and remains in Kenya. She is still devastated by the death of her father, Ferdinando, a famous Neapolitan poet who dominated her and others through the power of his words, but who, as the result of a brain tumor, died mute, devoid of language. Attracted to Africa as "a place that wouldn't remind me of him, a place full of emptiness, without a written history, where language had very little meaning" (Marciano, *Rules* 25), she moves in with Adam, the resourceful second-generation white Kenyan who makes a living leading wealthy foreigners on safaris in the bush. Esmé is at first attracted to him because "Adam and I didn't speak the same language, in any sense. By speaking in English to him I inevitably needed to force something out" (52). She also acknowledges that "by speaking my second language I was leaving behind a whole chunk of my history . . ." (52). Esmé finds that liberating, as does Marciano herself, who explained to an interviewer, "There are no witnesses if you write in another language" (Ermelino 34).

A passionate involvement with Hunter Reed, a rugged, cynical crisis correspondent who uses Nairobi as a safe base for journalistic forays into Somalia, Sudan, Rwanda, and other sites of atrocity, draws Esmé away from Adam. She at first serves as an interpreter when Hunter wants to interview an Italian liberationist priest who has been working with Kenya's poor and oppressed. But Esmé and Hunter are soon communicating in something more fundamental than Italian, English, Samburu, or Swahili—what she calls "the silent language of sex" (Marciano, *Rules* 237). Early in the novel, Esmé disdains the rich American tourists who arrive in Africa expecting everyone to speak their language, who ". . . usually came from the Midwest or the South, spoke with a nasal drawl, and insisted on talking to the Samburu with that thick accent, never for a second conceiving the possibility there could be humans on the planet who didn't speak English" (80). Yet *Rules of the Wild*, like Marciano's other books, is designed for readers who do speak English but are willing to use that language to imagine other possibilities.

Though her second novel, *Casa Rossa* (2002), is set largely in Italy and among Italians, Marciano wrote it, too, in English. Like *Bleak House*, *The House of the Seven Gables*, and *Howards End*, the book focuses on the vicissitudes of a homestead as an index to the fortunes of its inhabitants. During the final days before moving out of Casa Rossa, an ornate farmhouse in Puglia, in southern Italy, Alina Strada reflects on the seventy years in which her family has lived in it. Her grandfather, Lorenzo, a painter, moved to Puglia from Paris and bought and renovated the crumbling ruin of a dwelling that became the distinctively red-colored building, Casa Rossa. He brought with him a beautiful French-speaking Tunisian bride named Renée. However, after their daughter, Alba, is born, Renée abandons the family to join another woman in Germany. Alba grows up speaking French to her Swiss stepmother, Jeanne. After Alba's husband, a successful screenwriter named Oliviero Strada, commits suicide, Alba marries her lover, a wealthy businessman named Bruno, and she and her two daughters, Isabella and Alina, move in to his apartment in Rome. Alina, who remains loyal to her father and is convinced that her mother had a hand in his death, uses a linguistic metaphor to describe her sense of dislocation: "It was like having been kidnapped overnight and waking up in a foreign country where we didn't speak the language" (Marciano, *Casa* 102).

As a grownup, Alina ends up spending several years in a foreign country, the United States. She gets a job as assistant to Raimonda Morrison, the owner of an art gallery in New York's Soho. Because Raimonda is from Milan, Alina is able to speak Italian to her during her initial months in New York, when her English is still rudimentary and, she says, "I remember watching the news on TV and not being able to make out what they were going on about, or staring at a waitress in a coffee shop, unable to figure out what exactly was the special of the day" (Marciano, *Casa* 168). Yet Marciano renders conversations between Alina and Raimonda—like letters from Alina's sister, Isabella, in Italy as well as transcripts of testimony in an Italian court—in fluent English. So, too, are the headlines in the Italian newspapers that Alina buys at New York's Rizzoli Bookstore tacitly translated for the reader into English.

Those headlines convey news about political violence in Italy following the kidnapping and murder of former Prime Minister Aldo Moro during Italy's fearful *anni di piombo*, the so-called Years of Lead, from the late 1960s to the early 1980s. Isabella herself has joined a militant revolutionary faction and, captured hiding out in Casa Rossa, sends letters to Alina from solitary confinement in a maximum security prison in Voghera, in Northwest Italy. Meanwhile, Alina's experiment in becoming an American founders over her realization that the world of her lover, a magazine writer named Daniel Moore, remains irreducibly foreign to her. She returns from spending Thanksgiving, the quintessential American holiday, with his family, "having celebrated a festivity that meant absolutely nothing to me, pretending to be family with a bunch of strangers, speaking a strange language, warping my *r*'s, deluding myself that I could be this other person" (Marciano, *Casa* 212). Once again, language for a Marciano character is integral to identity, and Alina, who returns to the ancestral home—if only to pack things up after selling the property to an Australian family—feels most Italian when she is trying to speak English, the adopted language that Marciano deploys gracefully throughout *Casa Rossa*. Moving among rural Italy (Puglia), the national metropolis (Rome), and the country's penal citadel (Voghera), and through

World War II, the Years of Lead, and beyond, Marciano's novel embodies seventy momentous years of life in her native country. It is a Great Italian Novel—except that it was written in English.

Though Maria Galante, who narrates Marciano's third novel, *The End of Manners* (2008), lives in Milan, most of her story takes place in Afghanistan. A trip to that Central Asian country in 2004 in order to collect material for an Italian filmmaker led Marciano to reflect on the human rights of Afghan women. Maria, a thirty-two-year-old photographer, accompanies a swashbuckling journalist named Imo Glass on an assignment to investigate the mass suicides of Afghan women who have refused forced marriages. Imo, who speaks English, Spanish, French, and Russian, is a veteran of combat coverage in Sudan, Sierra Leone, and Kosovo. Maria marvels over how Imo, who was born in Medellín and grew up in London, "seemed able to effortlessly shift from one language to another, from one country to another, as if she were always swimming in the same water and consequently managed to feel at home just about everywhere" (Marciano, *End* 32). In Afghanistan, she and Maria mingle with a cosmopolitan coterie of war-hardened journalists, aid workers, contractors, and mercenaries from Britain, Canada, Sweden, France, Spain, the United States, and other parts of the world. Their Afghan guides provide translations—into English—from Pashto and Dari.

Though Maria is the daughter of a retired professor of Italian literature, Marciano renders all of her dialogue—even text messages back to her former lover Carlo in Milan—in English. Her late mother was Irish, but Maria notes that her mother was never comfortable in Italy or Italian: "She blushed when people didn't understand her pronunciation, or when she got the tenses wrong. No matter how many years she'd lived in Italy, she seemed never to belong" (Marciano, *End* 20). An award-winning photojournalist famed for her shots of child prostitutes in Bangkok, immigrants in Albania, and AIDS victims in Africa, Maria retired from the global chase after images of misfortune following a series of panic attacks. She instead settled into being a kind of culinary pornographer, photographing enticing images of *panna cotta*, orecchiette with broccoli, and tofu blueberry cheesecake for magazines such as *La Cucina Italiana*. However, appealing to her professional pride, her agent, Pierre Le Clerc, a Frenchman who lives in London, talks her into taking on the assignment in Afghanistan. Since it is a war zone, she must first go to Britain for a rigorous course in "hostile environment training."

The brutal treatment she experiences at the hands of the rugged ex-marines who administer the survival course seems devoid of manners, but it is designed to prepare her for unruly Afghanistan, which Imo Glass describes as "the place where all good manners have come to an end" (Marciano, *End* 132). The novel's title, *The End of Manners*, questions whether the protocols of civility might seem frivolous in a situation in which merely staying alive must take priority over the placement of a fork. However, for all the disdain that outsiders bring to the havoc that is Afghanistan, it is the condescending, tactless, and sometimes brutish outsiders who exhibit the worst manners. Central to the story Marciano tells is a series of ethical questions: Do Westerners have a responsibility to repair injustices even in a place as remote as Afghanistan? Do photographers have any obligation to the subjects of their photographs? (Toward the end of the novel, Maria notes the irony that she and Imo were so intent on exposing how women are generally abused in Afghanistan that they neglected to pay any attention to their guide's wife, whose pregnancy proves fatal to her. "What kills me," says Maria, "is that we were too busy doing a story on violence against women to pay attention to the fact that one of them was dying of childbirth" [*End* 252]). Is photojournalism inherently exploitative? Is peddling portraits of misery more reprehensible than photoshopping luscious images of tiramisu? Is reporting on the private lives of others a form of translation, hence of betrayal? Is English the proper medium for recounting an Italian woman's experiences in Afghanistan?

As its title suggests, language remains a central theme in Marciano's next volume, *The Other Language* (2014). The book's epigraph, a statement by Derek Walcott, "To change your language you must change your life," underscores the connection between translingualism and personal transformation emphasized throughout Marciano's oeuvre and in the arc of her own career. In the story collection's title piece, an Italian life is shaped at a crucial moment through contact with English. Just after the untimely death of his wife, a man referred to throughout only as "the father" takes their son and two daughters to spend the summer in a Greek village. Twelve-year-old Emma is struck by how her brother, thirteen-year-old Luca, develops a rapport with a Greek girl, Nadia; how, splashing merrily together in the sea "they no longer needed a common language to get along" (Marciano, *Other* 11). Emma herself is attracted to two older boys, Jack and David, who are visiting from England, but her lack of English keeps her at a distance from them.

"The Other Language" is the story of adolescent Emma's coming-of-age, specifically her sexual initiation, but it is remarkable how central language is to the entire experience. At first Emma, who lives in Rome and does not know any English, is frustrated in her tentative efforts to communicate with Jack and David. However, over the course of a few summers in which the Italian and English families return to the same Greek village, she acquires proficiency in the boys' language and a new sense of herself. Emma likens her acquisition of English to her newfound ability to swim out to an island in the Aegean: "That summer forever marked the moment when she swam all the way to the island and landed in a place where she could be different from whom she assumed she was. There were so many possibilities. She didn't know what she was getting away from, but the other language was the boat she fled on" (Marciano, *Other* 22). The other language—English—enables Emma to outgrow the miserable motherless Italian girl she once was. By the end of the story, grownup Emma has married an American and lives in the United States. "By then," we are told, "her English was fluent and flawless, and she hardly had a trace of an accent" (45). In her Whorfian belief that language determines identity, she feels that her metamorphosis is complete and beneficent and that it has been brought about through the agency of English: "She felt she had finally become the person she had always wanted to be. Someone who thought, dreamed and made love in a different language, who had acquired different habits and conformed to different rules of behavior" (44–45). Yet, the hint of incompatibility between Emma and her American husband in the story's final lines offers a soupçon of irony toward the triumphal project of personal transformation through language acquisition.

Most of the other stories in *The Other Language* also dramatize transcultural, transnational, and translingual contact. In "Big Island, Small Island," for example, Stella, an Italian biologist specializing in biodiversity, takes advantage of a conference in Dar es Salaam to pay a surprise visit to a former lover, Andrea, whom she has not seen in many years. He is now one of only two Europeans living on a remote, undeveloped Tanzanian island. Stella is shocked to find that Andrea has converted to Islam and gone native. Her conversations with him, rendered by Marciano in English of course, are belabored, in part because he has not spoken Italian in years, but mostly because he resists being drawn back into the mindset of a contemporary secular Italian. When Stella, who does not speak Swahili, tries to communicate with Andrea's wife, Farida, in what she assumes would be their lingua franca, she finds that Farida does not speak English. Stella is exasperated by the fact that she herself does, though, speak the same language as a glib, obnoxious developer, Carlo, who is visiting the island in order to convince the locals that the lucrative, invasive resort he wants to build there might benefit them.

In "The Presence of Men," Lara uses the money from a divorce settlement to buy and renovate a house in a bucolic village in Puglia. When her brother Leo, a successful movie agent, comes to visit, he brings along a presumptuous American movie star, ruining the village's rustic charms. Though Lara speaks English with the apparently monolingual American, when she is alone with her brother she uses their native tongue: "Switching to Italian with Leo made her feel more at ease, as it seemed to create the kind of intimacy she was craving" (Marciano, *Other* 130). However, Marciano renders the Italian conversations, like the English conversations and the entire narration, in English. Though "Chanel" and "Roman Romance" take place in Italy, the stories are recounted in English, as are "An Indian Soirée" (set in India), "The Club" (set in Kenya), "The Italian System" (set in the United States), and "Quantum Theory" (set in Kenya and the United States).

On occasion throughout her books, Marciano employs code-switching to provide some local color and to signal that English is not always—or ever—the language being spoken. In *Rules of the Wild*, for example, after Esmé proves as adept as the seasoned safari leaders in outrunning a pursuing elephant, one Kenyan says to another, "*Huyu, anaweza kukimbia sana*" (89). When Esmé replies, in English, "Of course I can run, what did you think?" it is a moment of triumph; not only has she escaped the dangerous elephant, but she has demonstrated that she understands the Swahili ("This woman can run very well") that the

African men assumed would exclude a greenhorn European from their private conversation.

In *Casa Rossa*, Raimonda, the owner of the art gallery in New York where Alina works, is fond of sprinkling adages into her conversation. Trying to console Alina over her sister's imprisonment for terrorism, Raimonda says, "Life goes on . . . that's the beauty of it. *Inutile piangere sul latte versato*" (Marciano, *Casa* 183). Since the two women are presumably speaking Italian to each other, it would have been more logical to render the entire speech in Italian. Or, since the entire novel is in English, Raimonda might have, instead, been quoted as saying, "There is no point in crying over spilled milk." However, the dictum in Italian adds a bit of pungency to the prose, even if it does break the narrative fourth wall, by alerting readers to the seams in the novel's linguistic medium.

In general, it would be difficult for a newcomer to Marciano's English prose to detect that her four books were not written by a native speaker. At times, she delivers a turn of phrase that is downright elegant, as when a character in the short story "Chanel" is said to think that ". . . time was beginning to feel like a fast express train that no longer stopped at all the stations" (*Other* 58) or when we are told that Peppino Esposito, an Italian movie mogul in *Casa Rossa* who speaks "very poor English," nevertheless ". . . could recognize talent, the way a dog smells a truffle" (*Casa* 59). However, even the translingual master Joseph Conrad (whose novels of exotic, treacherous travel Marciano repeatedly cites as an early influence) can sometimes nod, and it is possible to find a very few calques, instances in which Marciano, despite having been copyedited by one of the most prestigious publishing houses in the United States, might have been thinking in Italian and transposing literally into unidiomatic English. In *Casa Rossa*, for example, Alina says of the American Daniel Moore: "I love him but he has never become familiar to me" (*Casa* 232). The Italian *familiare*, with its connotations of domesticated, like family, would probably be more appropriate than its English cognate *familiar*. And in *The End of Manners*, Imo Glass is described as "standing abruptly, avoiding to make a comment on the story" (*End* 98). The standing might be abrupt, but the gerundive phrasing is awkward in a way that a native speaker would probably avoid.

In Marciano's short story "The Italian System," a woman from Rome has moved to New York, where she makes a living by teaching Italian. Despite her desire to become an assimilated American, she feels frustrated that after seven years she still feels like an outsider. She takes stock of the differences between Italy and the United States and sets about writing a manual for Americans, *The Italian System*, that pinpoints the civility and finesse that, she contends, sets her native culture apart. The irony in the story is that when she returns to Rome to visit her mother, she realizes that Italians are as coarse and materialistic as the Americans. Nevertheless, her book insists that *lightness* is the distinguishing genius of Italy. She writes the book in English, but she introduces the Italian term, *la leggerezza*, to suggest that the quality is distinctively Italian and untranslatable: "La leggerezza, *as we call it*," she writes, "*is the necessary quality to execute the flawless dive, the effortless pirouette. The nature of anything truly enchanting has to be as light as a whiff of air*" (Marciano, *Other* 240).

La leggerezza is the ideal to which Marciano's own limpid English prose aspires. Vladimir Nabokov provides an instructive contrast. Despite his mock self-pity for having to abandon "the infinitely docile Russian tongue for a second-rate brand of English, devoid of any of those apparatuses—the baffling mirror, the black velvet backdrop, the implied associations and traditions—which the native illusionist, frac-tails flying, can magically use to transcend the heritage in his own way" ("On a Book Entitled *Lolita*" 317), Nabokov delights in flaunting his own pyrotechnics—puns, anagrams, palindromes, and other verbal stunts that vaunt his mastery of an adopted language. If, according to Lawrence Venuti, foreignizing translation emphasizes differences from the source and domesticating translation erases those differences (*The Translator's Invisibility* 21), Nabokov is a foreignizing translingual, Marcioni a domesticating translingual. Apart from a rare calque or an instance of intrusive code-switching, her English sentences affect an effortless grace, whose translingual achievement is invisible. As much as *leggerezza*, Marciano's adopted English might be understood as what Baldesar Castiglione, coining a new term in 1528, called *sprezzatura*, "una certa sprezzatura, che nasconda l'arte e dimostri ciò, che si fa e dice, venir fatto senza fatica e quasi senza pensarvi" 'a certain nonchalance, so as to conceal all art and make whatever one does or says appear to be without effort and almost without any thought about it' (Castiglione, *Il Cortegiano* 1.26; Castiglione, *Book* 32). Marciano's translingual art conceals its own artistry: *ars est celare artem*.

Reflecting on elements that recur in her work, Marciano told an interviewer: "I tend to write stories about women who are kind of unhinged, who live in places which are home to others. I'm interested in the challenge that feeling poses and how this makes one particularly vulnerable. This is probably a recurring theme for me" (Vaugelas). A vital part of that challenge is speaking the language of others. Both Marciano and the women who populate her fiction feel particularly vulnerable but also particularly exhilarated by the trials of translingualism, abandoning the comfort and safety of a first language for an adopted one. "By writing in a language that is not my mother language," she explained, "no matter how fluent I feel I am, I still have less [calque alert!] tools than I would in my own language. And this, instead of being an obstacle has forced me to be very leaner and more spare because I don't control the language 101 percent. You know, there's always a fraction of the language that I feel I'm not in control of completely and that little insecurity that I have a) is a challenge, and b) forces me to—someone said it's like going on a hike with less gear. You still go up the mountain" ("Francesca Marciano").

For Marciano, writing in English is both liberating, exhilarating disorientation and productive discipline. It is akin to the "*long, immense et raisonné dérèglement de tous les sens*" 'the long, vast and rational *derangement of all the senses*' that Arthur Rimbaud prescribed as the recipe for creativity (Rimbaud). But it also resembles the rigorous regimen that Puerto Rican novelist Rosario Ferré claims that writing in English, rather than her native Spanish, imposes on her: "English makes me slow down. I have to think over what I'm going to say twice, maybe three times—which is often healthy because I can't put my foot, or rather my pen, in my mouth so easily. I can't be trigger-happy in English because words take too much effort" (137). At mid-career, Francesca Marciano cannot afford to put her foot in her mouth rather than on the path ahead as she continues, as she phrases it, to go up the mountain with less gear.

Hugo Hamilton's Language War

Translingual Trilemma

Hugo Hamilton's personal misfortune was that he grew up trilingual in a bilingual household. It would also be his literary asset, the inspiration behind two remarkable language memoirs. When she coined the term *language memoir* (life-writing in which the acquisition of a language shapes the narrative) in 1994, Alice Kaplan was composing *French Lessons*, her own account of falling in love with the language of Molière, Baudelaire, and Proust, and thereby with the way that French speakers filter experience. Among notable contributions to the genre of language memoir, by Ariel Dorfman, Eva Hoffman, Jhumpa Lahiri, Richard Rodriguez, Luc Sante, Ilan Stavans, and others, Hugo Hamilton's is unique in depicting a childhood that he describes as a "language war" (*Speckled* 279). In *The Speckled People* (2003) and its sequel, *The Sailor in the Wardrobe* (2006), Hamilton, who was born in 1953, recounts the linguamachy of a Dublin household in which Irish and German were the only two tongues permitted. Adopting the child's eye perspective of a youngster who simply echoes what adults tell him, Hamilton states, ". . . my father says your language is your home and your country is your language and your language is your flag" (*Speckled* 3).

For much of his childhood, Hamilton is confused about home, country, flag, and—especially—language. The subject of an autobiography is always a constructed self. In Hamilton's case, however, the protagonist is more clearly than most others constructed out of language and language choices. And that construction is, more than for most other language memoirists, a victory over linguistic division. In her empirical study of bilingual immigrants, Aneta Pavlenko found that 65 percent of her respondents reported distinct identities, that each language they spoke represented a separate, often incompatible, personality. Pavlenko calls this widespread tendency on the part of bilinguals to speak of discrete—if not conflicting—internal selves "the discourse of bilingualism as linguistic schizophrenia" (*The Bilingual Mind* 3). An example might be Rosario Ferré, the Puerto Rican novelist who sometimes publishes in Spanish and sometimes in English and contends that "a bilingual writer is really two different writers, has two very different voices, writes in two *different* styles, and, most important, looks at the world through two different sets of glasses. This takes a splitting of the self that doesn't come easily and can be dangerous" (138). Though he prefers the military metaphor of warfare to the psychological one of schizophrenia, Hamilton's two memoirs employ the discourse of trilingualism as internal linguistic combat.

Hamilton's mother, Irmgard née Kaiser Ó hUrmoltaigh, is a traumatized immigrant from Nazi Germany, and his abusive father, Séan Ó hUrmoltaigh, is an ardent Irish nationalist who punishes his children if they dare speak English, which they learn in school, at home. It is the language of their neighborhood but also of the despised conquerors of Eire. When Hamilton's father hears his older son, Franz, singing in English, the language of Ireland's oppressors, he is so furious that he breaks the boy's nose. As a merchant, he sacrifices income by refusing to accept checks made out to John Hamilton, the anglicized form of Séan Ó hUrmoltaigh. Hamilton's mother originally arrived in Ireland intending to learn English, but she and the Irish patriot she fell in love with dreamed of establishing a household that would be a principled oasis of Irish and German in the midst of English-speaking Dublin. Her son recalls Irmgard as proud of having created "an Irish-German family with lederhosen and Aran sweaters, so that we would not be afraid of being different" (*Sailor* 67). At the beginning of Hamilton's memoir, he presents that same image of sartorial exoticism and *métissage*: "So my brother and I ran out wearing lederhosen and Aran sweaters, smelling of rough wool and new leather, Irish on top and German below" (*Speckled* 2).

However, for much of his childhood, Hamilton is ashamed of being different, not least in the fact that he is mocked for speaking Irish, taunted for speaking German, and punished for speaking English. Whereas Jean-Jacques Rousseau begins his *Confessions* with a proud proclamation of utter uniqueness, in his own confessions Hamilton is initially a timorous outsider who is desperate to fit in. "Moi seul. Je sens mon cœur, et je connais les hommes," declares Rousseau. "Je ne suis fait comme aucun de ceux que j'ai vus; j'ose croire n'être fait comme aucun de ceux qui existent. 'Myself alone! I know the feelings of my heart, and I know men. I am not made like any of those I have seen; I venture to believe that I am not made like any of those who are in existence' (Rousseau 3). Hamilton probably has more claim to uniqueness than even Rousseau, but his distinctiveness is the source of confusion and anxiety as he grows up. The narrative arc of *The Speckled People*, the first of Hamilton's two memoirs, is a movement from dread of being different to an acceptance of his uniqueness. "I don't have to be like anyone else," he will finally declare (*Speckled* 295).

Fearful that the popular youth culture emerging in the 1960s will seduce their son and make him indistinguishable from the conformist mass of avid adolescent fans of rock and roll, Hamilton's parents insist on the importance of being different. "We don't want you to become a *Mitläufer*, a run-along," (*Sailor* 67) says his mother, who has experienced the deadly consequences of an entire society submissive to the leadership of Adolf Hitler. His father, Hamilton notes, says that "it's what happened to the Irish as well, when they started speaking English and were forced to run along after the British" (*Sailor* 67). Hamilton's father and mother want him to share their pride in standing apart. Beyond the portals of his peculiar domestic redoubt in Dún Laoghaire, a suburb of Dublin, Hamilton is unlike anyone he knows, though, despite his parents' admonition, he tries to resemble everyone he knows.

As a teenager, he takes a job assisting a fisherman at the city's harbor, but when his mother comes to see him, he hides, anxious to conceal his relationship with this odd-looking woman emitting guttural sounds. "I could not let anyone know that I had a German mother," Hamilton explains. "So I made her disappear out of my mind, out of my life completely. The language she was using was not my language" (*Sailor* 36–37). And yet German was his mother's tongue and, as the language most often spoken within his family, his mother tongue. Irmgard gives her son access to her diaries, written in German, in order to enable him to understand her experience growing up in Germany in a family that was persecuted for refusing to accept Nazism. They cultivated a form of passive resistance that Irmgard calls "the silent negative" (*Speckled* 84, 141, 152). In her case, the silent negative meant mentally injecting the word *not* into a mandatory pledge of allegiance to a figure she despised, saying, "I swear under oath that I will—NOT—serve the Führer as long as I live" (*Speckled* 84). The silent negative is a creative use of language that presages Hamilton's own strategies for resolving his linguistic trilemma. Though strictly forbidden to speak English in his Irish German home, he employs the silent negative by maintaining a running mental conversation with himself in the proscribed language.

In his account, Hamilton exaggerates his mother's lingering angst over the burdens of her German heritage. Examining Irmgard née Kaiser's six diaries, Dorothea Depner discovered that "her notebooks reinforce the impression of her as an ebullient, optimistic person, yet they contain few reflections on the Second World War and on German guilt, two major preoccupations attributed to her in *The Speckled People* and *The Sailor in the Wardrobe*. While Irmgard records her and her family's losses during the war (both of material possessions and, in her uncle's case, of status and employment, for which his widow was later compensated by the Federal Republic) and the hardships they suffered under Allied occupation, she makes no mention of the consequences of Nazi policies for others. She refers to Nazi crimes only twice, in the early 1960s, following Eichmann's trial, and both times she quotes the opinions expressed by others. Although Irmgard is occasionally critical of developments in contemporary Germany, noting the surge of materialism and the simultaneous disappearance of traditional values and religion from the lives of her German relatives and friends in the 1950s and '60s, there is no sense that she bore her German identity as a stigma" (11).

Nevertheless, young Hamilton's own command of his mother's problematic language endangers him when, targeted as a Nazi because he speaks German, he is attacked in the streets by neighborhood thugs who call him "Eichmann" and taunt him with cries of "*Sieg Heil*" (*Speckled* 4). Moreover, neither is Hamilton eager to be seen in public with his father, lest he be forced to speak Irish, a quaint, archaic tongue that is an embarrassment to him in 1960s Ireland.

Hamilton's trilingual dilemma makes him unlike any other author. Breyten Breytenbach, Kamala Das, Eugene Jolas, Vladimir Nabokov and others have also mastered three languages, but not the combination of Irish-German-English; and none has been as conflicted as Hamilton over language choice. He is an uneasy fit within the company of such Irish novelists as John McGahern, Edna O'Brien, and Roddy Doyle, nor, despite sharing their language, does he have much in common with German novelists such as Günter Grass, Peter Schneider, and Christa Wolf. However, Hamilton has noted his affinity with Heinrich Böll, the German novelist who did not settle in Ireland, like Irmgard Kaiser Ó hUrmoltaigh, but who spent some time there in the 1950s and wrote about it. In the introduction he contributed to the English translation of Böll's *Irish Journal*, Hamilton, who read the travel book, in German, shortly after it was published, notes, "When I got the book to read as a boy, it turned me into a visitor in my own country" (Introduction viii).

OUTSIDERS IN THE HAMILTON OEUVRE

To Hamilton, troubled by questions of nationality and language, it is problematic whether Ireland is more his own country than Germany or any other place. And his fiction often focuses on outsiders who cannot take culture or language for granted. That is certainly true of *Every Single Minute* (2014), a fictionalized account of the writer Nuala O'Faolain's first and last visit to Berlin while she is dying of cancer. *Surrogate City* (1990) is narrated by an Irishman who lives in Germany and counts other expatriates among his friends. An outsider himself, Hamilton set two other novels—*The Last Shot* (1991) and *The Love Test* (1995) in Germany.

But *Hand in the Fire* (2010) is probably the Hamilton novel that most resembles his memoirs in its defamiliarization of language and culture. Narrated by Vid Ćosić, a carpenter who has left Serbia for Ireland in hopes of erasing painful memories of the Yugoslav Wars, the novel depicts customs and conventions that Dubliners take for granted and makes them strange. Vid is often confounded by what passes for humor in Ireland. "Hard for me to know where the boundary lay between a joke and an insult," he observes (Hamilton, *Hand* 32). Because Serbian is his native language, he is cautious in his use of English. "I was eager not to be misunderstood or misled, so I stuck to the expressions that give me least trouble," he explains.

"I was reluctant to abbreviate. I never allowed myself to use puns or play with people's names. I tried to limit the amount of times I used words without meaning, such as 'like' or 'you know.' I was cautious with terms like 'mega' and 'sketchy' and 'leggin it' and 'literally glued to the television.' I didn't trust myself saying things like 'will you go away' or 'would you ever fuck off' because I'm always afraid people might take it to heart. Besides, I can never pronounce the word 'fuck' properly. I make it sound too genuine. You have so many different ways of saying it in this country, I've given up trying" (Hamilton, *Hand* 3). Composed in English, Hamilton's third language, *Hand in the Fire* is, like *The Speckled People* and *The Sailor in the Wardrobe*, written as if in translation.

THE TONGUE SET FREE

Hamilton told an interviewer, "My writing came from an attempt to explore that difficult issue of belonging. Was I Irish or was I German? Those were very troubled issues for me" (Randolph 34–35). However, the mathematics of Hamilton's childhood is more complicated and painful than the binary division suggested by *A Memoir of a Half-Irish Childhood*, the subtitle Hamilton gave to *The Speckled People*. His coming of age in the Republic of Ireland is both more and less than half-Irish; Irish, German, and English each compete to silence the other two. "We don't just have one language and one history," Hamilton says of his family. "We sleep in German and we dream in Irish. We laugh in Irish and we cry in German. We are silent in German and we speak in English" (*Speckled* 283). Years later, Hamilton would summarize the chaos of his primal linguistic situation: "It was a confusion of languages, confusion between the inside of the house and the outside of the house, between my father's idealism and my mother's memories. There's always been confusion in my life" (Hamilton and N'Duessan). Using the Irish word *breac*—"it means speckled, dappled, flecked, spotted, coloured" (*Speckled* 7)—Hamilton's father proclaims, "We're the speckled people . . . the 'brack' people . . ."

(*Speckled* 7). And *The Speckled People* becomes the apt title for the first volume of Hamilton's memoirs.

Hamilton begins that volume with an epigraph from Elias Canetti's own memoir. In the quoted passage, Canetti recounts a recurring childhood nightmare of elinguation, the excision of his tongue: "I wait for the command to show my tongue. I know he's going to cut it off, and I get more and more scared each time." Like Hamilton, Canetti—who wrote in German, his fifth language, after Ladino, Bulgarian, English, and French—was a translingual, an author who wrote in a language other than his native one. Both Canetti and Hamilton share profound anxiety over the prospect of losing one's tongue. However, each writer ultimately finds it liberating to live between languages, not to be confined to the prison-house of any single linguistic system. Canetti therefore titled the memoir from which Hamilton lifted his epigraph *Die Gerettete Zung* (literally *The Rescued Tongue*, though rendered in the published English translation as *The Tongue Set Free*). Hamilton, too, will eventually, by the conclusion of his memoir project, find a free space beyond Irish, German, and even English, the language of his own memoirs. However, Hamilton's autobiographical work testifies to the wrenching ordeal of translingualism.

"There is no language change without emotional consequences," Kaplan contends. "Principally: loss" ("On Language Memoir" 63). Hamilton's memoirs constitute a record of the ordeal entailed in switching languages, of forging an identity torn among the names Hugo, Johannes, Séan, and John. Because German was what in Irish would be called his *máthairtheanga*, his maternal language, in German his *Muttersprache*, and Irish his father's language, his *sermo patrius*, Hamilton's composition of his memoirs in English is an act of filial betrayal. They are the final assertion of linguistic freedom by an author bullied throughout childhood into shunning English, at the same time as they emphasize the spaces between languages and the inadequacy of any one language. Although Hamilton's trilingual triangulation constitutes a unique case, it raises pointed general questions about the relationships between language and personal and national identity and the uses of language to interrogate language.

Hamilton grows up with both gendered and politicized views of languages. He identifies himself as "the son of a German woman who was shamed in front of the world" (*Sailor* 7). The most traumatic personal memory that his mother passes on to him is of her rape by a Nazi businessman, and he associates their common language, German, with femininity and its violation. Though he is himself persecuted by neighborhood bullies as a presumed Nazi brute, German and Germany in his eyes belong to his vulnerable but loving mother's world. Irish is the language of his father, whom he most succinctly describes as "an Irishman who is refusing to surrender to the British" (*Sailor* 7). Séan Ó hUrmoltaigh is portrayed as an angry man who is quick to administer corporal punishment and was one of the founders of the Aiséirí, a quasi-fascist Irish nationalist movement inspired in part by Nazism. When, plotting to free Ulster from British rule, the movement embraces violence, Séan drops out, but his continued insistence on speaking Irish remains a vestige of his political defiance, one that he himself eventually comes to recognize is doomed to defeat. Thus, for their impressionable son, both father and mother speak languages of submission. "I know what it's like to lose," Hamilton writes, "because I'm Irish and I'm German" (*Speckled* 122).

Hamilton's father is ashamed of the memory of his own father, banishing all traces of the man from his household, except for an old photograph of him in a naval uniform that he hides away in a wardrobe; Hugo Hamilton's grandfather is "the sailor in the wardrobe" from whom the title of his second memoir is derived. Instead of resisting foreign domination, John Hamilton had acceded to English and even served in the British navy. Developing his own pubescent identity, Hugo Hamilton must learn to negotiate between maternal and paternal languages and the language of the Dublin streets. He will end up duplicating his grandfather's choice, changing his name from Johannes Ó hUrmoltaigh to Hugo Hamilton and forging a literary career in English.

In the Republic of Ireland in which Hamilton grows up, only a few decades after its independence, English, the colonial language, is the dominant form of communication, despite the proclamation in Article 8 of the Irish Constitution that "ós í an Ghaeilge an teanga náisiúnta is í an phríomhtheanga oifigiúil í" ("Bunreacht" 9)—that is, "the Irish language as the national language is the first official language" ("Bunreacht" 8). Yet, except for rural enclaves, called the *Gaeltacht*, where it persisted as the vernacular, the ancestral language was, during the 1950s and 1960s when Hamilton was growing up, on the verge of extinction. Even today, despite determined efforts by government and educational authorities to revive and promote the language, Irish is a national language whose nation venerates it too much to use. The website *Ethnologue: Languages of the World* now classifies Irish as a "threatened" language, with only 141,000 native speakers and 1,030,000 L2 users in Ireland ("Irish").

Flying by the Nets of Language and Nation

The point made by Hamilton's father that ". . . your language is your home and your country is your language and your language is your flag" (*Speckled* 3) is so important that the son later reiterates: "My father wants all the Irish people to cross back over into the Irish language so he made it a rule that we can't speak English, because your home is your language and he wants us to be Irish and not British" (*Speckled* 12). Still later, he repeats: ". . . it's important to work hard and invent lots of new things in Ireland and fight for small languages that are dying out. Because your language is your home and your language is your country" (*Speckled* 161). Hamilton's memoirs, composed in English, mark him as a troubled traitor who will not pledge unequivocal allegiance to the flag of his father's nation. "I always have to remember that I speak English most of the time," Hamilton told an interviewer. "It's the language that was forbidden to me as a child. So effectively I'm living in a foreign language. It's almost like a fictional language. It's as if I lived a version of myself that's made up" (Hamilton and N'Duessan). The sense that a translingual author creates a new self by adopting a new language is affirmed when Karen Blixen became Isak Dinesen in English, rather than her native Danish, and Shmuel Yosef Czaczkes became S. Y. Agnon in Hebrew, rather than his native Yiddish. Brian O'Nolan became Myles na gCopaleen in Irish and Flann O'Brien in English, and Felix Paul Greve became Frederick Philip Grove writing novels in English. All autobiographical writing is in effect a reconstruction of the self. However, composed in English, a language that was banished from his childhood, Hamilton's memoirs of growing up are even more poignantly factitious than most others. The language he uses to convey his childhood is not the languages in which he experienced it.

The possibility that language can be a choice and not a mere legacy is made vivid during a dinnertime scene about halfway through *The Speckled People*. The entire family—mother, father, and three children—is seated at the table, and Hamilton's mother serves something unusual, sliced tongue with cabbage. The metonymic association of cow's tongue with speech is made explicit when Hamilton's older brother Franz quips, ". . . if you eat a cow's tongue, will you start saying moo" (*Speckled* 162). The children dislike the rubbery taste of tongue, but their parents insist that they eat it anyway. However, it soon becomes clear that the parents do not care for the tongue either, and Irmgard tells the children they can leave the rest of the meat as long as they eat the cabbage. The chapter ends with Mother's promise "that we will never have to eat tongue as long as we live" (*Speckled* 163). It is not as easy for Hamilton to keep Irish and German out of his mouth.

In another of the most memorable episodes in *The Sailor in the Wardrobe*, Hamilton surreptitiously violates one of the household's most fearsome taboos. His father installs a state-of-the-art music system in order to be able to enjoy the German and Irish performances he loves. To ensure that no one tampers with it, Séan hides the key to the cabinet. One day, while his father is out of the house, Hamilton finds the key and plays the phonograph. However, not only does he risk his father's wrath merely for opening the music cabinet without permission; what he uses it to play is a Beatles song, "Don't Let Me Down," the B-side to the single "Get Back." Playing the song at high volume over and over again, Hamilton experiences guilty pleasure at hearing John Lennon's English words reverberate throughout a house in which that language is *verboten*. By playing "Don't Let Me Down," Hamilton is in effect letting his Anglophobic father down, but he revels in the naughty thrill of indulging in what has been forbidden.

When he has finished listening, Hamilton takes great care to remove any trace that he has gained access to his father's music system. However, later, at dinner, he realizes—too late—that he has forgotten one crucial incriminating detail; he left the Beatles record itself on Séan's precious turntable! When his father finds the record, he affects an air of forbearance toward "Na Ciaróga," as he calls the Beatles in Irish. Séan insists that father and son now listen together to "Don't Let Me Down." And then he plays his own recording of Elisabeth Schwarzkopf singing German lieder. Following that, Hamilton's father asks his son, "With your hand on your heart, which do you think is the better music?" (*Sailor* 69). When Hamilton chooses the Beatles over Schwarzkopf, his father, enraged, exclaims that "John Lennon is the last nail in the coffin for the Irish language" (*Sailor* 71). Séan is not convinced when his son, defending Lennon, points out that "he's half Irish. . . . His mother is Irish" (*Sailor* 69). Trying to minimize the importance of language, Hugo argues, "I know the songs are in English, but he's really singing in Irish underneath" (*Sailor* 70). He is hinting at a Chomskyan view that, at the deepest level, we all speak the same Ur-language.

A coal delivery provides another example of linguistic overlap. To ensure the accuracy of the price that the Ó hUrmoltaigh family is charged for the coal, the number of empty sacks is counted twice—once in German by Franz and Hugo and once in English by the deliveryman. As if the differences among English, German, and Irish are merely superficial, Hamilton is pleased to note that "it was the same number no matter what language" (*Speckled* 59). By contrast, Hamilton's father dreads the prospect of a world in which languages have ceased to be distinct. "One day there will be only one language and everybody will be lost" (*Speckled* 162), he laments, clinging to Irish as an obstacle to the Esperantization of global communications.

Polyglot from an early age, Hugo Hamilton has the freedom to choose among languages, if not within his father's household, at least within the theater of his own mind, where he continually conducts internal conversations in English. As a writer, he will choose English over Irish and German, for his autobiographies, the nine novels, and the collection of short stories he has thus far published. But ultimately, he aspires to a condition beyond any one language or country. It is because of Hamilton's linguistic and political homelessness that Aoileann Ní Éigeartaigh can declare that "Hamilton constitutes a fascinating example of a 'transcultural personality,' growing up in a family whose values and tropes of identity were unrecognised by, and unacceptable to, the surrounding culture" (114). If indeed "your language is your country," Hamilton is a cosmopolitan who yearns for a space between and beyond national boundaries, a utopia in the root sense of a state of mind that is no place.

Frustrated by having to choose between Lennon and Schwarzkopf, Hamilton wants both, but he is powerless to explain to his father the cosmopolitan urge to inhabit a realm defined by aesthetics, not linguistics or geopolitics: "I want to tell him that people like John Lennon and Ernest Hemingway and Franz Kafka are living in the same country now. It's the country I belong to as well, one without any flag" (*Sailor* 75). By the conclusion of *The Speckled People*, Hamilton has come to embrace the panlingual utopia of his imagination. "I'm not afraid any more of being German or Irish, or anywhere in between," he writes. "Maybe your country is only a place you make up in your own mind. Something you dream about and sing about. Maybe it's not a place on the map at all, but just a story full of people you meet and places you visit, full of books and films you've been to" (*Speckled* 295). Hamilton has rejected the *Vaterland* and the *Muttersprache*, the *athartha* and the *teanga athair*, in order to dwell in the domain of artistic expression. In English.

Hamilton's feckless father (who dies when attacked by a swarm of bees he was gathering in his apiary on the roof) is a failure at devising moneymaking schemes to sell crucifixes and toy trolleys. However, he is a trained engineer, and, when a problem develops with the national power grid, he is called in to solve it. No one can figure out why an English transformer cannot be made to work in series with a German transformer to generate electricity for Ireland. Séan spends many days pondering why one machine is unable to talk to the other. Rejecting any supernatural explanation that would attribute some devious motive to the transformers, he insists that machines are tools that will react predictably to human agency. "Under the right conditions, with no obstacles in the way," he explains to his family, "a machine will do as it is told in any language" (*Sailor* 235). Listening to that statement, the family is shocked to realize that, for the first time anyone can remember, Séan is speaking English within their house.

Part of the reason for slipping into English might simply be his excitement at figuring out exactly why the transformers are not running in tandem; both have dials, but the German one is set to run clockwise and the English counterclockwise. However, the insight that "a machine will do as it is told in any language" undercuts the rationale for cultivating different languages. Even an Irish patriot recognizes that English will do at least as well as Irish for discussing a technological problem. The scene helps prepare Hamilton for asserting his freedom from Ireland and Irish but, most importantly, his rejection of subservience to any particular nation or language. It is a faint echo of Ireland's most celebrated exiles, James Joyce and Samuel Beckett, who spent their careers in other countries speaking other languages. "I grew up with Joyce and Beckett," Hamilton told an interviewer. "It is very hard to avoid Joyce. He's in the atmosphere all around here even where I grew up" (Randolph 34).

Rebelling against the constrictions of an Irish identity, Joyce's Stephen Dedalus proclaims, "When the soul of a man is born in this country there are nets flung at it to hold it back from flight. You talk to me of nationality, language, religion. I shall try to fly by those nets" (Joyce 157). Like *A Portrait of the Artist as Young Man*, Hamilton's autobiographical volumes constitute a bildungsroman/künstlerroman that concludes with a declaration of independence. *A Portrait* opens, famously, with a young boy's perspective: "Once upon a time and a very good time it was there was a moocow coming down along the road and the moocow that was coming down along the road met a nicens little boy named baby tuckoo . . ." (Joyce 3). Like Joyce, Hamilton begins with a passive child's eye view. From the first sentence of *The Speckled People*—"When you're small you know nothing" (*Speckled* 1)—he recreates the perspective of a powerless boy who has no choice but to accept the political and linguistic dimensions of his universe. He is caught in the nets of nation and language. However, by the final page of the entire project, he is aspiring to a post-national, postlingual condition. At the end of *The Sailor in the Wardrobe*, Séan Ó hUrmoltaigh is dead, and his prodigal son has left Dublin for Berlin. Hugo Hamilton affirms, "Now I want to belong to the same country as Bob Dylan and Dostoevsky and Fassbinder" (*Sailor* 263). In the country he longs for, all conflicts between languages will be resolved and the separate selves pulling at Hugo Hamilton will be reconciled. Until then, the author keeps writing.

Jhumpa Lahiri
Goes Italian

Any casual runner knows how diabolically difficult it is to traverse 26.2 miles in under five hours. However, in 2011, James Gefke not only completed the 115th Boston Marathon in four hours, eighteen minutes, and twenty-nine seconds. In order to honor the memory of a fellow firefighter, Gefke did it while carrying thirty pounds of firefighting gear (Held). Similarly, anyone who has ever tried to write a book might agree with George Orwell's assessment that it is "a horrible, exhausting struggle, like a long bout of some painful illness" (Orwell 395). Why exacerbate the horror by contending with the additional burden of a foreign language's unfamiliar vocabulary and grammar? Joseph Conrad wrote remarkable fiction not in his native Polish or even his second language, French, but in English, a language he began studying seriously only after settling in England while in his twenties. Conrad likened his literary translingualism to arduous, dangerous labor. "I had to work like a coal-miner in his pit quarrying all my English sentences out of a black night" (Jean-Aubry 1927, 82), complained Conrad about the ordeal of expressing himself in his adopted English, a language he spoke with an accent so thick it was often unintelligible to his wife, Jessie.

Immigration is a common and compelling motive for switching languages. After news of the 1989 Tiananmen Square massacre convinced Ha Jin, who was studying in Boston at the time, not to return home to

China, it made sense to adopt the language of the country he ended up remaining in. Ten years later, he won the National Book Award for *Waiting*, a novel he wrote in English. Louis Begley, Edwidge Danticat, Ha Jin, Aleksandar Hemon, Viet Thanh Nguyen, and Luc Sante are among many other writers who adopted English after moving to the United States. Translingual transplants to France include Romain Gary, Nancy Huston, Milan Kundera, Alain Mabanckou, and Andreï Makine. Immigrants to Germany who have adopted German as their literary medium include Zehra Çirak, Wladimir Kaminer, Emine Sevgi Özdamar, and Feridun Zaimoğlu. However, many other writers abandoned the language of their homeland without leaving home; Chinua Achebe, Raja Rao, Léopold Senghor, and Wole Soyinka all adopted as literary medium the language of the European imperial power governing their country.

The case of Jhumpa Lahiri differs from all of these. Noting how the three most celebrated translingual authors—Samuel Beckett, Joseph Conrad, and Vladimir Nabokov—all had closer and longer ties to their adopted languages than she has to hers, Italian, Lahiri writes, in Italian, "Mi chiedo se ci siano altri come me" 'I wonder if there are others like me' (*In Other* 190; 191). There are not. Born in London to immigrants from Calcutta, she counts Bengali as her mother tongue, though she admits to an imperfect command of it. When she was two, the family moved to Rhode Island, where she grew up and where she began to cultivate a talent for writing in English. After receiving a BA in English literature from Barnard College, Lahiri continued to pursue her interest in English through two MAs, an MFA, and a PhD from Boston University. With two commercially successful collections of short fiction, *Interpreter of Maladies* (1999) and *Unaccustomed Earth* (2008), and two novels, *The Namesake* (2003) and *The Lowland* (2013), Lahiri has received some of the most prestigious accolades in the Anglophone literary world—a Pulitzer Prize, a PEN/Hemingway Award, and a National Humanities Medal, among others.

She now confesses to an aversion to speaking, reading, or writing English. "English denotes a heavy, burdensome aspect of my past," she writes, in Italian. "I'm tired of it" 'L'inglese significa un aspetto del mio passato pesante, ingombrante. Ne sono stanca' (*In Other* 167; 166). Her first book in Italian, a short series of reflections on the author's passion for the language, discards *inglese* in favor of *italiano*. Originally published in Milan in 2015 as *In Altre Parole*, it appeared in the United States in 2016 in a dual-language edition titled *In Other Words*. Lahiri's Italian text appears on the verso page, its English translation on the recto page. In the very brief "Author's Note" that, she points out, constitutes "the first formal prose I have composed in English since my last book, *The Lowland*, was completed, in 2012" (*In Other* xiii), Lahiri explains that she could not bring herself to translate her work into English. The task was instead entrusted to Ann Goldstein, acclaimed for her translations of Elena Ferrante and Primo Levi. Linguistic demographics suggest that Goldstein's text will be more widely read than Lahiri's.

In Other Words is a love story, the account of what followed Lahiri's initial infatuation with Italy and Italian during a visit to Florence at age twenty-five. Back in the United States, a succession of tutors feeds her passion for the language. Twenty years after her first encounter with Italy, she and her family move to Rome, and, during a two-year sojourn, she determines to express herself entirely in Italian. Symptoms of Lahiri's erotic fixation include separation pangs. During a month spent back in Massachusetts, surrounded entirely by English-speakers, she is distressed by the absence of her beloved. She is as smitten with Italian as the Russian émigré Andreï Makine is with French in his rhapsodic novel *Dreams of My Russian Summers* (1997) (*Le Testament français* [1995]). To find comparable ecstasy for the English language, one must look to the classic immigration memoir *The Promised Land* (1912), in which, erasing the tongue of her Russian Jewish childhood, Mary Antin extols English as beautiful, sweet, logical, and clear (164).

Lahiri describes her book as "una sorta di autobiografia linguistica, un autoritratto" 'a sort of linguistic autobiography, a self-portrait' (*In Other* 212; 213). It could also be categorized as what Alice Kaplan dubbed a "language memoir," autobiographical prose in which the focus is on the author's acquisition of a new language ("On Language Memoir"). Examples would be Kaplan's own *French Lessons: A Memoir* (1993), Nancy Huston's *Nord perdu* (2004), Eva Hoffman's *Lost in Translation: A Life in a New Language* (1989), and Ann Patty's *Living with a Dead Language: My Romance with Latin* (2016). Despite her fixation on French, Kaplan wrote her memoir in English, nor did Patty employ Latin to recount her love affair with the ancient language of Rome. However, Lahiri remains so beguiled by Italian that, despite her admission, "I have to accept that in Italian I'm partly deaf and blind" (*In Other* 179), she cannot imagine writing her memoir in any other language. *In Altre Parole* is so centered on Lahiri and Italian that there is no room for other characters; the author's husband and children remain shadowy, unnamed figures vaguely compliant with Lahiri's desire to immerse herself in Italy and Italian.

The gratuitousness of Lahiri's linguistic choices distinguishes her from most other language memoirists. Whereas some combination of immigration, imperialism, family ties, and market forces impels other translinguals to switch languages, Lahiri's choice of Italian—"a language that has nothing to do with my life" (*In Other* 29)—appears perverse. Early on, she admits, "I don't have a real need to know this language. I don't live in Italy, I don't have Italian friends. I have only the desire" (*In Other* 17). It seems bizarre to sacrifice the considerable advantages of her talent for writing in English to take up a language that is much less widely read. In 2020, English—as both native and acquired language—is the most widely spoken language in the world. It is the dominant language in the United States, the United Kingdom, Canada, Australia, India, South Africa, and more than fifty other countries. A talent for writing in English can provide access to the most influential publishing houses, book distributors, and reviewing media, as well as the largest number of readers and the most glittering prizes of any contemporary language. When Beckett gave up English to write in French, another prestigious language with global reach, he did not have to sacrifice as much cultural capital as Lahiri does when she chooses to write in Italian, the official language of Italy, Switzerland, San Marino, and the Vatican and only the fifteenth most widely spoken language in the world. *In Altre Parole* was awarded Italy's Premio Letterario Viareggio-Rèpaci, but its prestige is not nearly as lustrous internationally as the Man Booker Prize and the National Book Award, for both of which Lahiri's last book in English, *The Lowland*, was shortlisted.

Francesca Marciano is at a similar stage in her career to Lahiri's. She, too, has published four books of fiction—three novels, *Rules of the Wild* (1998), *Casa Rossa* (2004), and *The End of Manners* (2008), and one collection of short stories, *The Other Language* (2014). However, she seems an inverted image of Lahiri. While maintaining a successful career as a screenwriter for Italian cinema, Marciano, who lives in Rome, publishes all of her fiction not in her native Italian but in English. Lahiri is better known and recompensed than Marciano, but that would not be likely had she published all four of her previous books in Italian, not English. Hideo Levy, an American *gaijin* who writes all of his novels in Japanese (like Italian, a "minor" language in comparison with English, Chinese, and Spanish), might seem a parallel to Lahiri, though Levy's childhood as the son of a diplomat posted in various parts of Asia made Japanese a more natural choice for him than Italian is for Lahiri. However, Ann Patty's language memoir, *Living with a Dead Language*, offers perhaps the most instructive parallel to Lahiri's willful translingualism. Patty's subtitle, *My Romance with Latin*, emphasizes that, as with Lahiri, her relationship with Latin is, like Lahiri's with Italian, romantic. A retired book publisher, Patty recounts her midlife determination to master classical Latin, a "dead" language with no immediate worldly use except to fulfill her desire for a structure to her existence. At the end of four years of intensive study, Patty feels part of a small but worldwide community of Latinists. By contrast, though, Lahiri's embrace of Italian enhances her solitude. And though Patty writes her memoir in English, not Latin, it is an important part of Lahiri's linguistic project to hazard hers in Italian.

The ability to choose languages is a product of privilege. There are said to be more than sixty million refugees currently in the world, and few of those get to select their sanctuary, or its language. Similarly, passion for a particular language is rarely what drives translingual authors. It is not what led Eva Hoffman, wrenched by her parents out of her beloved Cracow at age thirteen and transported to North America, to live in English rather than the Polish she cherishes. However, Oscar Wilde's social status and education allowed him to write a play, *Salomé*, that scandalized contemporary London audiences, and he compounded the scandal by choosing to write it in French, further thumbing his nose at the English, oppressors of his native Ireland. During the Heian period in Japan, it was fashionable and a privilege of the aristocracy to write *kanshi*, poems composed in Chinese rather than their own Japanese.

Like Lahiri, Ribka Sibhatu switched to Italian, from her native Tigrinya. Like Lahiri, Sibhatu even published a dual-language edition of her literary work, titled *Aulò: Canto-Poesia dall'Eritrea* (1993). However, unlike Lahiri, Sibhatu created both texts, the Tigrinyan and the Italian, and she was drawn to Italy and Italian not out of some mystical attraction but because she was forced to flee violent oppression in her native Eritrea. The bestsellers that Lahiri published in English provided her the material security that enabled her to risk writing in Italian. Nevertheless, *In Altre Parole* is a brave, if not brazen, act, as foolhardy as the determination by Michael Jordan, at the height of his dazzling tenure with the Chicago Bulls, to retire from professional basketball and pursue a career as a major league baseball player. He failed and returned to the NBA, leading the Bulls to three more championships.

Lahiri anticipates that some readers might dismiss her excursion into Italian as "a dead end or, at best, a 'pleasant distraction'" (*In Other* 223). Expressing the hope that Lahiri would soon return to English, Dwight Garner in the *New York Times* did in fact dismiss *In Other Words* as "a soft, repetitive, self-dramatic and self-hobbled book" (Garner). However, disapproval might merely inspire Lahiri, who acknowledges the flaws in her Italian but proclaims, "Imperfection inspires invention, imagination, creativity. It stimulates. The more I feel imperfect, the more alive I feel" (*In Other* 113). Perfection, the kind for which her meticulous English style is often praised, thus becomes lethal, reason enough to grope her way through a strange new language. "If it were possible to bridge the distance between me and Italian," she contends, "I would stop writing" (*In Other* 95).

Lahiri abruptly and unexpectedly became famous when her first book, *Interpreter of Maladies*, sold hundreds of thousands of copies and won the Pulitzer Prize for Fiction. Celebrity was personally discomfiting and, for a writer who thrives on disappearing into her work, an aesthetic handicap. "I wanted to be anonymous and ordinary" ("Reflections"), she explained in an essay, in English, four years before *In Altre Parole*. Italian was an instrument of self-effacement, an exercise in humiliation, in reducing her proudest asset, command of language, to the level of a child's prattle. Echoing Beckett's famous explanation for his turn to French ("parce qu'en français c'est plus facile d'écrire sans style" 'because in French it's easier to write without style'), Lahiri declares, "In italiano scrivo seza stile, in modo primitivo" 'In Italian I write without style, in a primitive way' (*In Other* 58; 59). Disencumbering herself of the expectations created by her nuanced English style, she revels in a newfound freedom. In English, Lahiri cannot escape the burden of being a public figure, but in Italian, she can declare, "Scrivo per sentirmi sola" 'I write to feel alone' (*In Other* 184; 185).

Estranged from both Bengali and English, Lahiri fumbles her way to Italian. "Without a homeland and without a true mother tongue," she presents herself as "exiled even from the definition of exile" (*In Other* 133). In appropriating a statement by Nathaniel Hawthorne as the epigraph for her book *Unaccustomed Earth*, Lahiri underscored the creative stimulus provided by exile. The essay "The Custom-House," which serves as an introduction to *The Scarlet Letter*, compares human vitality to that of a potato: "Human nature will not flourish, any more than a potato, if it be planted and replanted, for too long a series of generations, in the same worn-out soil" (*Unaccustomed* epigraph). Lahiri's switch from English to Italian is a strategy for replenishing the soil. And her compounded exile—living in the language of Rome but admiring above all other poets Ovid, who was banished from Rome—is her literary ascesis, the mortification of her syntax "an act of demolition" (*In Other* 207). To restrain his playful prose, Georges Perec concocted a lipogrammatic novel, *La Disparition* (1969), that excludes the letter *e* from the entire volume. *In Altre Parole* is like an elaborate lipogram, one of those texts that arbitrarily avoid a particular letter of the alphabet. It is purged of all the nuances and felicities that Lahiri could count on in the use of English.

To translate is, for a writer, to pursue another discipline of self-effacement, by subordinating her own imagination to the text of another writer. Two years after publishing *In Altre Parole*, Lahiri returned to English, but only as the translator of an Italian novel, *Lacci* (2014), which, at the invitation of its author, Domenico Starnone, she Englished into *Ties* (2016). In her introduction to the translation, Lahiri says about her first reading of the novel while in Rome, "I was immersed in Italian, in a joyous state of self-exile from the language (English) and the country (the United States) that have marked me most significantly" (Starnone *Ties* 15). While expressing her admiration for *Lacci*, she describes the anxiety she felt about taking on the task of translating it. It would require a "return to English after a hiatus of not working with the language for nearly four years" (19). She feared that the project would distance her from Italian but discovered that the effect was quite the contrary. "If anything I feel more tied to it than ever," she states. "I have encountered countless new words, new idioms, new ways of phrasing things" (19). Lahiri's activity as translator furthers her ambition to immerse herself in the Italian language. In 2018, she went on to translate another Starnone work, his 2016 novel, *Scherzetto*, which she published as *Trick*. Her rendition was honored as a finalist for the National Book Award for Translated Literature. Asked by the *Paris Review* how translation has affected her work as a writer, Lahiri replied, "But even though I'm not writing as much in this phase, I know that the translation is feeding my creative work. Right now, I feel like my creative project is translation" (Piepenbring).

Lahiri continued that project when she edited *The Penguin Book of Italian Short Stories* (2019). In addition to writing the volume's introduction (in English), she translated into English six of the forty Italian stories—by Corrado Alvaro, Italo Calvino, Carlo Cassola, Goffredo Parise, Fabrizia Ramondino, Lalla Romano—she collected. A playful meditation on book covers she presented as a talk at the Festival degli Scrittori in Florence in June 2015 ended up as a sixty-two-page volume she titled *Il vestito dei libri* (*The Clothing of Books*). And she ventured back into original fiction with a short Italian novel she called *Dove mi trovo* (*Where I Find Myself*).

At the end of *In Altre Parole*, Lahiri is poised to leave Rome and return, reluctantly, to America and English. Recognizing her estrangement from English, a language in which she has ceased even to read, she wishes that she could remain in Italy and Italian. She confronts her ambiguous future with two questions: "Will I abandon English definitively for Italian? Or, once I'm back in America, will I return to English?" (*In Other* 119). Or will she take up the discipline of yet another strange, defamiliarizing language, such as Finnish or Amharic? Or might t'ai chi, sandpainting, or hatha yoga provide her with the self-transcending focus she found in taking up a foreign language? The only certainty is that if Lahiri, who currently teaches creative writing at Princeton, does return to fiction, it and she will never be the same, whether in English or Italian.

Linguaphobia and Its Resistance in America

From its very inception, the United States has been a multilingual society, one that expressed its founding principle in a Latin phrase: *E pluribus unum*. It is estimated that only 40 percent of the population of the original thirteen colonies was Anglophone at the time of the American Revolution (Shell "Afterword" 688). Later, when Thomas Jefferson purchased it from Napoleon, Louisiana was largely Francophone. At the time that they were absorbed into the United States, Texas, New Mexico, Arizona, and California were populated by speakers of Spanish and indigenous languages. Hawaiians spoke Hawaiian. Hundreds of non-European tongues were spoken throughout what is now the United States, which, over the centuries, has accumulated a rich body of literature in languages other than English. It includes poetry by Chinese immigrants detained on Angel Island; a slavery memoir written in Arabic by Omar Ibn Said; the earliest work of African American fiction, "Le Mulâtre," written in French by Victor Séjour; Navajo chants; *I de dage*, the classic frontier immigration novel, which its author, O. E. Rølvaag, co-translated from Norwegian as *Giants in the Earth*; *Dafydd Morgan*, a novel written in Michigan by R. R. Williams in Welsh; the Yiddish fiction of Isaac Bashevis Singer; and much, much more. A large and lively body of journalism has been published in the United States in Chinese, German, Spanish, Yiddish, and other non-English languages.

The United States is a nation of immigrants, refugees, and the descendants of people abducted from elsewhere. According to the 2010 Census, 12.9 percent of the population is foreign-born, which is not far below the historical high level set in 1890, when 14.8 percent of the population came from abroad (United States Census Bureau). Nevertheless, this country has also been the site of pervasive and persistent xenolinguaphobia, an animus against the use of any language but English. If the Holy Scriptures—like the Declaration of Independence—are in English, why do true Americans need any other language? Tongue depressors are those wooden implements used by physicians to examine the throat. However, the term *tongue depressor* could also describe those who feel so threatened by the ambient babel that they elevate monolingualism into a religious principle. Religious fundamentalists who, enlisting the authority of a translated Bible, insist on the supremacy, if not monopoly, of English, are just such tongue depressors.

On September 5, 1780, John Adams called for the creation of a national academy that would do for English what the Académie Française did for French: enforce standards of grammar, vocabulary, pronunciation, and spelling. Writing from Amsterdam to the president of the Continental Congress, Adams prophesied the global hegemony of his native language: "English is destined to be in the next and succeeding centuries more generally the language of the world than Latin was in the last or French is in the present age" (Mencken 8). If English becomes the world language, why bother to learn any other? It remained for the North American upstarts merely to Americanize, codify, and canonize the language. That was the lifelong mission of Noah Webster, who compiled a dictionary of what H. L. Mencken would later celebrate as "the American language," which Webster predicted would absorb and supplant all other tongues. Given the existence of an American language, it became logical, especially during wartime, for Theodore Roosevelt to equate Anglophone monolingualism with American patriotism. "We have room for but one language here," contended Roosevelt in 1917, "and that is the English language, for we intend to see that the crucible turns our people out as Americans, not as dwellers in a polyglot boarding house" (Roosevelt). More than any of his presidential predecessors, Roosevelt, himself a prolific author, was a patron of American literature, and, as Aviva F. Taubenfeld explains, welcomed immigrant writers—as long as they were European—to assimilate into it. Opposed to the eugenicist social engineering then coming into fashion, Roosevelt urged national unity based not on blood but language. Roosevelt's conception of American literature, like his conception of American culture in general, was of a linguistic melting pot, the collective creation of insiders and outsiders affirming their membership in "the English-speaking race" (Taubenfield 146). Roosevelt would not have accepted O. E. Rølvaag's *I de dage* (*Giants in the Earth*), Isaac Bashevis Singer's *Der kuntsnmakher fun Lublin* (*The Magician of Lublin*), or Tomás Rivera's . . . *y no se lo tragó la tierra* (. . . *and the earth did not devour him*) into the canon of American literature.

Before 1917, German was the most widely spoken second language in the United States, but during World War I, when sauerkraut was renamed "liberty cabbage" and Potsdam, Missouri, became Pershing, Missouri, it became illegal to teach the language of Goethe (and Kaiser Wilhelm) in many parts of the country. The governor of Iowa, William Harding, even went so far as to ban the use of *any* "foreign language" in public—not only in schools, but on the streets, in trains, even on the telephone. The First Amendment, he proclaimed, "is not a guaranty of the right to use a language other than the language of this country—the English language." Harding even insisted that God responded only to prayers uttered in English. As he explained to the Des Moines Chamber of Commerce, "Those who insist upon praying in some other language . . . are wasting their time for the good Lord up above is now listening for the voice of English." Before World War I, about 25 percent of high school students in the United States were studying German. By 1922, the figure had plummeted to .6 percent, and it has never recovered (Baron).

A popular teachers' guide published in 1921 offered suggestions on how to observe "Better English Week" by having students recite a pledge that included the affirmation "I love my country's language" (Elliott 41). Teachers were advised to encourage students to make posters with admonitions such as "Speak the Language of Your Flag" (Elliott 41). If the Stars and Stripes could speak, it would no doubt be in American English, but would it recite the Pledge of Allegiance to itself?

In 1919, reacting to the widespread dread of infection by enemy agents and uncouth immigrants, Nebraska passed the Siman Act, which stipulated that "no person, individually or as a teacher, shall, in any private, denominational, parochial, or public school teach any subject to any person in any language other than the English language." The law was upheld by Nebraska courts, but in 1923, a 7–2 decision by the United States Supreme Court declared the law a violation of the Due Process clause of the Fourteenth Amendment. Writing for the majority in the landmark *Meyer v. Nebraska* case, Justice James Clark McReynolds—who was otherwise one of the nastiest bigots in Court history (he refused to speak to fellow Justice Louis Brandeis because he was Jewish) and later a staunch foe of the New Deal—explained that "the protection of the Constitution extends to all, to those who speak other languages as well as to those born with English on the tongue" (*Meyer v. State of Nebraska*).

Of course, the Supreme Court did not—and could not—extirpate the virus of linguaphobia within the United States. Abducted into government boarding schools, American Indian children had their mouths washed out with astringent laundry soap for speaking their own languages. In the Southwest, it was not uncommon for Mexican American students to be spanked or even whipped if they were caught speaking Spanish. Gloria Anzaldúa recalls "being caught speaking Spanish at recess—that was good for three licks on the knuckles with a sharp ruler. I remember being sent to the corner of the classroom for 'talking back' to the Anglo teacher when all I was trying to do was tell her how to pronounce my name. If you want to be American, speak 'American.' If you don't like it, go back to Mexico where you belong" (53). An article in the *Chronicle of Higher Education* reports that "in Louisiana, first graders who spoke only Cajun French were forced to wet their pants until they learned how to ask to go to the bathroom in English" (Wheeler A16).

As late as 2018, a federal civil rights lawsuit alleged that employees at La Cantera, a posh resort in San Antonio, Texas, were forbidden to speak Spanish, even among themselves. The population of San Antonio, which, until the Texas Revolution of 1836, was part of Mexico, is more than 63 percent Latino, and, though not all Latinos speak Spanish, the language is widely spoken in the city. The punishment for speaking Spanish anywhere on the property of La Cantera (a Spanish word meaning *the quarry*) was, according to the brief filed in federal court by the U.S. Equal Employment Opportunity Commission, "harassment, excessive scrutiny, difficult work assignments, discipline, demotion, and termination." A manager allegedly disparaged Spanish as "a foul language," and when employees complained about the English-only policy, they were told, "This is America; so speak English! What's the problem?" (Fechter).

Advocates of English-only in America might take heart from the fact that currently the percentage of college students enrolled in language courses is at an all-time low and falling further. According to a recent study by the Modern Language Association, language enrollment has declined by 15.3 percent since 2009 (Looney and Lusin 2). While foreign language requirements were being gutted and majors even in Spanish, French, and German eliminated, monolingualism has become the norm for American college graduates. What Yasemin Yildiz calls "the monolingual paradigm" (Yildiz) and Viv Edwards calls "the monolingual mindset" (Edwards 3–5) seems stronger than ever in the United States.

According to an old witticism, someone who speaks three languages is trilingual. Someone who speak two languages is bilingual. But someone who speaks only one language is American. To be fair, linguaphobia is not exclusively either an American or a recent condition. The monolingual malaise is also endemic in England, Australia, and New Zealand. The Bible, whose Babel story in Genesis portrays multilingualism negatively, as a consequence of human sin, records reasons to be wary of strangers making unfamiliar sounds. Pronunciation of the word *shibboleth* in Judges 12 to distinguish Ephraimites from Gileadites had deadly consequences for the former. During World War II, American troops used pronunciation of the word *lollapalooza* to identify and kill Japanese infiltrators. In addition, during the Lebanese Civil War (1975–1990), strangers attempting to pass through a Phalangist Christian militia checkpoint were asked to pronounce the Arabic word for tomato. If they replied with *banadurra*, in the Lebanese pronunciation, they were given safe passage, but the Palestinian pronunciation, *bandora*, could mean a death sentence. In Chimamanda Ngozi Adichie's novel *Half of a Yellow Sun* (2006), set during the Biafran War among speakers of English, Ibo, Yoruba, and Hausa, characters are killed for speaking the wrong language in the wrong place. Linguistic differences have also turned violent in Belgium, Canada, Pakistan, and South Africa, among other countries.

In addition, language was a significant factor in Brexit, the decision by voters of the United Kingdom to cancel membership in the European Union. In the midst of the campaign to leave the EU, Nigel Farage, leader of that campaign and of the UK Independence Party, recounted a train trip from London to Kent during which he heard no English spoken. "In scores of our cities and market towns, this country in a short space of time has frankly become unrecognisable," Farage said, explaining his opposition to the free movement among EU nations that was resulting in an influx of newcomers speaking strange tongues. "Whether it is the impact on local schools and hospitals, whether it is the fact in many parts of England you don't hear English spoken any more. This is not the kind of community we want to leave to our children and grandchildren" (Sparrow).

To be precise, the problem is not exactly linguaphobia as much as xenolinguaphobia—hostility toward the language of the Other. Many regard the quaint system of sounds and symbols of their own culture as perfectly natural but dismiss any other system as grotesque, superfluous, and sinister. However, those who know only one language do not truly know that language. As Johann Wolfgang von Goethe, who had some facility in seven languages—German, Latin, Greek, French, Italian, English, and Hebrew—observed, "Wer fremde Sprachen nicht kennt, weiss nichts von seiner eigenen" 'If you do not know a foreign language, you know nothing of your own' (Goethe 41). Not only is one of the benefits of lifelong bilingualism, as found in a Canadian study, a delay in the onset of dementia by four years (Bialystok), but, perhaps more profoundly, the metalinguistic awareness that comes with knowing more than one language results not only in increased empathy and emotional resilience but also a greater appreciation for the elements of one's primary language. Monolingual Anglophones often stumble over the subjunctive, the conditional, the pluperfect, and even the differences between adjectives and adverbs. Their vocabularies, like their prospects for employment and their world views, are more limited.

Language is one of the most obvious ornaments of group identity. The categories of "Latino" and "Hispanic" are in fact linguistic in origin. They span racial, geographic, and religious categories and instead designate a Spanish-speaking heritage. The disintegration of a united Roman Europe and the rise of the post-Latin vernaculars collapsed linguistic and national identities, so that it was assumed that to be Latvian is to speak Latvian, to be Hungarian is to speak Hungarian, and to be Danish is to speak Danish. Speaking Provençal, Kurdish, or Basque becomes treasonable. Xenolinguaphobia became more virulent as national boundaries were drawn and reified. While nationalism inspired the Mexican muralists, Walt Whitman's *Leaves of Grass*, Adam Mickiewicz's *Pan Tadeusz*, and Bedrich Smetana's *The Moldau*, it also led to genocide. Albert Einstein diagnosed nationalism as "an infantile sickness. It is the measles of mankind" (Dukas and Hoffman 38). Today, humankind is suffering from a relapse, not only in the United States but in Hungary, Poland, Turkey, Romania, Greece, Italy, and elsewhere. When the natives are restless, they embrace nativism, a turbocharged form of nationalism. Nativists believe in the superiority of those born within the borders of their own country and harbor mistrust toward newcomers. To a nativist, Irving Berlin, Andrew Carnegie, and Li-Young Lee could never be authentically American. A strategy for discrediting a political opponent is to insist that he or she was born abroad, in an uncivilized country . . . perhaps Kenya. Xenolinguaphobia is one of nativism's most salient symptoms.

Latin America produces the most immigrants to the United States, and many of them are indistinguishable from white North Americans, until they start to speak. Spanish or even the trace of a Spanish accent becomes the shibboleth marking immigrants from south of the Rio Grande as imposters. Pride in one's own culture and language easily shades into abhorrence of outsiders. For Charles de Gaulle, nationalism was a pathologically misdirected form of patriotism. "Voilà ce qu'est le patriotisme," he explained, "c'est lorsque l'amour du people auquel vous appartenez passe en premier; le nationalisme c'est lorsque la haine des autres peuples l'emporte surtout" 'Patriotism is when love of your own people comes first: nationalism is when hate for people other than your own comes first' (Poncelet 107; Gary 29). In Richard Aldington's 1931 novel *The Colonel's Daughter*, a character named Reginald Purfleet attempts to draw a similar distinction. "Patriotism is a lively sense of collective responsibility," he contends. "Nationalism is a silly cock crowing on its own dunghill" (Aldington 49). To a true nativist, that crowing is acceptable only in the local language.

Thus, fearful of a backlash from nativists, some American leaders have been wary of using any language but English in public. When John Kerry ran for president in 2004, his fluency in French, acquired at a boarding school in Switzerland, became a political handicap, particularly after, angered over France's refusal to support the U.S. invasion of Iraq, the cafeteria in the House of Representatives renamed its French fries "freedom fries." Derided as "Jean Chéri," Kerry ceased giving interviews in French to reporters from Canada and France and, even later, after becoming secretary of state, made a point of not speaking French on American soil, where English is expected. Later, after leaving office and politics, Kerry accepted the title of Grand Officer of the French Legion of Honor. At the induction ceremony, Foreign Minister Jean-Marc Ayrault praised him as a Francophone and Francophile and the most Gallic of American leaders: "Francophone, francophile, vous êtes certainement le plus français des responsables américains." Hailing France, the United States, and French fries, Kerry proclaimed: "Vive les frites, vive la France, vive les Etats-Unis !" ("John Kerry reçoit").

During the 2012 presidential primaries, Mitt Romney similarly found that his knowledge of French, acquired during more than two years as a Mormon missionary in Paris and Bordeaux, was a liability. Newt Gingrich, Romney's opponent in the 2012 Republican primaries, ran an attack ad titled "The French Connection" that showed Romney speaking the foreign language and even likened him to Kerry. The insidious implication was that anyone who can converse in French is insufficiently American.

For Rick Santorum, another candidate in the 2012 Republican presidential primaries, the problem was Spanish. Puerto Rico was about to hold a referendum on whether to remain a commonwealth of the United States or seek statehood. Ignoring the fact that the Constitution says nothing about language and Congress has never passed a bill to specify a national language, Santorum advised: "Like any other state, there has to be compliance with this and any other federal law. And that is that English has to be the principal language. There are other states with more than one language such as Hawaii but to be a state of the United States, English has to be the principal language" ("Santorum"). This is a nation in which anything but Anglophone monolingualism is suspect. That became apparent on April 6, 2016, when Khairuldeen Makhzoomi, a political science major at the University of California, Berkeley, was removed from a Southwest Airlines flight from Los Angeles to Oakland because he was overheard speaking Arabic in a phone call to his uncle (Kim).

Donald Trump's third wife, Melania, is fluent in Slovenian, Serbo-Croatian, and English and also makes specious claims of facility in French, Italian, and German. But Trump himself speaks only a primitive form of English. If, according to Ludwig Wittgenstein's famous dictum, "the limits of my language mean the limits of my world" (Wittgenstein), he inhabits a very limited world. During the 2016 presidential campaign, he criticized Jeb Bush, his rival in the Republican primaries, for answering a reporter's questions in Spanish during a press conference in Miami. "I like Jeb," said Trump. "But he should really set the example by speaking English while in the United States" (Sevastopulo). Sarah Palin, the Republican vice-presidential candidate in 2012, doubled down on Trump's disdain for languages other than her own. She used an appearance on CNN's *State of the Union* to send this message to would-be immigrants: "When you're here, let's speak American. Let's speak English, and that's a kind of a unifying aspect of a nation is [sic] the language that is understood by all" (Feeney).

During a nationally televised presidential debate, Donald Trump, who began his presidential campaign stigmatizing Mexicans as "criminals" and "rapists," chided opponent Jeb Bush for responding in Spanish to a Spanish-speaking student. Trump proclaimed: "This is a country, where we speak English, not Spanish" ("Trump"). In contrast to other candidates, in 2016 and earlier, Trump did not advertise at all in the Spanish-language media (Goldmacher). And after he took office, the official website whitehouse.gov/espanol disappeared. The new president abandoned the practice—observed by his two predecessors—of posting information in Spanish. By contrast, the state-run Central News Agency of North Korea, perhaps the most isolated country in the world, maintains a Spanish-language website, as do the governments of China, Iran, and Russia, none of which has a sizeable Spanish-speaking population.

Of course, not all champions of English are xenophobes or bigots. One could make a plausible pedagogical case for opposing bilingual education and a political case for advocating a common language as a force for national cohesion. Antipathy, sometimes erupting in violence, by early Zionists toward Yiddish, a language of the Diaspora, derived in part from the desire to adopt Hebrew as the emblem and instrument of a new national unity. Some pro-English activists chafe at describing their movement as "English-only," when they insist that they do not oppose other languages—as long as they are in addition to English. However, ProEnglish, one of the most prominent groups advocating on behalf of the language most widely spoken in the United States, has also fought against other languages. Founded in 1994 under the name English Language Advocates, ProEnglish has so far failed in its quest to have English proclaimed the official language of the United States, though it has succeeded in enacting official-English statutes in several states. It has campaigned against not only bilingual education but also official documents, proceedings, and ballots in anything but English. In 2014, ProEnglish vehemently objected to a Coca-Cola ad aired during the Super Bowl in which "America the Beautiful" is sung in a variety of languages by people of a variety of ages and ethnicities. Marketing their product as the beverage of choice of a rainbow coalition of Americans obviously serves the corporate interests of the Coca-Cola Company, but ProEnglish complained that, by diminishing the role of English, the ad promoted national disunity. Citing the racist views of its founder, John Tanton, and the fact that its executive director, Robert Vandervoort, headed the Chicago chapter of the white supremacist organization American Renaissance, the Anti-Defamation League warned of the organization's "nativist agenda and xenophobic origins and ties" (Segal). The Southern Poverty Law Center has designated ProEnglish a hate group.

Hatred of other languages—that is, hatred of the Others' languages—reflects insecurity in one's primary language. French purists try to quarantine English because they perceive it as a threat to the language of Jean Racine, Gustave Flaubert, and Charles de Gaulle. Nativists, who define themselves through place of birth, often flaunt the language of that place as proof of their identity. An authentic Pole, insists the nativist, was born in Poland and speaks Polish. By contrast, the cosmopolitan, a citizen of the world, resists being defined only by geographical boundaries and insists on linguistic freedom. That freedom was proclaimed in the "Universal Declaration of Linguistic Freedom," drafted in Barcelona in 1996 and submitted to, but never formally adopted by, UNESCO. In 2011, on the fifteenth anniversary of the Declaration, PEN International updated and streamlined it in a text that was presented in Girona, Spain, and called the Girona Manifesto. The following are the most striking of its ten fundamental principles:

1. Linguistic diversity is a world heritage that must be valued and protected.
2. Respect for all languages and cultures is fundamental to the process of constructing and maintaining dialogue and peace in the world. . . .
7. It is desirable for citizens to have a general knowledge of various languages, because it favours empathy and intellectual openness, and contributes to a deeper knowledge of one's own tongue. (Girona Manifesto)

The value of linguistic diversity and the desirability of knowing multiple languages is self-evident and even banal to the cosmopolitan (and surely to anyone engaged in the study of comparative literature—i.e., the study of literature in ways that transcend national and linguistic boundaries). However, to the nativist, such sentiments are fighting words. Pursuing a Russification policy, Joseph Stalin not only deported non-Russian nationalities, such as Volga Germans, Crimean Tatars, and Chechens, to remote edges of the Soviet empire, but, though himself a Georgian, he also attempted to suppress the many non-Russian languages spoken throughout the Soviet Union. Stalin's campaign against what he labeled "rootless cosmopolitans" was often a thinly disguised attack on Jews, but it was more generally an attempt to extirpate alien influences, including languages, from Russian culture. An editorial in the state-run newspaper, *Pravda*, published on January 28, 1949, at the height of the purge of "non-Russian" elements, denounced theater critics for their "bourgeois aestheticism, sheltering an antipatriotic, cosmopolitan, and putrid treatment of Soviet art" ("About One").

"Cosmopolitans" are the avowed adversary of white supremacists in the United States, who share Stalin's nationalist chauvinism, though for them the supreme nation is American, not Russian. The term *cosmopolitan* shows up frequently on the websites of racist and anti-Semitic groups. But it also surfaced during a tense White House press conference in which CNN correspondent Jim Acosta expressed skepticism about a new immigration policy that would give preference to English-speakers. "Are we just going to bring in people from Great Britain and Australia?" he asked. In response, Stephen Miller, a top aide to President Trump, accused Acosta of a "cosmopolitan bias" (Kamisar). Miller, a Jew, presumably did not intend to evoke the anti-Semitic history of such accusations. However, alt-right commentators, who freely employ *cosmopolitan* as a term of abuse, often do.

In his book *Postcolonial Melancholia*, Paul Gilroy calls for "a cosmopolitan commitment," which he defines as "the principled and methodical cultivation of a degree of estrangement from one's own culture and history" (Gilroy 67). It is precisely that estrangement that disturbs nativists, who suffer anxiety over any distance between the homeland and themselves. Yet estrangement—*Verfremdungseffekt* for Bertolt Brecht, *ostranenie* for Viktor Shklovsky—is the governing principle of artistic perception. It is the foundation for the examined life that Socrates insisted is the only one worth living. It is the antithesis of *poshlost*. Only a turnip can enjoy an unreflective congruence with its own culture and history.

Learning an additional language is an act of resistance to the chauvinists of "America First," who usually also believe in English First, and often English only. Every language is, according to Frederic Jameson's metaphor, borrowed from Friedrich Nietzsche, a prison-house (Jameson), but the native language is probably the most constraining facility. It is too easy just to stay within its walls. Acquiring another language provides the ladder by which to scale those walls, although it means landing in another prison. The transfer broadens one's perspective, liberates one to think about penology. Translingualism—writing in an acquired language—and code-switching—mixing languages within a single text—are literary weapons in the war against monolithic thinking. The antidote to the monolingual mindset is a set of the dual-language Loeb Classical Library. Xenolinguaphobia is misdirected dread. Multilingualism conspires only against complacency. As the Anglophone United Kingdom's Royal Coat of Arms declares, "*Honi soit qui mal y pense*."

Omnilingual Aspirations: The Case of the Universal Declaration of Human Rights

In Book I of *The Republic*, Socrates makes a mockery of Thrasymachus's cynical contention that "justice is what is advantageous to the stronger." However, history, written by the conquerors, too often corroborates the claim. While the conclusion to World War II did not necessarily demonstrate that might makes *right*, it did provide the mighty an opportunity to make *rights*. The victorious powers that convened in San Francisco in 1945 to create the United Nations declared, in the preamble to its charter, that one of the new organization's principal objectives was "to reaffirm faith in fundamental human rights, in the dignity and worth of the human person, in the equal rights of men and women and of nations large and small." It was not until more than three years later, after painstaking deliberations and negotiations among its then fifty-eight members, that the UN got around to enumerating and defining those fundamental human rights, in a document titled "Universal Declaration of Human Rights."

The UDHR is, according to *Guinness World Records*, "the most translated document" in the world ("Most Translated Document"). It can be read in 520 distinct linguistic iterations, in languages ranging from Abkhaz to Zulu. However, these versions are not conceived as translations but rather as equivalences, alternate embodiments of identical tenets. The Bible has, according to the Global Alliance, been translated in part into 3,312 languages, as a whole into 670 (*Wycliffe*). However, in

THE CASE OF THE UNIVERSAL DECLARATION OF HUMAN RIGHTS   147

the case of the Bible, unlike the UDHR, it is meaningful to distinguish between the original and its derivatives. The Hebrew and Greek texts possess authority that English, Bengali, and Xhosa approximations do not. Nevertheless, although the Bible is *translated*, the UDHR is, through the theology of international governance, transubstantiated into multiple tongues. No version has priority; none is the urtext. In principle, each is equally valid, transparent, and interchangeable. The utopian—and moot—premise is not only that all humans possess inalienable rights but also that all languages are capable of expressing the same set of fundamental propositions.

The preamble to the UDHR proclaims that the Declaration provides "a common standard of achievement for all peoples and all nations." That standard is presumed to be the same whether expressed in Igbo, Korean, Quechua, Sanskrit, Welsh, Yiddish, or any of 514 other languages. In its English form, Article 5 proclaims that "no one shall be subjected to torture, or to cruel, inhuman, degrading treatment or punishment." But it is difficult enough within an exclusively Anglophone legal system to define the term *torture* and determine whether it applies, for example, to waterboarding. The difficulty is compounded when *torture*, which is prohibited by Article 5 of the UDHR, competes with *torturas* (Spanish), עינויים (*inuyim*, Hebrew), *Folter* (German), пытка (*pytka*, Russian), *cruciar* (Latin), изтезания (*iztezaniya*, Bulgarian), βασανιστήρια (*vasanistiria*, Greek), and *marteling* (Afrikaans) as the common standard of cruelty for all peoples and all nations.

The UDHR was conceived and created in the aftermath of atrocity, when it became urgent for people of good will to do something decisive to prevent the recurrence of genocide and global mayhem. The preamble evokes the enormity of the horrors perpetrated under the Nazi regime, the "barbarous acts which have outraged the conscience of mankind," as the motive for devising the Declaration. To the delegates of the United Nations General Assembly meeting temporarily in 1948 in the Palais de Chaillot in Paris—a city that had only three years earlier been liberated from German occupation—the Rape of Nanking, the conscription of Korean "comfort women," and the brutal war in the Pacific seemed less compelling than the reversion of European civilization to savagery. (A postwar consensus was also not as apparent in Tokyo as it was in

Nuremberg. One member of the International Military Tribunal for the Far East, Indian jurist Radhabinod Pal, issued a scathing dissent from the verdict of his colleagues. Pal voted to find each defendant not guilty, not because he denied that atrocities had been committed but because he challenged the legitimacy of the tribunal as an instrument of justice rather than retribution.) Whatever the impetus, when the leaders of the world met in Paris, they found it imperative to enumerate and affirm the inalienable rights possessed by all human beings of all eras and all cultures. Because uniformity of phrasing was less crucial than universal promulgation, the UN insisted that "no distinction" be made "between languages and dialects since all of them serve the purpose of global dissemination."

The UN actively encourages the creation of additional linguistic versions of the UDHR "to the end that every individual and every organ of society, keeping this Declaration constantly in mind, shall strive by teaching and education to promote respect for these rights and freedoms." In its English, French, and Spanish incarnations, the UDHR was adopted as Resolution 217 A (III) by unanimous vote (with eight abstentions, by five Soviet bloc nations plus Saudi Arabia and South Africa) on December 10, 1948. It immediately began proliferating throughout the planet—not only in the other official UN languages, Chinese and Russian; in Arabic, which became an official UN language in 1973; and in other widely spoken, government-sanctioned languages such as Bengali, Hindi, Japanese, and Portuguese; but also in stateless minority languages such as Aymara, Frisian, Hawaiian, Hmong, Mayan, Ojibwe, and Romani. The UDHR has been invoked explicitly in dozens of national constitutions adopted since 1948, as well as in hundreds of international treaties and conventions. It has also inspired the creation and continuing vigilance of such nongovernmental organizations as Amnesty International and Human Rights Watch. Implicitly, and often explicitly, it has haunted the war crimes trial of Serbian leader Slobodan Milošević, the extended house arrest of Burmese dissident Aung San Suu Kyi, the persecution by the Chinese government of practitioners of Falun Gong, and the use of "extraordinary rendition" by American authorities against suspected terrorists.

But the exceptionally wide diffusion of the UDHR challenges the document's ability to function as a common standard of achievement for all peoples and all nations. According to Talmudic legend, the Septuagint came into existence in the third century BCE when King Ptolemy II placed 72 scholars in 72 separate rooms and instructed them to produce a translation of the Hebrew Bible into Koine Greek. All 72 translations commissioned by Ptolemy were said to have been identical. An infinite number of monkeys with an infinite number of keyboards might eventually have tapped out those 72 identical iterations, but the Talmudic account (Tractate Megillah 9A) of the origins of the Septuagint seems as miraculous as the parting of the Red Sea. It is likely that even two translators working independently of each other would arrive at two distinct variants. The 520 versions of the UDHR have more in common with the childhood game of *telephone*, in which a message is passed down a line of participants and changes dramatically during transmission.

When a text asserts authority, we naturally seek to identify the author. The United Nations is the collective author of the UDHR, and the individuals who rendered the text into each language have, for the most part, vanished into that invisibility that is traditionally the goal—or at least the fate—of the translator. Most translators strive to domesticate their texts, and, for all their labor, few ever achieve fame or fortune. In only a very few instances does the website for the UDHR, which provides links, in impartial alphabetical order, to each of the 520 versions, credit an individual translator. Philippe Blanchet, for one, is listed as responsible for putting the UDHR into Provençal. Asked which text he used as his source, he replied, "Both English and French, I also had a look at the Italian version for some details" (Blanchet). Pamela Munro is credited with both the Chickasaw and the San Lucas Quiaviní Zapoteco texts, both of which she reports were derived from the English version. About the interchangeability of her translations with their source, she warns: ". . . there are different cultural conceptions of human rights. The UDHR is very much culturally anchored in Western postwar idealism" (Munro). Nor is there universal agreement within Western societies of what exactly those ideals mean and even whether they are worth pursuing. In 2018, the Trump administration withdrew the United States from the UN Human Rights Council. In calibrating his response to the murder of a dissident Saudi journalist, Jamal Khashoggi, within the Saudi consulate in Istanbul, Trump placed economic interests above human rights.

Aside from a few examples such as those, almost all the other versions of the UDHR are attributed to organizations rather than individuals. The Wolof text is credited to the United Nations Information

Centre, Senegal; the Urdu to the UNIC, Pakistan; the Catalan to the UNIC, Spain; and the Sanskrit to the UNIC, India. Several other texts, including those in Albanian, Arabic, Armenian, Dutch, Filipino, Hindi, Sudanese, Telugu, and Tiv, are listed as having been supplied by the United Nations Information Centre, New York. Amnesty International UK is credited with creating versions of the UDHR in Chinanteco, Even, Gagauz, Sardinian, and Scots, while responsibility for the Esperanto version is assigned to Universala Esperanto Asocio in Rotterdam. The effect of these corporate attributions is to emphasize that the document was created by agencies and to deflect attention from the personal agency involved in choosing words from one language to substitute for those of another language. The institutional generation of the UDHR's multiple versions is a form of self-translation similar to what happens when translingual authors such as Samuel Beckett, André Brink, Isak Dinesen, Ariel Dorfman, and Vladimir Nabokov transpose their own writings into another language. And it reinforces the illusion that the UDHR is spread impartially and equally across 520 languages, as if the *echt* Declaration exists not in any single version but rather in the entirety of its iterations. We are led to believe that the sum total of this babel is the consummate articulation of human rights. However, despite the institutional claims for parity, all versions of the UDHR except those in the official UN languages (and probably even a few of those) are translations. And the existence of translations and sources, derivatives and originals, implies a hierarchy of authenticity and authority.

Defining and proclaiming inalienable rights was one of the first priorities of the nascent United Nations after its founding late in 1945. The task was delegated to committees set up by the UN Human Rights Commission, an agency of the UN Economic and Social Council. During most of the painstaking deliberations that consumed two years, the working title for the project was the International Declaration of Human Rights. That name eventually morphed into the United Nations Declaration of Human Rights. However, during the final stage of drafting, the French delegation, preferring to deflect attention from the sponsors of the Declaration to its beneficiaries, convinced their colleagues to change the document's title again, to what it has been known as since (Morsink 33). "Universal Declaration of Human Rights" might seem a solecism, an instance of misplaced modification. Surely, despite the placement of the modifier, it is *human rights* that are universal, not the Declaration. Yet, even before the drafting process was complete, the UN Human Rights Commission was forced to defend its premise that certain rights are valid everywhere, independently of the milieux in which they are embedded.

In June 1947, the executive board of the American Anthropological Association sent a preemptive letter to the Commission warning about ethnocentric presumptions in "a statement of rights conceived only in terms of the values prevalent in the countries of Western Europe and America" (Glendon 222). While the drafting committee was wrestling with the wording of the UDHR, another UN agency, UNESCO, queried 150 prominent thinkers about whether it is indeed possible to identify any core values shared by all cultures. Among the respondents, who also included Benedetto Croce, Aldous Huxley, Richard McKeon, Salvador de Madariaga, and Pierre Teilhard de Chardin, Jacques Maritain was skeptical about finding common ground among widely diverse world views, noting that "the ideological contrast is irreducible and no theoretical reconciliation is possible" (Normand 183). More interested in responsibilities than rights, Mohandas Gandhi stated, "I learned from my illiterate but very wise mother that all rights to be deserved came from duty well done" (qtd. in Normand 184). Nevertheless, the UNESCO study concluded that, despite the fact that fundamental convictions throughout the world "are stated in terms of different philosophic principles and on the background of divergent political and economic systems" (Glendon 222), for practical purposes it is in fact possible to identify certain practices that are intolerably abhorrent in all human societies and others that elicit unanimous approbation.

Urging adoption of the document that she and others had been laboring over during more than eighty meetings in Europe and the United States, Eleanor Roosevelt, who chaired the UN Human Rights Commission, told the General Assembly: "This Declaration may well become the international Magna Carta of all men everywhere. We hope its proclamation by the General Assembly will be an event comparable to the proclamation of the Declaration of the Rights of Man by the French people in 1789, the adoption of the Bill of Rights by the people of the United States, and the adoption of comparable declarations at different times in other countries"

(Glendon 166). However, the Magna Carta, the Déclaration des droits de l'Homme et du Citoyen, and the Bill of Rights form part of a very specific Western political tradition, one that the framers of the UDHR consciously tried, with varying degrees of success, to enlarge. They were sensitive to the accusation of slighting values from other cultures and assuming the universality of their own. They pointed to the fact that the drafting committee consisted of delegates from eight far-flung nations—Australia, Chile, China, France, Lebanon, the Soviet Union, the United Kingdom, and the United States—and that many of the 50 other nations that in 1948 constituted the UN provided significant input into the thirty articles adopted as the final document. In 1993, forty-five years after its adoption, when 171 nations met in Vienna to reaffirm their commitment to the core principles of the UDHR, their official communiqué proclaimed: "The universal nature of these rights and freedoms is beyond question" ("Vienna Declaration").

Yet questions have in fact been raised from the very beginning, despite conscientious attempts to paper over political and linguistic discrepancies. The question of whether there are indeed cultural universals parallels the question of whether there are linguistic ones. A belief that human rights transcend the attitudes and mores of specific societies is not dissimilar from a Chomskyan conviction that deep structures common to all human languages are more significant than superficial differences in morphology, syntax, and phonology. *Universal*, the floating modifier in "Universal Declaration of Human Rights," points to its premise that both rights and writing transcend place and time. Though rational human beings might agree on some broad propositions, that premise is a mirage in both law and linguistics.

Intent on demonstrating how international and conscientious the project of creating the UDHR was, Charles Habib Malik, the delegate from Lebanon and a key figure during the drafting process, observed that "it may be that no other document in history, of the importance of the Universal Declaration, received the same world-wide, sustained consideration and scrutiny that this document did" ("Drafting" 19). Elsewhere, he recalled that ". . . every word and comma and semicolon was gone over most carefully several times by the chancelleries and representatives of some fifty-eight governments . . ." ("Human Rights" 275). However, precision in punctuation could not guarantee linguistic homology. English and French were the working languages of the committees that hammered out the wording of the UDHR, though Chinese, Russian, and Spanish were also at the time official languages of the UN. A month before the Declaration—in English, French, and Spanish texts—was submitted to a vote of the General Assembly, a subcommittee appointed at Malik's initiative was established "to ensure exact correspondence of the text in the five official languages of the UN" (Alfredsson 163). Of course, there can be no exact correspondence between Chinese and Russian or even between French and Spanish, and adding languages beyond those five has meant multiplying discrepancies. As Christopher Kuner notes, "The presumption of similar meaning is nothing more than a rule of convenience designed to reconcile the practice of providing authentic versions of treaties in as many as five or six languages with the general unwillingness to interpret treaties in a truly multilingual fashion" (Kuner 962).

In international relations as in poetry, translation is indeed betrayal, if unavoidable. The initial draft of the UDHR was prepared by John Peters Humphrey, a legal scholar from Canada who served as head of the UN Secretariat on Human Rights. Though bilingual in English and French, he worked primarily in English. Humphrey's draft was revised by René Cassin, a prominent French jurist whose command of English was shaky. He confessed in his memoir that, confused over what was being said during one meeting, he inadvertently voted in favor of a measure he actually opposed: "I failed to understand, and thus let pass, proposals and resolutions that did not correspond to my own views" (Normand 196).

Neither English nor French was a problem for the Lebanese Malik, a philosopher who had written his doctoral dissertation under Alfred North Whitehead at Harvard University and later taught at the American University of Beirut. Nor was it for the drafting committee's vice chairman, Peng-chun Chang, the Chinese delegate who had earned his PhD under John Dewey at Columbia University. The Indian delegate, Hansa Mehta, had translated *Hamlet*, *The Merchant of Venice*, and *Gulliver's Travels*, as well as *Le Bourgeois Gentilhomme* and *Tartuffe*, into Gujarati. Carlos P. Rómulo, the delegate from the Philippines, had earned an MA from Columbia University, served as chairman of the Department of English at the University of the Philippines, and received a Pulitzer

Prize for his English-language journalism. Eleanor Roosevelt, who patiently and deftly guided the UDHR from conception to adoption, was of course, like William Hodgson of Australia and Charles Dukes of the United Kingdom, an Anglophone. However, she was fluent enough in French that once, when Cassin spoke so long without pausing for translation that the interpreter left the room in tears, she was able to provide an English summary of his speech (Glendon 31). Of the core members of the drafting team, only Hernán Santa Cruz of Chile and Alexei Pavlov of the Soviet Union might have had to rely on translators to understand and be understood during the course of the proceedings.

The specific choice of words in a UN text is a matter of more than merely stylistic interest. A statement on human rights created and endorsed by the world body has real-life implications and consequences. Nevertheless, anxious not to get bogged down further in disputes over definition and jurisdiction, the framers of the UDHR agreed to defer questions of implementation and enforcement. The visionary document that the UN adopted in 1948 was designed to provide a set of guiding principles for all people for all time. It is not legally binding the way that the UN Covenant on Civil and Political Rights and the UN Covenant on Economic, Social, and Cultural Rights, both ratified in 1976, are, but it has had a wider influence through its moral force as "a common standard of achievement for all peoples and all nations." Beyond its widespread incorporation into subsequent national and international law, the UDHR has inspired millions throughout this imperfect world with a forthright statement of how things ought to be.

The framers aimed for lucidity and economy, and most accounts of the drafting of the UDHR discuss the language of the document not in terms of the incommensurability of Italian, Persian, and Thai but rather in terms of how, aiming for precision, concision, and simplicity, delegates fretted over their choice of words, subjecting parts of the document to fourteen hundred separate committee votes before the General Assembly finally adopted it in toto. Alert to redundancies, the architects of the UDHR pared the forty-nine articles in Humphrey's first draft down to thirty in the final version. Most agreed with Chang that the Declaration "should be as simple as possible and in a form which was easy to grasp" (Morsink 34). Though Article 46 in the Humphrey draft, which guaranteed the right to expression, education, and litigation in an individual's own language, disappeared from later versions, its principle of linguistic equality was assumed to be implicit in the rest of the document. And language as the medium of the UDHR itself was never far from the deliberations.

Some friction among the drafters over the wording of rights was ideological rather than linguistic, though the English word *right* does not translate perfectly into the Russian *право* (*prava*) the Chinese 權 (*quán*), or the Hindi सही (*sahī*). The Greek word δικαιώματα (*dikaiómata*) and זכויות (*zkhuyot*), the Hebrew word, lack any authoritative association with the dominant right hand found in the words *rights, droits, derechos, and Rechte*. Western delegates, heirs to an Enlightenment emphasis on the individual as an independent moral agent, were most intent on affirming civil and political principles (freedom of speech, assembly, and belief; presumption of innocence), while delegates from the Soviet bloc and Latin America emphasized economic and social ones (the right to employment, education, health care, and housing). Franklin D. Roosevelt's 1941 "Four Freedoms" speech, proclaiming freedom of expression and belief as well as freedom from want and fear, provided a basis for consensus, and the UDHR ended up accommodating both libertarian and communitarian orientations toward rights. Disagreement over the wording of religious rights focused on the possibility of conversion. To Muslim delegates, Article 18's guarantee of the freedom to switch religions translated into Arabic not as a freedom but as مرتد (murtad), apostasy. That and Article 16's guarantee of equal rights in marriage led Saudi Arabia to abstain on the final vote to adopt the document.

During discussion of Article 2's insistence that everyone, without distinction, is entitled to the rights set forth in the Declaration, M. H. Klevkovkin, the Ukrainian delegate, recommended specifying that those rights apply regardless of social status. He suggested inserting the term *сословие* (sosloviye), a Ukrainian and Russian word meaning, roughly, "estate." However, because historical Eastern European social categories do not translate easily into other languages, *сословие* did not make it into the final English draft, which guarantees human rights regardless of "race, colour, sex, language, religion, political or other opinion, national or social origin, property, birth or other status." A variant of *сословие* does show up in the Russian version, but not in the Ukrainian.

Article 4, which prohibits slavery, originally stated: "No one shall be held in slavery or involuntary servitude," though the French version simply stated: "Nul ne sera ... tenu en servitude," omitting the adjective "involontaire" (Verdoodt 103). When A. F. Canas, the delegate from Costa Rica, pointed out the discrepancy, Cassin—ignoring a landmark in French political theory, Etienne de la Boétie's *Discours de la servitude volontaire* (1549)—observed that in French *all* servitude is involuntary. Though in English it is possible to describe certain military and occupational commitments as "voluntary servitude," the phrase "involuntary servitude," Cassin insisted, does not have any meaning in French. To repair this disparity between the English and French texts, the committee voted 17–15, with 4 abstentions, to delete the word "involuntary" from the final English text.

The English version of Article 12, guaranteeing that "no one shall be subjected to arbitrary interference with his privacy," was rendered into French as "nul ne sera l'objet d'immixtions arbitraires dans sa vie privée," into Spanish as "nadie será objeto de injerencias arbitrarias en su vida privada," and into German as "niemand darf willkürlichen Eingriffen in sein Privatleben." However, some communal cultures do not valorize or even recognize privacy, and their languages lack a term to denote it. Russian lacks a satisfactory equivalent for *privacy, vie privée, vida privada,* or *Privatleben,* and its version of Article 12, "Никто не может подвергаться произвольному вмешательству в его личную ...," instead affirms the protection of the *personal* (*личную, lichnuyu*), which is not quite the same as *privacy*.

It is possible to go through the entirety of the Declaration, from the Preamble to the conclusion of Article 30, noting divergences created by the fact that no two languages are identical. However, a glance at Article 1, a statement of the fundamental premises on which the entire document is based, might suffice for a sense of how cacophonous is the polyglot polytext that the United Nations sent off into the world. The draft that Cassin submitted in June 1947 begins "Tous les hommes sont frères. Comme êtres doués de raison et membres d'une seule famille, ils sont libres et sont égaux en dignité et en droits." He was clearly borrowing from the 1789 Déclaration des droits de l'Homme et du Citoyen, whose first article begins "Les hommes naissent et demeurent libres et égaux en droits" 'Men are born and remain free and equal in rights.' The English rendition of Cassin's text submitted to the committee was "All men, being members of one family, are free, possess equal dignity and rights, and shall regard each other as brothers." In French, English, Spanish, and many other European languages, "men" can function as synecdoche for "human beings," though since 1948 it has grown increasingly suspect as sexist.

However, a Soviet delegate, Vladimir Koretzsky, objected, contending that the phrase "All men" is one of those "historical atavisms which preclude us from an understanding that we men are only one-half of the human species" (Glendon 68). Although she called herself a feminist, Roosevelt defended the commonplace conflation of "men" with "human beings." After considerable discussion, the drafting committee eliminated the masculine subject, making the opening of Article 1 read "Tous les êtres humains naissent libres et égaux en dignité et en droits" / "All human beings are born free and equal in dignity and rights." Nevertheless, in Basque, it is necessary to distinguish between male and female, and, instead of making the subject of the sentence in Article 1 generic, the Basque version of the UDHR had to substitute a compound subject: "Gizon-emakume guztiak aske jaiotzen dira" 'All men and women are born free.' The second sentence of Article 1 still calls for "a spirit of brotherhood," and the French version, echoing the revolutionary call for *liberté, égalité, et fraternité*, similarly demands a spirit of *fraternité*. The German version likewise refers to *Geiste der Brüderlichkeit* and the Hebrew to רוח של אחווה.

Again avoiding a masculine bias, the Basque version calls for all human beings to behave toward one another *artean senide*—as if within the family. One hopes that Basque families are not abusive. The name of the document—in English, "Universal Declaration of Human Rights"; in Spanish, "Declaración Universal de Derechos Humanos"; in Russian, "Всеобщая декларация прав человека"; in Chinese, "世界人权宣言"; and in Arabic, "الإعلان العالمي لحقوق الإنسان"—is generic, but the French version, "Déclaration universelle des droits de l'homme," is not. It declares the rights of *man*, not *humans*. It echoes the hallowed "Déclaration des droits de l'Homme et du Citoyen" and demonstrates how, even if their syntax and vocabularies are similar, languages bear different historical freight.

Similarly, inclusion of the word *dignity* in the English version of Article 1 is a legacy of the European Enlightenment, during which Immanuel Kant insisted that rational human beings are ends in themselves, not means toward an end, that they possess an inherent dignity, what in his *Kritik der praktischen Vernunft* (1788) he called *Würde*. While Kant's French contemporaries were still using *dignité* to refer to the respect and privilege claimed by persons of high position, the French text of the UDHR leveled the meaning of *dignité*, to proclaim that all human beings possess inherent value. The English version of Article 1 might have done better to assert that all human beings are equal in *worth* or *value*, since the word *dignity* in English evokes the fusty image of starched collars and walking sticks. Surely the UDHR is not intended as an accessory to vanity or as a prohibition against satirists such as Jon Stewart or Stephen Colbert from deflating the self-esteem of the sanctimonious and the hypocritical. Nor is *dignity* exactly commensurate with αξιοπρέπεια (*axioprépeia*), dignidade, כבוד (*kavod*), *waardigheid*, or достоинство (*dostoinstva*).

Chang, the vice chairman of the drafting committee, suggested inserting the Chinese word 仁 (*rén*) into Article 1. He explained that, as a combination of the characters 人 (man) and 二 (two), it meant something like "two man-mindedness" (qtd. in Glendon 67). Its English equivalent might be *empathy*. However, the commission instead ended up asserting that human beings are endowed not with 仁, but with *reason* and *conscience*, terms that are themselves each problematic in English and possess imprecise equivalents in other languages. The French text also employs the word *conscience* (just as the Spanish text uses *conciencia* and the Italian *coscienza)*, but the meaning is somewhat different in the Romance languages, closer to *consciousness*. Nor did 仁 (*rén*) make it into the final Chinese version, which employs the term 良心 (*liángxīn*) instead. 良心 (*liángxīn*) is usually rendered in English as *conscience*.

While it is the most ambitious, the UDHR is certainly not the earliest instance of a transnational plurilingual text. Versions of a peace treaty that ended hostilities between the Egyptian Pharaoh Ramesses II and the Hittite King Hattušiliš III in 1271 BCE have been preserved in both Egyptian hieroglyphics and Hittite cuneiform (Šarčević 23). According to the book of Esther, when Haman determined to exterminate all the Jews in the polyglot Persian empire, he prepared an edict in the name of King Ahasuerus and dispatched it "to the rulers of every people of every province, according to the writing thereof, and to every people after their language" (*The Holy Bible*, Esth. 3:12). Ahasuerus rescinded the death decree by sending out countermanding orders in each of those same languages (8:9). The Treaty of Versailles that concluded World War I was drafted simultaneously in French and English and taken to possess primary and equal authority in each. In 1969, as linguistically parallel versions of international agreements were multiplying, the Vienna Convention on the Law of Treaties attempted to codify their status in international law. Article 1 of the Vienna Convention states that "when a treaty has been authenticated in two or more languages, the text is equally authoritative in each language, unless the treaty provides or the parties agree that, in case of divergence, a particular text shall prevail" (Kuner 454 n.5). That has not silenced controversy among legal scholars about whether, in applying plurilingual documents to particular situations, one text is sufficient or it is necessary to consider all authoritative linguistic versions.

Furthermore, ascribing authority is one thing, but Article 3 of the Vienna Convention goes on to make the linguistically absurd claim that "the terms of the treaty are presumed to have the same meaning in each authentic text." *The Unnamable* (1958) could not possibly have the same meaning as *L'Innomable* (1953), even if Beckett had attempted to make his English text a perfect facsimile of his French novel. It is as naive to assume perfect congruence between the English and Russian texts of the Nuclear Non-Proliferation Treaty ("the English, Russian, French, Spanish, and Chinese texts of which," according to its Article XI, "are equally authentic") as between *Lolita* and *Лолита*, even if Nabokov had not consciously reconceived his novel between its publication in English in 1955 and in Russian in 1967.

When they were signed in Uccialli in 1889, it was agreed that the Amharic and Italian versions of the Treaty of Friendship and Commerce between Italy and Ethiopia possessed equal authority (Tabory 5). In

Amharic, Article 17 stated that Emperor Menelik II *was permitted* to use the services of the Italian government to conduct foreign relations. However, when the emperor discovered that the Italian text stated that he *was obliged* to use the services of the Italian government to conduct foreign relations, he was furious at the attempt to erase Ethiopia's sovereignty through linguistic legerdemain. By 1896, the discrepancy between the two texts had led to a war in which Italian troops suffered more than five thousand casualties. Because the Italian and Amharic texts were incompatible, Italy was eventually forced to pay an indemnity of ten million lire and to renounce, in no uncertain terms, any claims to Ethiopian territory.

Similarly, many years after the conclusion of the 1967 Six Day War, contemporary tensions in the Middle East remain exacerbated by the fact that the two authoritative versions of United Nations Security Council Resolution 242 do not say quite the same thing. Israel has accepted the English wording of Article 1, which calls for "withdrawal of Israel armed forces from territories occupied in the recent conflict." However, the government of the state of Israel rejects the French text, which calls for "retrait des forces armées israéliennes des territoires occupés lors du récent conflit" 'withdrawal of Israeli armed forces from the (or some of the) territories occupied in the recent conflict.' Because French, unlike English, requires an article or a partitive before a noun, it was impossible to use the phrase "retrait des forces armées israéliennes *de* territoires occupés lors du récent conflit." But because "retrait des forces armées israéliennes des territoires" could mean withdrawal from *the* (i.e., *all the*) territories, Israeli officials found the resolution acceptable only in its vaguer English wording.

Belgium, Canada, India, South Africa, and Switzerland are among contemporary nations that recognize multiple official languages and generate legally binding, parallel texts in each. But the closest analogy to the linguistic pluralism of the UDHR is probably found in the *Official Journal of the European Union*. Published every working day at considerable expense, the *Journal* appears in identical formats in each of the official languages of the European Union. At present, the EU certifies twenty-three languages as "official and working" (English, French, and

German are the "procedural languages" of the European Commission), with more likely to come as its membership expands to include such nations as Albania, Iceland, and Turkey. However, even if the EU ends up having to employ translators to cover as many as thirty languages, its purposes would still seem modest in comparison to those of the UDHR, which aspires to speak about essential things to everyone everywhere.

The UDHR imagines an ideal planet in which hunger, torture, homelessness, unemployment, arbitrary arrest, exploitation, and tyranny do not exist. It projects a utopian vision of the best of all possible worlds created in reaction to a global crisis in which the worst were filled with passionate intensity and the best floundered in the absence of an international mechanism to prevent unprecedented carnage. Of necessity, as a proclamation of general principles, the UDHR abounds with abstract terms such as *freedom, liberty, dignity, justice, equality,* and *rights,* all of which are problematic within just English and impossible to find exact equivalents of in other languages. Philippe Blanchet, who struggled to translate the lofty French and English of the document into Provençal, a language that he insists favors concreteness, noted that: ". . . we don't express things in abstract terms in Provençal and . . . I had to try and find a way to turn it into a more pragmatic and familiar way of saying it, which is very important in the Provençal culture and sociolinguistics rules." Not only did he find it difficult to represent the abstractions in the Declaration, but he reports that Provençal concepts such as *lou parage,* which means the condition of living together as equal beings, simply have no equivalent in French and English (Blanchet).

Moreover, the UDHR adopts the European Enlightenment model of personhood, of the individual human being as a rational, sovereign moral agent. Rights do not exist unless they can be asserted, and they cannot be asserted if they are not articulated. Using the tools of distinct first-, second-, and third-person pronouns as well as the ascription of causality through subject-verb agreement, English and French are efficient mechanisms for delineating the kinds of human rights that did not exist under fascism. Might different linguistic systems in the Amazon rain forest and Papua New Guinea express human relationships very differently? Of course, it is a truism of anthropology that human relationships vary considerably from culture to culture, and a key to all cultures might seem chimerical, attained not empirically but mystically. However, in the first chapter of *De Interpretatione*, Aristotle contends that "affections of the soul" (16^{a}3) are universal, though expressed differently in different languages. For Roosevelt and the other members of the committee convened by the UN after World War II, human rights were indeed what Aristotle would call "affections of the soul," and if a common language does not exist in which to express them, we must stretch all the languages we have to accommodate discourse about rights. An opponent of essentialism, John Rawls would use the term "overlapping consensus" (421) to avoid assumptions about universality. The strategy might seem useful for discussions of human rights. However, in order to understand the overlap, we still need a shared language. And if there is indeed an overlap, we might as well call it universal. The cosmopolis of perfect communication in which every human being is accorded respect persists as a fond fantasy.

In practice, we as social creatures inhabit interpretive communities, in which we are forever negotiating meanings among complementary and colliding texts. Translingual treaties are collective fictions that derive their authority from the premise that we can make languages work for us interchangeably. Like literary criticism, legal hermeneutics is a matter of floating consensus. However, when we decide to accept Stephen Mitchell's "We cannot know his legendary head / with eyes like ripening fruit" instead of, or in addition to, Robert Bly's "We have no idea what his fantastic head / was like, where the eyeballs were slowly swelling" as a substitute for Rainer Maria Rilke's "Wir kannten nicht sein unerhörtes Haupt, / darin die Augenäapfel reiften" (the opening of "Archaïscher Torso Apollos"), it is ultimately a matter of taste. But how we decide to translate and apply "Everyone has the right to an education," in Article 26 of the UDHR, has very practical consequences. Linguistic communities often readjust their reading of *education*—as well as *right* and *everyone*.

The task of the translator is, according to Walter Benjamin's famous essay by that name, to aim to attain the impossible, a pure language that is the consummation of the thousands of actual human tongues. "It is the task of the translator," he wrote, "to release in his own language that pure language which is exiled among alien tongues, to liberate the language imprisoned in a work in his re-creation of that work. For the sake of the pure language, he breaks through decayed barriers of his own language" (Benjamin 261). There may or may not be a Universal Grammar—of human rights or of human language. But each of the 520 versions of the "Universal Declaration of Human Rights" aspires to that ideal language and ideal human condition for which we still lack perfect words.

* * *

As a demonstration of the daunting challenge of achieving linguistic universality, following is the entirety of Article 1 of the UDHR in twenty officially recognized iterations.

English: All human beings are born free and equal in dignity and rights. They are endowed with reason and conscience and should act towards one another in a spirit of brotherhood.

Arabic:
يولد جميع الناس أحرارًا متساوين في الكرامة والحقوق. وقد وهبوا عقلاً وضميرًا وعليهم أن يعامل بعضهم بعضًا بروح الإخاء.

Basque: Gizon-emakume guztiak aske jaiotzen dira, duintasun eta eskubide berberak dituztela; eta ezaguera et a kontzientzia dutenez gero, elkarren artean senide legez jokatu beharra dute.

Chinese: 人人生而自由，在尊严和权利上一律平等。他们赋有理性和良心，并应以兄弟关系的精神相对待。

Esperanto: Ĉiuj homoj estas denaske liberaj kaj egalaj laŭ digno kaj rajtoj. Ili posedas racion kaj konsciencon, kaj devus konduti unu al alia en spirito de frateco.

Finnish: Kaikki ihmiset syntyvät vapaina ja tasavertaisina arvoltaan ja oikeuksiltaan. Heille on annettu järki ja omatunto, ja heidän on toimittava toisiaan kohtaan veljeyden hengessä.

French: Tous les êtres humains naissent libres et égaux en dignité et en droits. Ils sont doués de raison et de conscience et doivent agir les uns envers les autres dans un esprit de fraternité.

German: Alle Menschen sind frei und gleich an Würde und Rechten geboren. Sie sind mit Vernunft und Gewissen begabt und sollen einander im Geiste der Brüderlichkeit begegnen.

Greek: Όλοι οι άνθρωποι γεννιούνται ελεύθεροι και ίσοι στην αξιοπρέπεια και τα δικαιώματα. Είναι προικισμένοι με λογική και συνείδηση, και οφείλουν να συμπεριφέρονται μεταξύ τους με πνεύμα αδελφοσύνης.

Hebrew:
כל בני האדם נולדו בני חורין ושווים בערכם ובזכויותיהם. כולם חוננו בתבונה ובמצפון, לפיכך חובה עליהם לנהוג איש ברעהו ברוח של אחווה.

Hungarian: Minden. emberi lény szabadon születik és egyenlő méltósága és joga van. Az emberek, ésszel és lelkiismerettel bírván, egymással szemben testvéri szellemben kell hogy viseltessenek.

Latin: Omnes homines liberi aequique dignitate atque juribus nascuntur. Ratione conscientiaque praediti sunt et alii erga alios cum fraternitate se gerere debent.

Malay: Semua manusia dilahirkan bebas dan samarata dari segi kemuliaan dan hak-hak. Mereka mempunyai pemikiran dan perasaan hati dan hendaklah bertindak di antara satu sama lain dengan semangat persaudaraan.

Maori: Ko te katoa o nga tangata i te whanaungatanga mai e watea ana i nga here katoa; e tauriterite ana hoki nga mana me nga tika. E whakawhiwhia ana hoki ki a ratou te ngakau whai whakaaro me te hinengaro mohio ki te tika me te he, a e tika ana kia meinga te mahi a tetahi ki tetahi me ma roto atu i te wairua o te noho tahi, ano he teina he tuakana i ringa i te whakaaro kotahi.

Nahautl: Nochi tlakamej uan siuamej kipiaj manoj kuali tlakatisej, nochi san se totlatechpouiltilis uan titlatepanitalojkej, yeka moneki kuali ma timouikakaj, ma timoiknelikaj, ma timotlasojtlakaj uan ma timotlepanitakaj.

Norwegian: Alle mennesker er født frie og med samme menneskeverd og menneskerettigheter. De er utstyrt med fornuft og samvittighet og bør handle mot hverandre i brorskapets ånd.

Russian: Все люди рождаются свободными и равными в своем достоинстве и правах. Они наделены разумом и совестью и должны поступать в отношении друг друга в духе братства.

Spanish: Todos los seres humanos nacen libres e iguales en dignidad y derechos y, dotados como están de razón y conciencia, deben comportarse fraternalmente los unos con los otros.

Turkish: Bütün insanlar hür, haysiyet ve haklar bakımından eşit doğarlar. Akıl ve vicdana sahiptirler ve birbirlerine karşı kardeşlik zihniyeti ile hareket etmelidirler.

Zulu: Bonke abantu bazalwa bekhululekile belingana ngesithunzi nangamalungelo. Bahlanganiswe wumcabango nangunembeza futhi kufanele baphathane ngomoya wobunye.

Glossary

Calque: A word or other expression formed by transposing literally from another language

Code switching: The practice of alternating between two or more languages or varieties of language

Compound bilinguals: Learned their languages in a single environment and, consequently, have a single underlying and undifferentiated conceptual system linked to the two lexicons

Coordinate bilinguals: Learned their languages in distinct environments and have two conceptual systems associated with their two lexicons

Creole: A pidgin that has become the native language of a speech community

Defamiliarization (*ostranenie*): In Russian Formalist theory, aestheticizing perception by "making strange," forcing a fresh take on familiar experiences

Domesticating: A translation in which both the translator and the fact of translation become invisible

Foreignizing: A translation that calls attention to the fact that it is a transposition from another language

Isolingual: Pertaining to an author who writes in only one language

L1: A speaker's or writer's primary language, sometimes called native language or "mother tongue"

L2: A speaker's or writer's first acquired language
Omnilingual: The aspirational condition of knowing all languages
Panlingual: Embracing all languages
Subordinate bilinguals: Learned the second language via the first, typically in a classroom, and have a single system where the second-language lexicon is linked to conceptual representations through first-language words
Translingualism: The phenomenon of writing in more than one language or in a language other than one's primary language.
Xenolinguaphobia: Fear of or aversion to foreign languages

Works Cited

Abish, Walter. *Double Vision: A Memoir*. Knopf, 2004.
"About One Anti-Patriotic Group of Theatre Critics." *Pravda*, 28 Jan. 1949, translated by P. K. Volkov, p. 3, http://www.cyberussr.com/rus/kritikov-e.html.
"About the Universal Declaration of Human Rights Translation Project." *Office of the High Commissioner for Human Rights*, http://www.ohchr.org/en/udhr/pages/introduction.aspx. Accessed 27 May 2018.
"About Three Percent." *Three Percent*, http://www.rochester.edu/College/translation/threepercent/about/.
Aciman, André. *Out of Egypt: A Memoir*. Farrar, Straus & Giroux, 1994.
Adichie, Chimamanda Ngozi. *Half of a Yellow Sun*. Knopf, 2006.
Ælfric. "Preface to Ælfric's Translation of Genesis." Translated by Jonathan Wilcox. *Translation—Theory and Practice: A Historical Reader*, edited by Daniel Weissbort and Astradur Eysteinsson, Oxford UP, 2006, pp. 40–41.
Aesop. *The Classic Treasury of Aesop's Fables*. Running Press, 1999.
Agosín, Marjorie. *The Alphabet in My Hands: A Writing Life*. Rutgers UP, 2000.
Ahmed, Leila. *A Border Passage: From Cairo to America—A Woman's Journey*. Farrar, Straus & Giroux, 1999.
Alameddine, Rabih. *An Unnecessary Woman*. Grove, 2014.
Aldington, Richard. *The Colonel's Daughter*. Doubleday, 1931.
Alexander, Meena. *Fault Lines*. Feminist Press, 1993.
Alfredsson, Gudmundur, and Asbjørn Eide, editors. *The Universal Declaration of Human Rights: A Common Standard of Achievement*. Kluwer Law International, 1999.

Alvarez, Julia. "Leaving English." *The Woman I Kept to Myself*, Algonquin, 2011, p. 111.
Antin, Mary. *From Plotzk to Boston: A Young Girl's Journey from Russia to the Promised Land*. 1894. Markus Wiener, 1996.
———. *The Promised Land*. 1912. Introduction and notes by Werner Sollors, Penguin, 1997.
Antunes, António Lobo. *The Return of the Caravels*. Translated by Gregory Rabassa, Grove, 2002.
Anzaldúa, Gloria. *Borderlands/La Frontera: The New Mestizo*. Spinsters/Aunt Lute, 1987.
Apter, Emily. *The Translation Zone: A New Comparative Literature*. Princeton UP, 2006.
Arana, Marie. *American Chica: Two Worlds, One Childhood*. Dial, 2005.
Aristotle. *Categories and De Interpretatione*. Translated by J. L. Ackrill, Oxford UP, 1963.
Asayesh, Galareh. *Saffron Sky: A Life Between Iran and America*. Beacon, 1999.
Assouline, Pierre. *Gaston Gallimard: Un demi-siècle d'édition française*. Balland, 1984.
Bakhtin, M. M. *The Dialogic Imagination: Four Essays*. Translated by Caryl Emerson and Michael Holquist, edited by Michael Holquist, U of Texas P, 1981.
Baron, Dennis. "America's War on Language." *The Web of Language*, 3 Sept. 2014, https://blogs.illinois.edu/view/25/116243.
Barthes, Roland. "The Death of the Author." *Image-Music-Text*, translated by Stephen Heath, Hill and Wang, 1977, pp. 142–48.
———. *Fragments d'un discours amoureux*. Le Seuil, 1977.
Beauchamps, Pierre François Godart de. *Histoire du Prince Apprius*. Constantinople, 1728.
Beaujour, Elizabeth Klosty. *Alien Tongues: Bilingual Russian Writers of the "First" Emigration*. Cornell UP, 1989.
Bell, Anthea. "Translation: Walking the Tightrope of Illusion." *The Translator as Writer*, edited by Susan Bassnett and Peter Bush, Continuum, 2006, pp. 58–70.
Benjamin, Walter. "The Task of the Translator." *Selected Writings: Volume 1, 1913–1926*, edited by Marcus Bullock and Michael W. Jennings, Harvard UP, 1996, pp. 253–63.
Beowulf. Translated by Seamus Heaney, W. W. Norton, 2001.
Bernabé, Jean, Patrick Chamoiseau, and Raphaël Confiant. *Eloge de la Créolité*. Gallimard, 1989.
Bertran, Antonio. "Califican de estético arresto de Pinochet," *Reforma*, 14 Nov. 1998, p. 2.
Besemeres, Mary. "Language and Emotional Experience: The Voice of Translingual Memoir." *Bilingual Minds: Emotional Experience, Expression, and Rep-

resentation, edited by Aneta Pavlenko, Multilingual Matters, 2006, pp. 34–58.
Bhabha, Homi K. *The Location of Culture*. 1994. Routledge Classics, 2004.
Bialystok, Ellen, F. Craik, and M. Freedman. "Bilingualism as a Protection against the Onset of Symptoms of Dementia." *Neuropsychologia*, vol. 45, no. 2, 2007, pp. 459–64.
Birnbaum, Robert. Interview with Julia Alvarez. *Identity Theory*, 22 May 2006, http://www.identitytheory.com/julia-alvarez/.
Blanchet, Philippe. Email to the author. 22 May 2011.
Bok, Edward W. *The Americanization of Edward Bok: The Autobiography of a Dutch Boy Fifty Years After*. Charles Scribner's Sons, 1920.
"Box Office Business for *Abre los ojos*." *Internet Movie Database*, https://www.imdb.com/title/tt0125659/?ref_=nv_sr_1?ref_=nv_sr_1. Accessed 30 Sept. 2019.
"Box Office Business for *Pearl Harbor*." *Box Office Mojo*, https://www.boxofficemojo.com/movies/?id=pearlharbor.htm. Accessed 30 Sept. 2019.
"Box Office Business for *3 Men and a Baby*." *Internet Movie Database*, https://www.imdb.com/title/tt0094137/. Accessed 30 Sept. 2019.
"Box Office Business for *Trois hommes et un couffin*." *Internet Movie Database*, https://www.imdb.com/title/tt0090206/. Accessed 30 Sept. 2019.
"Box Office Business for *Vanilla Sky*." *Internet Movie Database*, https://www.imdb.com/title/tt0259711/?ref_=nv_sr_1?ref_=nv_sr_1. Accessed 30 Sept. 2019.
"Box Office Business for *Y tu mamá también*." *Box Office Mojo*, https://www.boxofficemojo.com/movies/?id=ytumamatambien.htm. Accessed 30 Sept. 2019.
Brecht, Bertolt. *Brecht on Theatre: The Development of an Aesthetic*. Edited and translated by John Willett, Hill and Wang, 1964.
Breytenbach, Karen. "Prize-Winning Poet Accused of Plagiarism." *Cape Times*, 12 Aug. 2005, https://www.iol.co.za/news/south-africa/prize-winning-poet-accused-of-plagiarism-250665.
Browning, Elizabeth Barrett. "Sonnets from the Portuguese." *Poems*, vol. III, Chapman and Hall, 1850, pp. 188–232.
Bulosan, Carlos. *America Is in the Heart: A Personal History*. Harcourt, Brace & Company, 1946.
"Bunreacht na hÉireann/The Constitution of Ireland." *Roinn an Taoisigh: Department of the Taoiseach*, http://www.taoiseach.gov.ie/eng/Historical_Information/The_Constitution/Bunreacht_n_h%C3%89ireann_October_2015_Edition.pdf.
Cameron, Deborah. *Verbal Hygiene*. Routledge, 1995.
Campbell, Roy. *Collected Works IV: Prose*. Edited by Peter Alexander, Michael J. F. Chapman, and Marcia Leveson, A. D. Donker, 1988.

Camus, Albert. *Carnets II Janvier 1942–Mars 1951*. Gallimard, 1964.
Canetti, Elias. *Das Augenspiel: Lebensgeschichte 1931–1937*. Carl Hanser, 1985.
———. "The Play of the Eyes." *The Memoirs of Elias Canetti: The Tongue Set Free, The Torch in My Ear, The Play of the Eyes*, translated by Ralph Mannheim, Farrar, Straus & Giroux, 1999, pp. 585–34.
Castiglione, Baldesar. *The Book of the Courtier: The Singleton Translation*. Translated by Charles S. Singleton, W. W. Norton, 2002.
———. *Il Cortegiano*. Edited by Bruno Maier, Unione Tipografica Editrice Torinese, 1983.
Chaucer, Geoffrey. "The Knight's Tale." *The Riverside Chaucer*, edited by N. F. Robinson, 3rd ed., Oxford UP, 1988, pp. 37–65.
Chauffier, Louis Martin. "Ma patrie, la langue française." *Domaine Français: Messages 1943*, edited by Jean Lescure, Editions des Trois Collines, 1943, pp. 61–68.
Cimino, Michael. *Big Jane*. Translated by Anne Derouet (Laetitia Devaux), La Noire, 2001.
Cioran, E. M. *Aveux et Anathèmes*. Gallimard, 1987.
Cisneros, Sandra. *Caramelo, or, Puro Cuento*. Knopf, 2003.
Clavel, André. "L'intransigeant amoureux de la France." *L'express*, 3 Apr. 2003, p. 4.
Cocco De Filippis, Daisy. *Desde la diáspora: selección bilingüe de ensayos/A Diaspora Position: A Bilingual Selection of Essays*. Ediciones Alcance, 2003.
Codrescu, Andrei. *An Involuntary Genius in America's Shoes (And What Happened Afterwards)*. Black Sparrow, 2002.
Conrad, Joseph. *The Secret Agent: A Simple Tale*. Penguin, 1986.
Coudé-Lord, Michelle. "Son album en anglais." *Le Journal de Montréal*, 6 June 2012, https://www.journaldemontreal.com/2012/06/06/son-album-en-anglais.
Courtivron, Isabelle de, editor. *Lives in Translation: Bilingual Writers on Identity and Creativity*. Palgrave Macmillan, 2003.
Crèvecoeur, J. Hector St. John de. *Letters from an American Farmer and Sketches of Eighteenth Century America*. 1782. Penguin, 1981.
Cuddy, Lois A. "The Influence of Latin Poetics on Emily Dickinson's Style." *Comparative Literature Studies*, vol. 13, no. 3, 1976, pp. 214–29.
Dagnino, Arianna. *Transcultural Writers and Novels in the Age of Global Mobility*. Purdue UP, 2015.
Dante Alighieri. *The Inferno*. Translated by Robert and Jean Hollander, Doubleday, 2000.
Das, Kamala. "Introduction." *Switching Languages: Translingual Writers Reflect on Their Craft*, edited by Steven G. Kellman, U of Nebraska P, 2003, pp. 5–6.

Delisle, Jean, and Judith Wordsworth. *Translators Through History*. John Benjamins, 1995.

Depner, Dorothea. "The Ruins of Identity: Memory, Postmemory and Belonging in the Works of Christabel Bielenberg and Hugo Hamilton." *Nordic Irish Studies*, vol. 13, no. 1, 2014, pp. 129–47.

Derrida, Jacques. *Le Monolinguisme de l'autre—ou la prothèse de l'origine*. Galilée, 1996.

———. "The Retrait of Metaphor." *Enclitic*, vol. 2, no. 2, 1978, pp. 5–33.

Djebar, Assia. *Ces Voix qui m'assiègent . . . en marge de ma francophonie*. Les Presses de l'Université de Montréal, 1999.

———. "Writing in the Language of the Other." *Lives in Translation: Bilingual Writers on Identity and Creativity*, edited by Isabelle de Courtivron, Palgrave Macmillan, 2003, pp. 19–28.

Doloughan, Fiona J. "Translating the Self: Ariel Dorfman's Bilingual Journey." *Language and Intercultural Communication*, vol. 2, no. 2, 2002, pp. 147–52.

Donoso, José. *Taratuta and Still Life with Pipe: Two Novellas*. Translated by Gregory Rabassa, W. W. Norton, 1994.

Dorfman, Ariel. "Footnotes to a Double Life." *The Genius of Language: Fifteen Writers Reflect on Their Mother Tongues*, edited by Wendy Lesser, Pantheon, 2004, pp. 206–17.

———. *Heading South, Looking North: A Bilingual Journey*. Farrar, Straus & Giroux, 1998.

———. "If Only We All Spoke Two Languages." *New York Times*, 24 June 1998, p. A25, https://www.nytimes.com/1998/06/24/opinion/if-only-we-all-spoke-two-languages.html.

———. *Koers Zuid, richting noord: Een reis in twee talen*. Translated by Sjaak Commandeur, De Bezige Bij, 1999.

———. *Kurs nach Süden, Blck nach Norden: Leben zwischen zwei Welten*. Translated by Gabriele Gockel, Barbara Reitz, and Maria Zybak, Europa-Verlag, 1998.

———. *Kurs syd, mod nord: en rejse imellem to sprog*. Translated by Rigmor Kappel Schmidt, Tiderne Skifter, 2001.

———. *Rumbo al sur, deseando el norte: Un romance bilingüe*. Planeta, 1998.

———. *Um vida em transito: memórias de un homem entre duas culturas*. Translated by Ana Luiza Borges, Objectiva, 1998.

———. *Verso sud, guardando a nord: l'avventura di un doppio esilio*. Translated by Paolo Croci, Ugo Guanda, 1999.

———. "The Wandering Bigamists of Language." *Lives in Translation: Bilingual Writers on Identity and Creativity*, edited by Isabelle de Courtivron, Palgrave Macmillan, 2003, pp. 9–37.

"Dorfman Explores Reality in His New Novel." *The Herald-Sun*, 20 July 2001, p. C6.

Dostoevsky, Fyodor. *Crime and Punishment*. Translated by Constance Garnett, Heinemann, 1914.

Dukas, Helen, and Banesh Hoffman, editors. *Albert Einstein, the Human Side: New Glimpses from His Archives*. Princeton UP, 1979.

Dumas, Firoozeh. *Funny in Farsi: A Memoir of Growing Up Iranian in America*. Villard, 2003.

Eco, Umberto. *Experiences in Translation*. Translated by Alastair McEwen, U of Toronto P, 2001.

Edwards, Viv. *Multilingualism in the English-Speaking World: Pedigree of Nations*. Wiley Blackwell, 2004.

Éigeartaigh, Aoileann Ní. "Homesick While at Home: Hugo Hamilton and *The Speckled People*." *Exploring Transculturalism: A Biographical Approach*, edited by Wolfgang Berg and Aoileann Ní Éigeartaigh, Verlag für Sozialwissenschaften, 2010, pp. 113–30.

Eliot, T. S. "Tradition and the Individual Talent." *Selected Prose of T. S. Eliot*, edited by Frank Kermode, Harcourt, 1975, pp. 37–44.

Elliott, Charles H., and Charles S. Crow, editors. *Sample Materials for the Junior and Senior High School*. State U of New Jersey, 1921.

Ellmann, Richard. *Oscar Wilde*. Knopf, 1988.

Erard, Michael. *Babel No More: The Search for the World's Most Extraordinary Language Learners*. Free Press, 2012.

Ermelino, Louisa. "All Roads Lead to . . . Rome?" *Publishers Weekly*, vol. 261, no. 12, 24 March 2014, pp. 33–34.

Evagrius. "Prologue to *The Life of St. Anthony*." Translated by L. G. Kelley. *Translation—Theory and Practice: A Historical Reader*, edited by Daniel Weissbort and Astradur Eysteinsson, Oxford UP, 2006, p. 27.

Everett, Daniel. *Don't Sleep, There Are Snakes: Life and Language in the Amazonian Jungle*. Pantheon, 2008.

"Facts and Figures about Refugees." *United Nations High Commissioner for Refugees*. https://www.unhcr.org/en-us/teaching-about-refugees.html#facts.

Faulkner, William. *Absalom, Absalom!* 1936. Vintage International, 1990.

———. *Las palmeras salvajes*. Translated by Jorge Luis Borges, Siruela, 2007.

Fechter, Joshua. "Lawsuit: La Cantera Resort & Spa Managers Threatened to Fire Employees Who Spoke Spanish at Work." *San Antonio Express-News*, 25 Sept. 2018, https://www.expressnews.com/business/local/article/Lawsuit-La-Cantera-managers-threatened-to-fire-13256731.php?utm_campaign=mysa&utm_source=article&utm_medium=https%3A%2F%2Fwww.mysanantonio.com%2Fbusiness%2Flocal%2Farticle%2FLawsuit-La-Cantera-managers-threatened-to-fire-13256730.php.

Feeney, Nolan. "Sarah Palin Wants Immigrants to 'Speak American.'" *Time*, 7

Sept. 2015, http://time.com/4024396/sarah-palin-speak-american-energy-de partment/.

Ferré, Rosario. "Bilingual in Puerto Rico." *Switching Languages: Translingual Writers Reflect on Their Craft*, edited by Steven G. Kellman, U of Nebraska P, 2003, pp. 135–38.

Fish, Stanley. "Literature in the Reader: Affective Stylistics." *New Literary History*, vol. 2, no. 1, 1970, pp. 123–62.

Fishkin, Shelley Fisher. *Was Huck Black? Mark Twain and African American Voices*. Oxford UP, 1993.

Fitch, Brian T. *Beckett and Babel: An Investigation into the Status of the Bilingual Work*. U of Toronto P, 1988.

"Foreign Films Translate into Growing Revenue Stream." *U.S. Census Bureau News*, 12 Dec. 2007, http://www.census.gov/PressRelease/www/releases /archives/service_industries/011070.html. Accessed 2008.

Forster, E. M. *Two Cheers for Democracy*. Harcourt, Brace & Company, 1951.

"Francesca Marciano at the New York State Writers Institute in 2014." 16 Apr. 2014, https://www.youtube.com/watch?v=hAHoYc92Q5Y.

Friedman, Amelia. "America's Lacking Language Skills." *The Atlantic*, 10 May 2015, https://www.theatlantic.com/education/archive/2015/05/filling-amer icas-languageeducation-potholes/392876/.

Frost, Robert. "Conversations on the Craft of Poetry." *Robert Frost on Writing*, edited by Elaine Barry, Rutgers UP, 1973.

Fruman, Norman. *Coleridge, the Damaged Archangel*. George Braziller, 1971.

García, Cristina. *Dreaming in Cuban*. Knopf, 1992.

García Márquez, Gabriel. *One Hundred Years of Solitude*. Translated by Gregory Rabassa, Harper & Row, 1970.

Garner, Dwight. "A Writer's Headlong Immersion into Italian." *New York Times*, 10 Feb. 2016, p. C1.

Gary, Romain. "To Mon Général." *Life*, vol. 66, no. 18, 9 May 1969, pp. 26–29.

Gaus, Günter. *Zur Person: Porträts in Frage und Antwort*. Deutscher Taschenbuch Verlag, 1987.

Gauvin, Lise. *L'écrivain francophone à la croisée des langues: entretiens*. Karthala, 1997.

Gellius, Aulus. *The Attic Nights of Aulus Gellius*. Translated and edited by John C. Rolfe, vol. 2, Harvard UP, 1982.

Gilroy, Paul. *Postcolonial Melancholia*. Columbia UP, 2005.

"The Girona Manifesto: Encapsulating the Universal Declaration of Linguistic Rights." 13 May 2011, https://pen-international.org/news/the-girona-manifesto -encapsulating-the-universal-declaration-of-linguistic-rights.

Glendon, Mary Ann. *A World Made New: Eleanor Roosevelt and the Universal Declaration of Human Rights*. Random House, 2001.

Goethe, Johann Wolfgang von. *Goethe's Maximen und Reflexionen: A Selection*.

Edited by R. H. Stephenson, Scottish Papers in Germanic Studies, 1986.

Goldmacher, Shane. "Trump's English-Only Campaign." *Politico*, 23 Sept. 2016, https://www.politico.com/story/2016/09/donald-trumps-english-only-campaign-228559.

Gombrowicz, Witold. *Ferdydurke*. Translated by Eric Mosbacher, Harcourt, Brace & World, 1961.

Granger, Colette A. *Silence in Second Language Learning: A Psychoanalytic Reading*. Multilingual Matters, 2004.

Grossman, Edith. *Why Translation Matters*. Yale UP, 2010.

Guilleragues, Gabriel-Joseph de Lavergne, comte de. *Lettres portugaises*. Cl. Barbin, 1669.

Hamburger, Michael. *String of Beginnings: Intermittent Memoirs 1924–1954*. Carcanet, 1973.

Hamilton, Edith. "On Translating." *Three Greek Plays*. Translated by Edith Hamilton, W. W. Norton, 1937, pp. 9–16.

Hamilton, Hugo. *Every Single Minute*. Fourth Estate, 2014.

———. *Hand in the Fire*. Fourth Estate, 2010.

———. Introduction. *Irish Journal*. 1967. By Heinrich Böll. Translated by Leila Vennewitz, Melville House, 2011, pp. vii–xiv.

———. *The Last Shot*. Faber and Faber, 1991.

———. *The Love Test*. Faber and Faber, 1995.

———. *The Sailor in the Wardrobe*. Harper Perennial, 2006.

———. *The Speckled People: A Memoir of a Half-Irish Childhood*. Harper Perennial, 2004.

———. *Surrogate City*. Faber and Faber, 1990.

——— and Kouadio N'Duessan. "*The Speckled People*—A Conversation with Hugo Hamilton." *La Clé des Langues*, ENS de LYON/DGESCO, 10 June 2013, http://cle.ens-lyon.fr/anglais/litterature/entretiens-et-textes-inedits/the-speckled-people-a-conversation-with-hugo-hamilton. Accessed 20 Sept. 2016.

Hawthorne, Nathaniel. *Nathaniel Hawthorne's Tales*. Edited by James Mcintosh, W. W. Norton, 1987.

Heidegger, Martin. *Über den Humanismus*. 1949. Vittorio Klostermann, 2000.

Held, Tom. "Glendale Firefighter Finishes Boston Marathon in Full Gear." *Milwaukee Journal Sentinel*, 18 Apr. 2011, http://www.jsonline.com/blogs/lifestyle/120070364.html.

Hejmadi, Padma. *Room to Fly: A Transcultural Memoir*. U of California P, 1999.

Hever, Hannan. "Hebrew in an Israeli Arab Hand: Six Miniatures on Anton Shammās's Arabesques." *Cultural Critique*, vol. 7, 1987, pp. 47–76.

Hoffman, Eva. *Lost in Translation: A Life in a New Language*. Penguin, 1989.

Hoffman, Jascha. "Data; Comparative Literature." *New York Times*, 15 Apr. 2007,

https://archive.nytimes.com/query.nytimes.com/gst/fullpage-9A06E3D8163F
F936A25757C0A9619C8B63.html.

Hokenson, Jan Walsh, and Marcella Munson. *The Bilingual Text: History and Theory of Literary Self-Translation*. St. Jerome, 2007.

The Holy Bible: King James Version. Hendrickson, 2011.

Huston, Nancy. *Nord perdu: suivi de Douze France*. Actes Sud, 2004.

Huston, Nancy, and Leila Sebbar. *Lettres parisiennes: Histoires d'exil*. Bernard Barrault, 1986.

Hutton, Christopher M. *Linguistics and the Third Reich: Mother-Tongue Fascism, Race, and the Science of Language*. Routledge, 1999.

Incubus. Movie Fanatic, incubusthefilm.com/esperanto.html. Accessed 2008.

Incubus. Written and directed by Leslie Stevens, performance by William Shatner and Allyson Ames, Winstar, 1965.

"The International Migration Report 2017 (Highlights)." *United Nations Department of Economic and Social Affairs*. 18 Dec. 2017, https://www.un.org/development/desa/publications/international-migration-report-2017.html.

"Irish." *Ethnologue: Languages of the World*. http://www.ethnologue.com/language/gle.Accessed 16 Oct. 2019.

Jalali, Wasfia. "Can't Feel at Home in English: Coetzee." *Outlookindia.com*, 24 Jan. 2011, https://www.outlookindia.com/newswire/story/cant-feel-at-home-in-english-coetzee/709589.

James, Henry. "Letter to Urbain Mengin, November 27, 1894." *The Selected Letters of Henry James*, edited by Leon Edel, Stratford Press, 1955.

Jameson, Frederic. *The Prison-House of Language: A Critical Account of Structuralism and Russian Formalism*. Princeton UP, 1972.

Jandl, Ernst, and Rosemarie Waldrop. *Reft and Light: Poems by Ernst Jandl with Multiple Versions by American Poets*. Burning Deck, 2000.

Jarvis, Charles. "Translator's Preface." *The Life and Exploits of Don Quixote de la Mancha*, by Miguel de Cervantes Saavedra. Translated by Charles Jarvis, vol. 1, J. & B. Williams, 1828, pp. 3–36.

Jean-Aubry, Georges. *Joseph Conrad Life and Letters*. Vol. 2, Doubleday, 1927.

Jenkin, Guy, director and writer. *The Sleeping Dictionary*. Fine Line Features, 2003.

Jin, Ha. "Exiled to English." *New York Times*, 30 May 2009, https://www.nytimes.com/2009/05/31/opinion/31hajin.html.

"John Kerry reçoit la Légion d'honneur des mains de Jean-Marc Ayrault." *Ouest France*, 10 Dec. 2016, https://www.ouest-france.fr/europe/france/john-kerry-recoit-la-legion-d-honneur-des-mains-de-jean-marc-ayrault-4671077.

Johnson, Barbara. "Taking Fidelity Philosophically." *Difference in Translation*, edited by Joseph F. Graham, Cornell UP, 1985, pp. 142–48.

Johnson, Samuel. *Samuel Johnson: Selected Poetry and Prose*. Edited by Frank Brady and William Wimsatt, U of California P, 1977.

Jonson, Ben. "To the Memory of My Beloved Master, the Author Mr William Shakespeare." *The Complete Poetry*, edited by George Parfitt, Penguin, 1988, 263.

Joyce, James. *A Portrait of the Artist as a Young Man*. Wordsworth Editions, 1992.

Kadare, Ismail. *Agamemnon's Daughter*. Translated by David Bellos, Arcade, 2006.

———. *The Concert*. Translated by Barbara Bray, Morrow, 1994.

———. *The File on H*. Translated by David Bellos, Arcade, 1998.

———. *The Palace of Dreams*. Translated by Barbara Bray, Arcade, 1996.

———. *The Pyramid*. Translated by David Bellos, Vintage, 1996.

———. *Spring Flowers, Spring Frost*. Translated by David Bellos, Arcade, 2002.

———. *The Successor*. Translated by David Bellos, Arcade, 2008.

Kamisar, Ben. "Trump Aide Miller Blasts CNN Reporter for 'Cosmopolitan Bias.'" *The Hill*, 2 Aug. 2017, https://thehill.com/homenews/administration/345012-wh-aide-blasts-cnn-reporter-for-cosmopolitan-bias.

Kaplan, Alice. *French Lessons*. U of Chicago P, 1993.

———. "On Language Memoir." *Displacements: Cultural Identities in Question*, edited by Angelika Bammer, Indiana UP, 1994, pp. 59–70.

Keats, John. "On First Looking into Chapman's Homer." *Complete Poems*, edited by Jack Stillinger, Harvard UP, 1982, p. 34.

Keeley, Edmund. *Borderlines: A Memoir*. White Pine Press, 2005.

Keene, Donald. *Chronicles of My Life: An American in the Heart of Japan*. Columbia UP, 1989.

Kellman, Steven G., editor. *Switching Languages: Translingual Writers Reflect on Their Craft*. U of Nebraska P, 2003.

———. *The Translingual Imagination*. U of Nebraska P, 2000.

Kellman, Steven G., and Natasha Lvovich, editors. "Selective Bibliography of Translingual Literature." *L2 Journal*, vol. 7, no. 1, 2015, pp. 152–66, https://escholarship.org/uc/item/86m2x5x9.

Kennedy, John F. *A Nation of Immigrants*. Anti-Defamation League of B'nai B'rith, 1959.

Kerney, Michael P. "Biographical Sketch of Edward Fitzgerald." *Rubáiyát of Omar Khayyám*, translated by Edward Fitzgerald, Houghton Mifflin, 1884, pp. 47–61.

Kim, Soo. "Man Kicked Off Flight After Being Overheard Speaking Arabic." *The Telegraph*, 18 Apr. 2016, https://www.telegraph.co.uk/travel/news/man-kicked-off-southwest-airlines-flight-for-speaking-arabic/.

Kosinski, Jerzy. *Conversations with Jerzy Kosinski*. Edited by Tom Teicholz, UP of Mississippi, 1993.
Kraft, Scott. "A Ray of Hope for S. Africa." *Los Angeles Times*, 17 Apr. 1990, http://articles.latimes.com/1990-04-17/news/vw-1426_1_south-africa/2.
Kramsch, Claire J. *Context and Culture in Language Teaching*. Oxford UP, 1993.
Kundera, Milan. *Jacques et son maître: hommage à Denis Diderot en trois actes*. Gallimard, 1981.
———. *L'Art du roman*. Gallimard, 1986.
Kuner, Christopher. "The Interpretation of Multilingual Treaties: Comparison of Texts versus the Presumption of Similar Meaning." *International and Comparative Law Quarterly*, vol. 40, no. 4, Oct. 1991, pp. 953–64.
Lahiri, Jhumpa. *Dove mi trovo*. Ugo Guanda, 2018.
———. *In Other Words*. Translated by Ann Goldstein, Knopf, 2016.
———. *Interpreter of Maladies*. Houghton Mifflin Harcourt, 2000.
———. *The Lowland*. Bloomsbury, 2013.
———. *The Namesake*. Houghton Mifflin, 2003.
———, editor. *The Penguin Book of Italian Short Stories*. Penguin, 2019.
———. "Reflections: Trading Stories, Notes from an Apprenticeship." *The New Yorker*, 13 June 2011, http://www.newyorker.com/magazine/2011/06/13/trading-stories.
———. *Unaccustomed Earth*. Knopf, 2008.
———. *Il vestito dei libri*. Ugo Guanda, 2017.
Lefevere, André, editor. *Translation/History/Culture: A Sourcebook*. Routledge, 1992.
Lefevre, Raoul. *The Recuyell of the Historyes of Troye*. Translated by William Caxton, William Caxton, 1474.
Leland, John. "Adventures of a Teenage Polyglot." *New York Times*, 11 Mar. 2012, p. MB1.
Lem, Stanislaw. *Solaris*. Translated by Joanna Kilmartin and Steve Cox, Walker & Co., 1970.
Lesser, Wendy, editor. *The Genius of Language: Fifteen Writers Reflect on Their Mother Tongue*. Pantheon, 2004.
Levine, Suzanne Jill. *The Subversive Scribe: Translating Latin American Fiction*. Graywolf, 1991.
Levy, Hideo. *The Room Where the Star Spangled Banner Cannot Be Heard: A Novel in Three Parts*. Translated by Christopher D. Scott, Columbia UP, 2011.
———. *Seijouki no kikoenai heya*. Kodansha, 1992.
Levý, Jiří. "From *Literary Translation as an Art Form*." *Translation—Theory and Practice: A Historical Reader*, edited by Daniel Weissbort and Astradur Eysteinsson, Oxford UP, 2006, pp. 337–45.

Lewis, Philip E. "The Measure of Translation." *Difference in Translation*, edited by Joseph F. Graham, Cornell UP, 1985, pp. 31–62.
Li, Yiyun. "To Speak Is to Blunder." *The New Yorker*, 2 Jan. 2017, pp. 31–33, https://www.newyorker.com/magazine/2017/01/02/to-speak-is-to-blunder.
Lim, Shirley Geok-lin. *Among the White Moon Faces: An Asian-American Memoir of Homelands*. Feminist Press, 1996.
Lima, José Lezama. *Paradiso*. Translated by Gregory Rabassa, Dalkey Archive, 2000.
Lindgren, Astrid. *Pippi Longstocking*. Puffin, 1997.
Lionnet, Françoise. *Autobiographical Voices: Gender, Race and Self-Portraiture*. Cornell UP, 1989.
Looney, Dennis, and Natalia Lusin. "Enrollments in Languages Other Than English in United States Institutions of Higher Education, Summer 2016 and Fall 2016: Preliminary Report." *Modern Language Association*, 2018, https://www.mla.org/content/download/83540/2197676/2016-Enrollments-Short-Report.pdf.
Louÿs, Pierre. *Les Chansons de Bilitis*. Librairie de l'Art Indépendant, 1894.
Lowell, Robert. Introduction. *Imitations*, Farrar, Straus & Giroux, 1961, pp. xi–xiii.
Lvovich, Natasha. *The Multilingual Self: An Inquiry into Language Learning*. Lawrence Erlbaum, 1997.
Macpherson, James. *Fingal, An Ancient Epic Poem, in Six Books: Together with Several Other Poems, Composed by Ossian the Son of Fingal*. R. Fitzsimons, 1762.
Mahfouz, Naguib. *Children of the Alley*. Translated by Peter Theroux, Doubleday, 1996.
Mair, Elizabeth Floyd. "Language Choices." *Albany Times Union*, 3 Apr. 2014, http://www.timesunion.com/living/article/Language-choices-5374338.php.
Maisonnat, Claude. "Le français dans l'écriture conradienne." *Cahiers victoriens et édouardiens*, vol. 78, 2013, https://cve.revues.org/959.
Malik, Charles. "The Drafting of the Universal Declaration of Human Rights." *United Nations Bulletin of Human Rights*, vol. 86, no. 1, 1978, pp. 18–26.
———. "Human Rights in the United Nations." *International Journal*, vol. 6, no. 4, Autumn 1951, pp. 275–80.
"Manifesto de Prago." *Manifesto de Prago pri la internaci lingvo Esperanto*, 1996, http://lingvo.org/prago.
Mann, Thomas. *Der Zauberberg*. S. Fischer, 1924.
———. *The Magic Mountain*. Translated by John E. Woods, Knopf, 2005.
Marchand, Leslie A. *Byron: A Portrait*. Knopf, 1970.
Marciano, Francesca. *Casa Rossa*. Vintage, 2003.
———. *The End of Manners*. Vintage, 2009.

———. *The Other Language: Stories*. Pantheon, 2014.
———. *Rules of the Wild: A Novel of Africa*. Vintage, 1999.
Markham, James M. "Arab Novelist Falls in Love with French." *New York Times*, 25 Nov. 1987, p. A7.
Martin, Rachel. "Characters Try on Different Cultures in 'Other Language.'" NPR *Weekend Edition Sunday*, 13 Apr. 2014, http://www.npr.org/2014/04/13/302532201/characterstry-on-different-cultures-in-other-language.
McMillin, Arnold. "Bilingualism and Word Play in the Work of Russian Writers of the Third Wave of Emigration: The Heritage of Nabokov." *The Modern Language Review*, vol. 89, no. 2, 1994, pp. 417–26.
Memmi, Albert. *Le Racisme: description, définition, traitement*. Gallimard, 1982.
Ménage, Gilles. *Ménagiana*. Vol. 4, Florentin Delaulne, 1715.
Mencken, H. L. *The American Language*. 4th ed., Knopf, 2006.
Meyer v. State of Nebraska. Legal Information Institute, https://www.law.cornell.edu/supremecourt/text/262/390.
Mignolo, Walter D. *Local Histories/Global Designs: Coloniality, Subaltern Knowledges, and Border Thinking*. Rev. ed., Princeton UP, 2012.
"Missing Parrot Turns Up Minus British Accent and Speaking Spanish." *The Guardian*, 17 Oct. 2014, https://www.theguardian.com/lifeandstyle/2014/oct/17/missing-parrot-british-accent-speaking-spanish-california.
Morsink, Johannes. *The Universal Declaration of Human Rights: Origins, Drafting, and Intent*. U of Pennsylvania P, 1999.
"Most Translated Document." *Guinness World Records*, 2009, https://www.guinnessworldrecords.com/world-records/most-translated-document.
Munro, Pamela. Email to the author. 19 May 2011.
Murakami, Haruki. *Gefährlichte Geliebte*. Translated by Giovanni Bandini and Ditte Bandini, DuMont, 2000.
Nabokov, Vladimir. *Лолита*. Phaedra, 1967.
———. "On a Book Entitled *Lolita*." 1956. *The Annotated Lolita: Revised and Updated*, 2nd ed., edited by Alfred Appel, Jr., Vintage International, 1991, pp. 311–18.
———. *Pale Fire*. G. P. Putnam's Sons, 1962.
———. *Pnin*. 1957. Knopf, 2004.
———. *Speak, Memory: An Autobiography Revisited*. G. P. Putnam's Sons, 1966.
———. "Translator's Foreword." *A Hero of Our Time*, by Mihail Lermontov. Translated by Vladimir Nabokov with Dmitri Nabokov, Doubleday, 1958, pp. vii–xix.
Némirovsky, Irène. *Suite Française*. Translated by Sandra Smith, Knopf, 2006.
No Man's Land: New German Literature in English Translation. www.no-mans-land.org.

Normand, Roger, and Sarah Zaidi. *Human Rights at the UN: The Political History of Universal Justice*. Indiana UP, 2008.

Orwell, George. "Why I Write." *The Orwell Reader: Fiction, Essays, and Reportage*. Harcourt, 1984, pp. 390–96.

Øverland, Orm, editor. *Not English Only: Redefining "American" in American Studies*. Vu UP, 2001.

Patty, Ann. *Living with a Dead Language: My Romance with Latin*. Viking, 2016.

Pavlenko, Aneta. *The Bilingual Mind and What It Tells Us about Language and Thought*. Cambridge UP, 2014.

———. "Bilingual Selves." *Bilingual Minds: Emotional Experience, Expression, and Representation*, edited by Aneta Pavlenko, Multilingual Matters, 2006, pp. 1–33.

———. "Language Learning Memoirs as a Gendered Genre." *Applied Linguistics*, vol. 22, no. 2, 2001, pp. 213–40.

Paz, Octavio. *The Labyrinth of Solitude: Life and Thought in Mexico*. Translated by Lysander Kemp, Grove, 1961.

Pérez Firmat, Gustavo. *Bilingual Blues: Poems, 1981–1994*. Bilingual Press, 1995.

———. *El año que viene estamos en Cuba*. Arte Publico, 1997.

———. *Life on the Hyphen: The Cuban-American Way*. Rev. ed., U of Texas P, 2012.

———. *Next Year in Cuba: A Cubano's Coming-of-Age in America*. Anchor, 1995.

———. *Tongue Ties: Logo-Eroticism in Anglo-Hispanic Literature*. Palgrave Macmillan, 2003.

Philcox, Richard. "Fidelity, Infidelity, and the Adulterous Translator." *Australian Journal of French Studies*, vol. 47, no. 1, 2010, pp. 29–35.

Piepenbring, Dan. "The Tragedy of Going Back: An Interview with Jhumpa Lahiri." *Paris Review*, 18 Apr. 2018, https://www.theparisreview.org/blog/2018/04/18/the-tragedy-of-going-back-jhumpa-lahiri-on-her-work-as-a-translator/.

Poncelet, Christian, editor. *Charles de Gaulle et la nation: Actes du colloque organisé à Paris, sous le patronage de Christian Poncelet, président du Sénat, les 30 novembre et 1er décembre 2000*. Guibert, 2002.

Proust, Marcel. *Against Sainte-Beuve and Other Essays*. Translated by John Sturrock, Penguin, 1994.

———. *Contre Sainte-Beuve*. Edited by P. Clarac, Bibliothèque de la Pléiade, 1971.

Pushkin, Aleksandr. *Eugene Onegin*. Translated by Vladimir Nabokov, Princeton UP, 1964. 4 vols.

Rabassa, Gregory. *If This Be Treason: Translation and Its Dyscontents*. New Directions, 2005.

Randolph, Jody Allen. "Hugo Hamilton." *Close to the Next Moment: Interviews from a Changing Ireland*. Carcanet, 2010, pp. 33–49.

Rao, Raja. "Raja Rao." *Interviews with Writers of the Post-Colonial World*, edited by Feroza Jussawalla and Reed Way Dasenbrock, UP of Mississippi, 1992, pp. 140–55.

Ravage, Marcus Eli. *An American in the Making*. 1917. Edited by Steven G. Kellman, Rutgers UP, 2009.

Rawlings, Marjorie. "Translator's Foreword." *Phèdre*, by Jean Racine, translated by Marjorie Rawlings, E. P. Dutton, 1961, pp. 9–16.

Rawls, John. "The Idea of an Overlapping Consensus." *Collected Papers*, edited by Samuel Freeman, Harvard UP, 1999, pp. 421–48.

Reston, James. *Collision at Home Plate: The Lives of Pete Rose and Bart Giamatti*. HarperCollins, 1991.

Rilke, Rainer Maria. *Briefe an einen jungen Dichter*. Insel, 1967.

———. *Letters to a Young Poet*. Translated by Joan M. Burnham, New World Library, 2000.

Rimbaud, Arthur. "Letter to Paul Demeny, May 15, 1871." *Lettres d'Arthur Rimbaud dites "du Voyant,"* http://www.mag4.net/Rimbaud/Documents1.html.

Roche, Paul. "Translator's Preface." *Sophocles: The Complete Plays*. Translated by Paul Roche, New American Library, 2001, pp. xv–xviii.

Roosevelt, Theodore. "Roosevelt's Last Message." *The Independent . . . Devoted to the Consideration of Politics, Social and Economic Tendencies, History, Literature, and the Arts (1848–1921)*, vol. 97, no. 3658, 18 Jan. 1919, p. 70.

Rorato, Laura. "Memoria e oblio in *Casa Rossa* di Francesca Marciano." *Narrativa*, vol. 25, 2003, pp. 157–68.

Rose, Julie. "Translator's Preface." *Les Misérables*, by Victor Hugo. Translated by Julie Rose, Modern Library, 2008.

Rosenwald, Lawrence. "Language Traitors, Translation, and *Die Emigranten*." *German? American? Literature? New Directions in German-American Studies*, edited by Winifried Fluck and Werner Sollors, Peter Lang, 2002, pp. 249–62.

Rousseau, Jean-Jacques. *The Confessions of Jean-Jacques Rousseau*. Translated by anonymous, Wordsworth Editions, 1996.

Said, Edward. *Reflections on Exile: And Other Essays*. Harvard UP, 2001.

Saint-Exupéry, Antoine de. *Ang Munting Prinsipe*. Translated by Lilia F. Antonio, Phoenix, 1969.

Saint-Onge, Kathleen. *Bilingual Being: My Life as a Hyphen*. McGill-Queen's UP, 2013.

Salinger, J. D. キャッチャー・イン・ザ・ライ (*The Catcher in the Rye*). Translated by Haruki Murakami, Hakusuisha, 2003.

———. *Der Fänger im Roggen*. Translated by Heinrich Böll, Diana, 1954.

———. *El guardián entre el centeno*. Translated by Carmen Criado, Alianza, 1997.
Salten, Felix. *Bambi, Eine Lebensgeschichte aus dem Walde*. Ullstein, 1923.
———. *Bambi: A Life in the Woods*. Translated by Whittaker Chambers, Pocket Books, 1956.
Sándor, Márai. *Embers*. Translated by Carol Brown Janeway, Knopf, 2001.
Sante, Luc, *The Factory of Facts*. Pantheon, 1998.
Santiago, Esmeralda. *Cuando Era Puertorriqueña*. Vintage, 1994.
———. *When I Was Puerto Rican*. Vintage, 1993.
"Santorum to Puerto Rico: Speak English if You Want Statehood." *Reuters*, 14 Mar. 2012, https://www.reuters.com/article/us-usa-campaign-puertorico/santorum-to-puerto-rico-speak-english-if-you-want-statehood-idUSBRE82D16Z20120314.
Šarčević, Susan. *New Approach to Legal Translation*. Kluwer Law International, 1997.
Schlegel, August Wilhelm von. "Nachschrift des Übersetzers an Ludwig Tieck." *Athenaeum: eine Zeitschrift*, edited by Curt Grützmacher, vol. 2, Rowohlt, 1969, pp. 105–09.
Schleiermacher, Friedrich. "On the Different Methods of Translating." 1813. *The Translation Studies Reader*, 3rd ed., edited by Lawrence Venuti, translated by Susan Bernofsky, Routledge, 2012, pp. 43–63.
———. "Ueber die verschiedenen Methoden des Uebersetzens." *Dokumente zur Theorie der Übersetzung antiker Literatur in Deutschland seit 1800*, edited by Josefine Kitzbichler, Katja Lubitz, and Nina Mindt, Walter de Gruyter, 2009, pp. 59–82.
Scholz, Martin. "Dieses Wort 'Heimat' gehört ja auch zu uns." *Welt*, 24 June 2018, https://www.welt.de/kultur/article178083246/Martin-Suter-und-Stephan-Eicher-Dieses-Wort-Heimat-gehoert-ja-auch-zu-uns.html.
Segal, Oren. "ProEnglish Attacks Super Bowl Ad Promoting America's Diversity." *Anti-Defamation League*, 5 Feb. 2014, https://www.adl.org/blog/proenglish-attacks-super-bowl-ad-promoting-americas-diversity.
Senghor, Léopold Sédar. "Le français langue de culture." *Liberté I: Négritude et humanism*, editions du Seuil, 1964, pp. 358–63.
Sevastopulo, Demetri. "Teflon Trump Chastises Jeb Bush for Speaking Spanish." *Financial Times*, 3 Sept. 2015, FT.com.
Shammās, Anton. "My Case Is Hopeless." Interview by Anne Zusy. *New York Times Book Review*, 17 Apr. 1988, p. 48.
———. שטח הפקר [Shetakh Hefker]. Hakibbutz Hameuchad, 1979.
———. "Three Poems." *Banipal: Magazine of Modern Arab Literature*, 3 Oct. 1998, http://www.banipal.co.uk/selections/17/165/anton-shammas/.
Shaw, Bernard. "Maxims for Revolutionists." *Man and Superman: A Comedy*

and a Philosophy, edited by Dan H. Laurence, Penguin, 2000, pp. 251–65.

Shell, Marc. Afterword. *The Multilingual Anthology of American Literature: A Reader of Original Texts with English Translations*, edited by Marc Shell and Werner Sollors, New York UP, 2000, pp. 684–92.

———, editor. *American Babel: Literatures of the United States from Abnaki to Zuni*. Harvard UP, 2002.

———, and Werner Sollors, editors. *The Multilingual Anthology of American Literature: A Reader of Original Texts with English Translations*. New York UP, 2000.

Shklovsky, Viktor. "Art as Technique." *Russian Formalist Criticism: Four Essays*, edited and translated by Lee T. Lemon and Marion J. Reis, U of Nebraska P, 1965, pp. 3–24.

Sibhatu, Ribka. *Aulò: Canto-Poesia dall'Eritrea*. Sinnos, 1993.

Skinner, John. *The Stepmother Tongue: An Introduction to New Anglophone Fiction*. St. Martin's, 1998.

"S. Korea Moviegoers Decreased 5 Percent Last Year." *Yonhap News Agency*, 15 Jan. 2009.

"Sleeping dictionary." *Oxford English Dictionary*. 2nd ed., 1989, http://www.oed.com/view/Entry/181615. Accessed 8 June 2012.

Snyder, Gary. *Regarding Wave*. New Directions, 1970.

Sollors, Werner, editor. *Multilingual America: Transnationalism, Ethnicity, and the Languages of American Literature*. New York UP, 1998.

Sparrow, Andrew. "Nigel Farage: Parts of Britain Are 'Like a Foreign Land.'" *The Guardian*, 28 Feb. 2014, https://www.theguardian.com/politics/2014/feb/28/nigel-farage-ukip-immigration-speech.

Spurr, David. *The Rhetoric of Empire: Colonial Discourse in Journalism, Travel Writing, and Imperial Administration*. Duke UP, 1993.

Spyri, Johanna. *Heidi*. Wilder, 2007.

Starnone, Domenico. *Ties*. Translated and introduction by Jhumpa Lahiri, Europa Editions, 2016.

———. *Trick*. Translated and introduction by Jhumpa Lahiri, Europa Editions, 2018.

Stavans, Ilan. *On Borrowed Words: A Memoir of Language*. Viking, 2001.

Steiner, George. *After Babel: Aspects of Language and Translation*. 3rd ed., Oxford UP, 1998.

———. *Extraterritorial: Papers on Literature and the Language Revolution*. Atheneum, 1971.

———. *My Unwritten Books*. New Directions, 2008.

Stenport, Anna Westerstahl. *Locating August Strindberg's Prose: Modernism, Transationalism, and Setting*. U of Toronto P, 2010.

Svevo, Italo. *La Coscienza di Zeno*. Licinio Cappelli Editore, 1923.

Tabory, Mala. *Multilingualism in International Law and Institutions.* Sijthoff & Noordhoff, 1980.
Taubenfield, Aviva F. *Rough Writing: Ethnic Authorship in Theodore Roosevelt's America.* New York UP, 2008.
Tawada, Yoko. *Exophony: Traveling Out of One's Mother Tongue.* Iwanami Shoten, 2003.
Tolstaya, Tatiana. "Love Story: Dreams of My Russian Summers." *New York Review of Books*, 20 Nov. 1997, pp. 4–5.
Tomasi di Lampedusa, Giuseppe. *The Leopard.* Translated by Archibald Colquhoun, Pantheon, 2007.
Triolet, Elsa. *La Mise en mots.* Albert Skira, 1969.
"Trump: We Speak English Here, Not Spanish." *YouTube*, 16 Sept. 2015: https://www.youtube.com/watch?v=eNjcAgNu1Ac.
Turner, Victor. *In the Forest of Symbols.* Cornell UP, 1967.
TV Guide. Incubus, https://www.tvguide.com/movies/incubus/review/102059/.
Umpierre, Luz María. "Unscrambling Allende's '*Dos palabras*': The Self, the Immigrant/Writer, and Social Justice." *MELUS*, vol. 27, 2002, pp. 129–36.
United States Census Bureau. "The Foreign Born Population in the United States." https://www.census.gov/newsroom/pdf/cspan_fb_slides.pdf.
"The Universal Declaration of Human Rights Is the Most Universal Document in the World." *Office of the High Commissioner for Human Rights*, https://www.ohchr.org/EN/UDHR/Pages/WorldRecord.aspx.
Untermeyer, Jean Starr. *Private Collection.* Knopf, 1965.
Vasconcelos, José. *The Cosmic Race/La raza cósmica. A Bilingual Edition.* 1925. Translated by Didier T. Jaén, Johns Hopkins UP, 1997.
Vaugelas, Laure de. "Francesca Marciano—Rome, Italy—Novelist, Screen Writer." *Aloud*, 23 May 2011, https://aloudblog.wordpress.com/2011/05/23/francesca-marciano-rome-italy-novelist-screen-writer/.
Venuti, Lawrence. "Lawrence Venuti." *Translation—Theory and Practice: A Historical Reader*, edited by Daniel Weissbort and Astradur Eysteinsson, Oxford UP, 2006, 546–57.
———, editor. *The Translation Studies Reader.* 2nd ed., Routledge, 2004, pp. 369–88.
———. *The Translator's Invisibility: A History of Translation.* Routledge, 1995.
Verdoodt, Albert. *Naissance et signification de la Déclaration Universelle des Droits de l'Homme.* Nauwelaerts, 1963.
Vian, Boris. *J'irai cracher sur vos tombes.* Scorpion, 1946.
"Vienna Declaration and Programme of Action." World Conference on Human Rights, 1993, http://www.ohchr.org/EN/ProfessionalInterest/Pages/Vienna.aspx. Accessed 10 June 2018.
Voltaire. *Candide, ou l'Optimisme.* Cramer, 1759.

———. "Letter to Madame la Marquise Du Duffand." 23 Apr. 1754. *Selected Letters of Voltaire*, edited by L. C. Syms, BiblioLife, 2008, pp. 118–20.

Vonnegut, Kurt. *Timequake*. Berkley Trade, 1998.

Wagner, Stephen. "Incubes et Succubes!" http://cabinet.auriol.free.fr/Documents/ParalysieSommeil/incubes.htm.

Walkowitz, Rebecca L. *Born Translated: The Contemporary Novel in an Age of World Literature*. Columbia UP, 2015.

Walpole, Horace. *The Castle of Otranto*. Thomas Lownds, 1764.

———. *The Castle of Otranto*. 3rd ed., John Murray, 1769.

Wanner, Adrian. *Out of Russia: Fictions of a New Translingual Diaspora*. Northwestern UP, 2011.

Warren, Robert Penn. *Talking Interviews 1950–1978*. Edited by Floyd C. Watkins and John T. Hiers, Random House, 1980.

Webster, Noah. *American Spelling Book*. Teachers College Press, 1962.

Wechsler, Robert. *Performing Without a Stage: The Art of Literary Translation*. Catbird, 1998.

West, Kevin. "Translating the Body: Towards an Erotics of Translation." *Translation and Literature*, vol. 19, no. 1, 2010, pp. 1–25.

Wheeler, David L. "The Death of Languages." *Chronicle of Higher Education*, 20 Apr. 1994, pp. A8, A9, A16, A17.

Whitman, Walt. "Slang in America." 1895. *Prose Works 1892, Volume 2: Collected and Other Prose*, edited by Floyd Stovall, New York UP, 1964, pp. 572–77.

Wirth-Nesher, Hana. *Call It English: The Languages of Jewish American Literature*. Princeton UP, 2006.

Wittgenstein, Ludwig. *Tractatus Logico-Philosophicus*. 1921. Edited and translated by C. K. Ogden, Routledge & Kegan Paul, 1981.

Wolfson, Louis. *Le schizo et les langues*. Gallimard, 1970.

Wright, Peter. *Spycatcher: The Candid Autobiography of a Senior Intelligence Officer*. Viking, 1987.

Wycliffe Global Alliance. http://www.wycliffe.net/statistics. Accessed 29 May 2018.

Yeats, William Butler. *The Countess Kathleen and Various Legends and Lyrics*. T. F. Unwin, 1892.

Yezierska, Anzia. *Hungry Hearts*. Penguin, 1997.

Yildiz, Yasemin. *Beyond the Mother Tongue: The Postmonolingual Condition*. Fordham UP, 2012.

INDEX

A

Abre los ojos (1997 film), 68
"abusive translation," Philip E. Lewis, 37
Académie Française, 3, 29, 135
Achebe, Chinua, 2, 8, 127
Aciman, André, 2, 78; *Out of Egypt*, 80
Acosta, Jim, 144
Adams, John, 135
Adelbert von Chamisso Prize, 3
Adichie, Chimamanda Ngozi, 78; *Half of a Yellow Sun*, 138
Ælfric, 68–69
Aesop, *The Classic Treasury of Aesop's Fables*, 64
Agnon, S. Y. (Shmuel Yosef Czaczkes), 3, 15, 42, 121
Agosín, Marjorie, 47; *The Alphabet in My Hands*, 88
Ahasuerus, 159
Ahmed, Leila, *A Border Passage*, 80
Akkadian, 4
Alameddine, Rabih, 2, 78; *An Unnecessary Woman*, 12, 71
Alarcón, Daniel, 2

Alas sobre el Chaco (1935 film), 91
Alexakis, Vassilis, 3
Alexander, Meena, *Fault Lines*, 80
Aldington, Richard, *The Colonel's Daughter*, 140
Alfau, Felipe, 78
Allen, Woody, 96
Allende, Salvador, 55
Allende, Taty, 53, 54
Alvarez, Julia, 2, 13, 24–25, 78
Alvaro, Corrado, 133
ambilingual translinguals, 13
American Anthropological Association, 151
American Renaissance (white supremacist organization), 143
"America the Beautiful," 143
Ames, Allyson, 94, 96, 97–98
Amichai, Yehudah, 3
Amnesty International, 148, 150
Amore e morte (1932 film), 91
Andrewes, Lancelot, 60
Angel Island poetry, 134
Anniversary, The (2003 film), 91
Anti-Defamation League, 143

Antin, Mary: *From Plotzk to Boston*, 82–83; *The Promised Land*, 49, 82–83, 84–85, 128
Antonio, Lilia F., 71
Antonioni, Michelangelo, 89
Anzaldúa, Gloria, 20, 30, 137; *Borderlands/La Frontera*, 27
Apocalypto (2006 film), 91–92
Appelfeld, Aharon, 3, 13, 14, 18, 100
Apuleius, 78
Arabic language, 4
Aramaic language, 11
Arana, Marie, 23
Arendt, Hannah, 25
Aristeas, 60
Aristotle, *De Interpretatione*, 162
Arnaz, Desi, *I Love Lucy*, 21
Arndt, Walter M., 69
Asayesh, Galareh, *Saffron Sky*, 80
Asimov, Isaac, 78
Athaniu of Alexandria, *Life of St. Anthony*, 68
Atmar, Ann, 93
Auerbach, Eric, 42
Augustine, Saint, 78
Aulus Gellius, 40
Ausonius, 78
Ayrault, Jean-Marc, 141

B
Babel, 138
Bach, Johann Sebastian, *Amore Traditore*, 35
Bailey, Keith, 92
Bak, Joshua, 76
Bakhtin, Mikhail, "dialogic imagination," 11–12, 57–58
Balboa, Vasco Núñez de, 76
banadurra, pronunciation of during the Lebanese Civil War, 138
Bancroft, Anne, 90
Bandini, Ditte, 71
Bandini, Giovanni, 71

Barnay, Inez, 101
Barthes, Roland, 33–34; *La Mort de l'auteur*, 61
Baudelaire, Charles, 75
Beauchamps, Pierre François Godard de, *Histoire du prince Apprius*, 74
Beaujour, Elizabeth Klosty, *Alien Tongues*, 13, 17
Beckett, Samuel, 2, 10, 14, 15, 16, 23, 47, 102, 125, 127, 131–32, 150; *l'Innomable/The Unnamable*, 159; *Molloy*, 5
Begley, Louis, 2, 18, 78, 127
Behros, Fateme, 3
Bell, Anthea, 61
Bellos, David, 71
Bellow, Saul, 42
Benjamin, Walter, "The Task of the Translator," 162–63
Ben Jelloun, Tahar, 3, 34–35
Beowulf, 67
Bergman, Ingmar, 89
Berlin, Irving, 78, 140
Bernabé, Jean, 30
Berra, Yogi (Lawrence), 57
Bertolucci, Bernardo, 89
Besemeres, Mary, 16
Bhabha, Homi K., 19
Bialik, Chaim Nachman, 3
Bianciotti, Hector, 3
Bible, 146–47
bilinguals, Aneta Pavlenko on, 13–14; compound, 13; coordinate, 13–14; subordinate, 14
Bill of Rights, 151–52
Blanchet, Philippe, 149, 161
Bly, Robert, 162
Boccaccio, Giovanni, 100; *Teseida delle nozze di Emilia*, 65
Bok, Edward W., 17
Böll, Heinrich, 67; *Irish Journal*, 117
Borges, Jorge Luis, 67, 75
Brandeis, Louis, 137

Index   191

Bray, Barbara, 71
Brecht, Bertolt, *Verfremdungseffekt*, 53, 145
Brenner, Yosef Chaim, 3
Brexit, 138–39
Breytenbach, Breyten, 14, 78, 117
Bridge on the River Kwai, The (1957 film), 90
Brink, André, 13, 47, 102, 150
Brodsky, Joseph, 42, 79
Broken Arrow (1950 film), 90
Brooks, Mel, 90
Broome, William, 76
Browning, Elizabeth Barrett, *Sonnets from the Portuguese*, 73
Browning, Robert, 73; translation of Aeschylus's *Agamemnon*, 25
Budé Collection, 70
Bulosan, Carlos, 78; *America Is in the Heart*, 80–81, 84
Buridan's paradox, 25
Burnham, Joan M., 66–67
Bush, Jeb (John Ellis), 142
Byron, Lord George Gordon, 44

C

Cahan, Abraham, 78
Cajun French language, 137
Calvino, Italo, 133; *Se una notte d'inverno un viaggiatore*, 13
Cameron, Deborah, "verbal hygiene," 29
Campbell, Roy, 36
Camus, Albert, 20
Canas, 154
Canetti, Elias, 40, 42; *Die Gerettete Zung*, 119
Cantínflas (Mario Moreno), 56
Capote, Truman, 8
Capriolo, Ettore, 61
Carnegie, Andrew, 79, 140
Carver, Raymond, 8
Casanova, Giacomo, 34, 100
Cassin, René, 64, 153, 154, 156–57

Cassola, Carlo, 133
Castiglione, Baldesar, *sprezzatura*, 111–12
Castro, Brian, 101
Catherine the Great (Catherine II), 89
Caxton, William, 63
Celan, Paul, 17, 18
Central News Agency of North Korea, 142
Cervantes, Miguel de, 15, 55–56; *Don Quixote*, 13, 69, 75
Chambers, Whittaker, 65
Chamoiseau, Patrick, 30
Chang, Peng-chun, 153, 154, 158
Chan Is Missing (1982 film), 91
Chaplin, Charles, 98
Chardin, Teilhard de, 151
Chaucer, Geoffrey, "The Knight's Tale," 65
Chauffier, Louis Martin, 20
Chin, Marilyn, 78
Chinese language, 4
Chinglish language, 29
Cicero, *De oratore*, 65
Cimino, Michael, *Big Jane*, 66
Cioran, E. M., 77
Çirak, Zehra, 3, 127
Cisneros, Sandra, *Caramelo*, 25
Ciudad (The City), La (1998 film), 91
Cixous, Hélène, 3
Clarke, Charles Crowden, 75
Clay Sanskrit Collection, 70
Coca-Cola, 143
Cocco De Filippis, Daisy, 19
Codex Argenteus, 1
Codrescu, Andrei, 79; *An Involuntary Genius in America's Shoes*, 80
Coetzee, J. M., 20, 101
Colbert, Stephen, 158
Coleridge, Samuel Taylor, *Biographia Literaria*, 66
Colquhoun, Archibald, 66
compound bilinguals, 13

compound translinguals, 14
Condé, Maryse, 34
Confiant, Raphaël, 30
Conrad, Joseph (Józef Teodor Konrad Nalécz Korzeniowski), 2, 10, 11, 15, 16, 39, 110, 126, 127; *The Secret Agent*, 11
conscience, 158
Contra la corriente (1935 film), 91
Cook, Thomas L., 66
coordinate bilinguals, 13–14
coordinate translinguals, 14
Cortez (Hernán Cortés), 76
cosmopolitans, 143–45
Cossa, Paolo, 97
Costello, Elvis, *Blood and Chocolate*, 98
Cowper, William, 76
Cox, Steve, 71
creolization, 30
Crèvecoeur, Michel-Guillaume-Jean de, *Letters from an American Farmer*, 78
Croce, Benedetto, 151
¿Cuándo te suicidas? (1931 film), 91
Cuarón, Alfonso, 89
Curtiz, Michael, 89

D

Dances with Wolves (1990 film), 90
Dante, Alighieri, 15, 33, 43–44, 100; *Convivio*, 44; *De Vulgari Eloquentia*, 44
Danticat, Edwidge, 2, 13, 24, 78, 127
Das, Kamala, 4, 77, 102, 117
Déclaration des droits de l'Homme et du Citoyen, 151, 156–57
Deffand, Madame du (Marie de Vichy-Chamrond), 72–73
de Gaulle, Charles, 140
Denham, Sir John, 63
Depner, Dorothea, 116
De Quincey, Thomas, 66
Derrida, Jacques, *Le Monolinguisme de l'autre*, 21–22; "The Retrait of Metaphor," 37

Desai, Anita, 14
Descartes, René, 14; *Meditationes de prima philosophia*, 3
Deutschrussich, 29
Devaux, Laetitia (pseuds. Anne Derouet; L.), 66
"dialogic imagination," Mikhail Bakhtin, 11–12, 57–58
día que me quieras, El (1936 film), 91
Diaz, Junot, 2, 78
Dickens, Charles, *Bleak House*, 104
Dickinson, Emily, 9
Dietrich, Marlene, 89
Dinesen, Isak (Karen Blixen), 77, 102, 121, 150; *Out of Africa/Den afrikanske farm*, 4
Dion, Céline, 20
Djebar, Assia, 3, 13, 19, 39
Dolet, Etienne, 61
Doloughan, Fiona J., 52
"domesticating translation," Lawrence Venuti, 61–62
Doner, Timothy, 44
donna bianca, La (1930 film), 91
Donoso, José, *Tarantula and Still Life with Pipe*, 66
Dorfman, Ariel, 2, 12, 39, 46–58, 113, 150; *Heading South, Looking North*, 6, 23–24, 46–47, 49–58, 80, 85–87; *Kurs nach Süden*, 51; *Para leer al Pato Donald*, 48; *Rumbo al sur, deseando el norte*, 6, 46–47, 49–58
Dostoevsky, Fyodor, *Crime and Punishment*, 69
Dukes, Charles, 154
Dumas, Firoozeh, *Funny in Farsi*, 80, 88

E

Eat a Bowl of Tea (1989 film), 91
Eco, Umberto, *Experiences in Translation*, 70
Edwards, Viv, "monolingual mindset," 138
Eggers, Dave, 66

Éigeartaigh, Aoileann Ní, 123
Einstein, Albert, 140
Eliot, T. S., 9; "Tradition and the Individual Talent," 74
Emigranten, Die (1882 play), 28
English language, 30–31
Enheduanna, 4
Erard, Michael, *Babel No More*, 44–45
Esperanto language, 64, 92–93, 95–97, 98, 99
Esther (book of), 159
eta knabino, La (1997 film), 98
Evagrius of Antioch, 68
Everett, Daniel, 10
exophony, 2

F
Falun Gong, 148
Farage, Nigel, 138–39
Faulkner, William, 9–10; *Absalom, Absalom!*, 10; *Las palmeras salvajes*, 67
Federer, Roger, 38
Ferguson, Miriam "Ma," 60
Ferrante, Elena, 128
Ferré, Rosario, 6, 7, 112, 114
Fish, Stanley, 22
Fishkin, Shelley Fisher, 9
Fitch, Brian T., 23
Fitzgerald, Edward, "The Rubaiyat of Omar Khayyam," 65
Fitzgerald, F. Scott, 8
foreign films, 67–68. See also individual film titles
"foreignizing translation," Lawrence Venuti, 53, 61–62, 111
Forman, Miloš, 89
Forster, E. M., 42–43; *Howards End*, 104
Fraker, William, 96
Franglais, 29
French language, 31, 140–41; Cajun French, 137

Freud, Sigmund, 41
Frost, Robert, 75
Fruman, Norman, 66

G
Gabriel, J. Philip, 71
García, Cristina, 2, 78; *Dreaming in Cuban*, 79
García Márquez, Gabriel, *One Hundred Years of Solitude*, 66
Garner, Dwight, 131
Garnett, Constance, 69
Gary, Romain, 3, 17, 127
Gattaca (1997 film), 98
Gauvin, Lise, 26
Gefke, James, 126
George, Stefan, 75
German language, 136
Ghalib, Mirza, 16, 47
Ghandi, Mohandas, 151
Ghérasim, Luca, 26
Gibson, Mel, 91–92
Gilroy, Paul, *Postcolonial Melancholia*, 145
Gingrich, Newt, 141
Girona Manifesto, 144
Goethe, Johann Wolfgang von, 11, 15, 22, 139
Gogol, Nikolai, 101
Goldberg, Leah, 77
Goldoni, Carlo, 100
Goldstein, Ann, 128
Gombrowicz, Witold, *Ferdydurke*, 70
Goncourt, Edmond de, 43
González Iñárritu, Alejandro, 89
Graduate, The (1967 film), 45
Granger, Colette A., 18
Great Dictator, The (1940 film), 98
Greek language, 4, 11, 40
Green, Julien, 96
Greenberg, Uri Zvi, 16
Grobler, Melanie, "Stad," 65–66
Grossman, Edith, *Why Translation Matters*, 70

Grove, Frederick Philip (Felix Paul Greve), 121
Grushin, Olga, 2
Guilleragues, Gabriel Joseph de Lavergne, vicomte de, *Lettres portugaises*, 74
Guo, Xiaolu, 78
Gustafsson, Lars, 10

H

Haitian Creole, 10
Ha Jin, 3, 16, 43, 79, 100, 126–27
Hall, Conrad, 95, 98
Haman, 159
Hamburger, Michael, *Strings of Beginnings*, 70
Hamid, Mohsin, 78
Hamilton, Edith, 74
Hamilton, Hugo (Johannes Ó hUrmoltaigh), 12, 113–25; *Every Single Minute*, 117; *Hand in the Fire*, 117–18; *The Last Shot*, 117; *The Love Test*, 117; *The Sailor in the Wardrobe*, 116, 118, 119–20, 122–25; *The Speckled People*, 26, 114, 115, 116, 118–19, 120–24; *Surrogate City*, 117
Hamilton, Irmgard (Irmgard née Kaiser Ó hUrmoltaigh), 114, 115, 117, 119–20
Hamilton, John (Séan Ó hUrmoltaigh), 115, 120, 124, 125
Harding, William, 136
Hardt, Eloise, 94, 98
Hart-Cellar Act, 87
Hassel, Stéphane, 64
Hattušiliš III, 159
Hawthorne, Nathaniel: "The Custom-House," 132; *The House of the Seven Gables*, 104; "Rappaccini's Daughter," 75
Heaney, Seamus, 67
Hebrew, 142–43
Hegi, Ursula, 3, 78
Heidegger, Martin, 21

Hejmadi, Padma, *Room to Fly*, 85
Hemingway, Ernest, 9
Hemon, Aleksandar, 3, 78, 127
Hernandez, José, *Martin Fierro*, 56
Herzog, Werner, 89
"heterophobia," Albert Memmi, 30
Hitler, Adolf, *Mein Kampf*, 98
Hobbes, Thomas, 76
Hodgson, William, 154
Hoffman, Eva, 12, 113, 130; *Lost in Translation*, 6–7, 18, 19, 79–80, 83–85, 128
Hollis, Roger, 59
Hombres armados (*Men with Guns*, 1998 film), 91
Homer, 75–76
Hosseini, Khaled, 78
Hugo, Victor, *Les Misérables*, 62, 74
human rights, universality of, 151–52, 155, 161–62
Human Rights Watch, 148
Humphries, John Peters, 64, 153, 154
Huston, Nancy, 3, 23, 127; *Noir perdu*, 128
Hutton, Christopher M., 42
Huxley, Aldous, 151
hyperpolyglots, 44–45

I

Igarashi, Hitoshi, 61
"illusionist translation," Jiří Levý, 60–62
immigrant memoirs, 77–88
Incubus (1965 film), 92–99; curse of, 97–98
initiation ritual, 18
Institute of the Czech Language, 29
International Military Tribunal for the Far East, 148
Ionesco, Eugène, *La Leçon*, 12
Irish language, 120–21
Irving, Washington, 9
isolingual writers, 11, 13
Italian language, 100
Iyer, Pico, 101

J

Jackson, Michael, *Redeeming Eastern Europe*, 98
James, Henry, 9, 38–39
Jameson, Frederic, 145
Jandl, Ernst, *Reft and Light*, 62
Janeway, Carol Brown, 70
Japanese language, 8
Jara, Victor, 55
Jarvis, Charles, 69
Jasienko, Jean-Michel, 71
Jefferson, Thomas, 134
Jenkin, Guy, 37
Jewish multilingualism, 42
Jhabvala, Ruth Prawer, 77
Jimeno, Claudio, 54
Jolas, Eugene, 117
Johnson, Barbara, 35
Johnson, Samuel, 8, 38; "The Vanity of Human Wishes," 65
Jonson, Ben, 8, 75
Jordan, Michael, 131
Joyce, James, 125; *A Portrait of the Artist as a Young Man*, 125
Joy Luck Club, The (1993 film), 91
Judas Iscariot, 43
Judges (book of), 29, 138

K

Kadare, Ismail, 71
Kalelkar, Kaka, 47
Kallifatides, Theodor, 3
Kaminer, Wladimir, 127
kanshi, 130
Kant, Immanuel, 158
Kaplan, Alice, 16; *French Lessons*, 113, 128; "On Language Memoir," 119, 128
Kapovich, Katia, 77
Kappus, Franx Xavier, 41
Keats, John, "On First Looking into Chapman's Homer," 75–76
Keeley, Edmund, *Borderlines*, 70
Keene, Donald, *Chronicle of My Life*, 70
Kennedy, John F., *A Nation of Immigrants*, 78
Kerry, John, 140–41
Khashoggi, Jamal, 149
Kilmartin, Joanna, 71
Kim Il-sung, 8
Kim Jong-il, 8
Kim Jon-un, 8
Kingdom of Heaven (2005 film), 89
King James Version (Bible), 42, 60
Kissinger, Henry, 78
Klevkovkin, M. H., 155
Koestler, Arthur, 17
Koretzsky, Vladimir, 157
Kozinski, Jerzy, 7, 13, 17, 79
Kramsch, Claire J., 19
Krebs, Emil, 44
Kundera, Milan, 3, 36, 39, 127; *Jacques et son maître*, 36

L

La Boétie, Etienne de, *Discours de la servitude volontaire*, 156
La Cantera civil rights lawsuit, 137–38
Lahiri, Jhumpa, 113, 126–33; *Dove mi trovo*, 133; *In Other Words/In Altre Parole*, 127, 128, 129, 131, 132, 133; *Interpreter of Maladies*, 127, 131; *The Lowland*, 127, 129; *The Namesake*, 127; ed., *The Penguin Book of Italian Short Stories*, 133; as translator, 132–33; trans. *Ties*, 132–33; trans. *Trick*, 133; *Unaccustomed Earth*, 127, 131; *Il vestito dei libri/The Clothing of Books*, 133
Lam, Andrew, 3
Lang, Fritz, 89
language as home, 19–22
"language traitor," Lawrence Rosenwald, 28–29
Last Temptation of Christ, The (1988 film), 90
Latin language, 3, 9, 11, 40, 78

Latini, Brunetto, 44
Latvian State Language Center, 29
Laugier, Henri, 64
Lee, Ang, 89
Lee, Li-Young, 3, 78, 140
Lefevere, André, 61
Lefevre, Raoul, *Recuyell of the Historyes of Troye*, 63
Leibniz, Gottfried Wilhelm, 73
Lem, Stanislaw, *Solaris*, 71
Lennon, John, 122–24
Lermontov, Mikhail, *A Hero of Our Time*, 62
Lessing, Gotthold Ephraim, 22
Levi, Primo, 128
Levine, Suzanne Jill, *The Subversive Scribe*, 70
Levy, Hideo, 130; *Seijouki no kikoenai heya* (*A Room Where the Star Spangled Banner Cannot Be Heard*), 3
Levý, Jiří, "illusionist" and "anti-illusionist" translation, 60–62
Lewis, Philip E., "abusive translation," 37
Lezama Lima, José, *Paradiso*, 66
Lim, Shirley Geok-lin, 3, 79; *Among the White Moon Faces*, 88
Lindgren, Astrid, *Pippi Longstocking*, 64
linguistic purity, 29–30
Lionnet, Françoise, 30
Li Po, 15, 65
Lisowski, Georges, 70
Littell, Jonathan, 3
Livius Andronicus, 78
Li, Yiyun, 3, 77–78
Lobo Antunes, António, *The Return of the Caravels*, 66
Loeb Classical Library, 145
lollapalooza, pronunciation of during World War II, 138
Longfellow, Henry Wadsworth, 9
Louÿs, Pierre, *Les Chansons de Bilitis*, 74

Lowell, Robert, *Imitations*, 62
Lubitsch, Ernst, 89
Lucan, 78
Lucian, 36
Luehr, Rick, 92
Luther Bible, 60
Lvovich, Natasha, 17, 19

M

Maalouf, Amin, 3
Mabanckou, Alain, 3, 127
Macpherson, James, 76; *Fingal*, 72
MAD magazine, 56
Madariaga, Salvador de, 151
Magna Carta, 151–52
Magnolo, Walter D., 28
Mahfouz, Naguib, *Children of the Alley*, 66
Mahloujian, Azar, 3
Maisonnat, Claude, 11
Makhzoomi, Khairuldeen, 141
Makine, Andreï, 3, 127; *Le Testament français*, 12, 28, 128
Malik, Charles Habib, 64, 152, 153
man, use of as generic term, 157–58
Manguel, Alberto, 101
Mann, Klaus, 17
Mann, Thomas, 46; *Doktor Faustus*, 46; *Der Erwählte*, 46; *Der Zauberberg*, 7
Marciano, Francesca, 100–12, 129–30; *La bestia nel cuore*, 102; calques, 110; *Casa Rossa*, 101, 103, 104–06, 110, 130; *The End of Manners*, 103, 106–07, 110, 130; *Euforia*, 102; *Io e te*, 102; *Io non ho paura*, 102; *The Other Language*, 107–09, 111, 130; *Rules of the Wild*, 103–04, 109–10, 130; self-translation of, 102–03; her *sprezzatura*, 111–12; *Viaggio sola*, 102
Maria Full of Grace (2004 film), 91
Maritain, Jacques, 64, 151
Markovic, Goran, 99
Martial, 78

Index

Matar, Hisham, 3, 78
McCarthy, Charlie, 56
McCarthy, Joseph, 56
McEwen, Alastair, 70
McKeon, Richard, 151
McReynolds, James Clark, 137
Mehta, Hansa, 153
Melville, Herman, 9; *Moby-Dick*, 55
Memmi, Albert, "heterophobia," 30
Ménage, Gilles, 36
Mencken, H. L., 135
Mendele Mocher Sforim (S. J. Abramowitch), 13, 47
Menelik II, 160
Mengestu, Dinaw, 3
Mengin, Urbain, 38
Mervius, 92
Meyer v. Nebraska, 137
Mezzofanti, Cardinal Guiseppe, 44
Michaels, Anne, "There Is No City That Does Not Dream," 65–66
Mickiewicz, Adam, *Pan Tadeusz*, 140
Miller, Stephen, 144
Milos, Milos, 94, 96, 97–98
Milošević, Slobodan, 148
Miłosz, Czesław, 20
Milton, John, 8, 42
Mirele Efros (1939 film), 91
Mitchell, Stephen, 66, 162
"monolingual mindset," Viv Edwards, 138
"monolingual paradigm," Yasemin Yildiz, 4, 31, 138
monolingual translinguals, 13
Montale, Eugenio, 75
Morante, Elsa, 101
Moravia, Alberto, 101
More, Sir Thomas, *Utopia*, 3
Morrice, James, 76
Mosbacher, Eric, 70
mother tongue, 38–39, 42
Mu Dan (Zha Liangzheng), 75
Mukherjee, Bharati, 77
Munro, Pamela, 148

Murakami, Haruki, 8, 67; *South of the Border, West of the Sun*, 71

N

Nabokov, Vladimir, 2, 4, 10, 15, 16, 24, 39, 102, 111, 117, 127, 150; trans. *Eugene Onegin*, 69, 72; trans. *A Hero of Our Time*, 62; *Лолита*, 159; *Lolita*, 35, 159; *Pale Fire*, 12, 69, 72; *Pnin*, 52; *Speak, Memory*, 82
Nafisi, Azar, 79
nationalism vs. patriotism, 140
Ndembu (of Zambia), 18
Némirovsky, Irène, 3, 13; *Suite Française*, 66
Nessin, Azis, 61
Newton, Sir Isaac, *Principia Mathematica*, 3
Ngũgĩ wa Thiong'o, 13, 101
Nguyen, Viet Thanh, 79, 127
Nietzsche, Friedrich, 145
Nigel (parrot), 14
no man's land, 25–26, 32
No Man's Land: New German Literature in English Translation, 26
Norte, El (1983 film), 91
Nuclear Non-Proliferation Treaty, 159
Nyggard, William, 61

O

Obreht, Téa, 3, 77
O'Faolain, Nuala, 117
Official Journal of the European Union, 160–61
Ogilby, John, 76
O'Higgins, Bernardo, 57
O'Nolan, Brian (Myles na gCopaleen; Flann O'Brien), 121
Oldisworth, William, 76
Orwell, George (Eric Blair), 126
Oscan, 11
ostranenie, Viktor Shklovsky, 12, 145
Øverland, Orm, 91

Özdamar, Emine Sevgi, 3, 127
Ozell, John, 76

P
Pal, Radhabinod, 148
palimpsest, 1
Palin, Sarah, 142
panlingualism, 31
Papavrami, Tedi, 71
Parise, Goffredo, 133
Parks, Tim, 101
Parra, Violeta, 55
Parsley Massacre, 29
Passion of the Christ, The (2004 film), 90
Pasternak, Boris, 75
patriotism vs. nationalism, 140
Patty, Ann, *Living with a Dead Language*, 128–29, 130
Pavlenko, Aneta, 13; *The Bilingual Mind*, 14, 114
Pavlov, Alexei, 154
Paz, Octavio, *El laberinto de la soledad*, 54
Pearl Harbor (2001 film), 93
Pelecanos, George, 66
PEN International, 143–44
Penkov, Miroslav, 78
Perec, Georges, *La Disparition*, 132
Pérez Firmat, Gustavo, 21, 87; *Life on the Hyphen*, 24–25; "logo-eroticism," 39; *Next Year in Cuba*, 80
Perrot d'Ablancourt, Nicolas, 36
Pessoa, Fernando, 13, 15, 47
Peter, Saint, 43
Petrarch, 16, 47, 100
Philcox, Richard, 34–35
Phoenicians, 3–4
pillow dictionary, 37–38
Pinochet, Augusto, 55
Pirahã people of the Amazon, 10
Plato, 41; *The Republic*, 146
Polanski, Roman, 89
Pope, Alexander, 76

Pound, Ezra, 9; "The River Merchant's Wife," 65
Prague Manifesto, 93
Premchand, Munshi (Dhanpat Rai Shrivastava), 13
presidio, El (1930 film), 91
ProEnglish, 143
Proust, Marcel, 10; *A la recherche du temps perdu*, 13, 15
pseudotranslation, 72–75
Ptolemy II, 148–49
Puerto Rico, 141
Pushkin, Alexander, 15

Q
Quevedo, Francisco de, 56
Quintilian, 78

R
Rabassa, Gregory, 66; *If This Be Treason*, 70
Racine, Jean, *Phèdre*, 69
Rahimi, Atiq, 3
Rameses II, 158
Ramondino, Fabrizia, 133
Rand, Ayn, 13, 79
Rao, Raja, 2, 5–6, 127
Ravage, M. E., *An American in the Making*, 81–82
Rawicz, Piotr, 17
Rawlings, Marjorie, 69–70
Rawls, John, 162
religious freedom, 155
Renoir, Jean, 89
Rilke, Rainer Maria, 15, 41, 162; *Letters to a Young Poet*, 66
Rimbaud, Arthur, 112
Rivera, Tomás, *. . . y no se lo tragó la tierra*, 136
Robe, The (1953 film), 90
Roche, Paul, 69
Rodo, José Enrique, *Ariel*, 49
Rodrigues da Silva, Guilem, 3
Rodriguez, Richard, 113

Rølvaag, Ole Edvart, *I de dage/Giants in the Earth*, 134
Romano, Lalla, 133
Romney, (Willard) Mitt, 141
Rómulo, Carlos P., 153–54
Ronsard, Pierre de, "Quand vous serez bien vieille," 65
Roosevelt, Eleanor, 64, 151, 154, 157, 162
Roosevelt, Franklin Delano, 155
Roosevelt, Theodore, 135–36
Rose, Julie, 62, 74
Rosenberg, Julius, 59–60
Rosenwald, Lawrence, "language traitor," 28–29
Rousseau, Jean-Jacques, 115
Royal Coat of Arms, United Kingdom, 145
Rushdie, Salman, *The Satanic Verses*, 61
Russian Synod Bible, 60

S

Sabatini, Rafael, 12–13, 16
Said, Edward, 20–21
Said, Omar ibn, 134
Saint-Exupéry, Antoine de, *The Little Prince*, 71
Saint-Onge, Kathleen, *Bilingual Being*, 24
Salinger, J. D.: *Der Fänger im Roggen*, 67; *El guardián entre el centeno*, 67; キャッチャー・イン・ザ・ライ, 67
Salten, Felix, *Bambi*, 64–65
San Antonio, Texas, 137
Sándor, Márai, *Embers*, 70
Sanskrit language, 4
Santa Cruz, Hernán, 154
Santayana, George, 77
Sante, Luc, 3, 12, 113, 127; *The Factory of Facts*, 6, 80, 87
Santiago, Esmeralda: *Cuando era puertorriqueña*, 87–88; *When I Was Puerto Rican*, 87–88
Santorum, Rick, 141
Sarraute, Nathalie, 13
Saturday Evening Post, 56
Scarlet Empress, The (1934 film), 89
Schelling, Friedrich, 66
Schlegel, August Wilhelm von, 34, 66
Schleiermacher, Friedrich, 4; "Ueber die verschiedenen Methoden des Uebersetzens," 2, 53; *verfremdende Übersetzung*, 53
Schwarz-Bart, André, 3
Schwarzkopf, Elizabeth, 123
second-degree translation, 70–72
Séjour, Victor, 134
Semiramis, 33
Semprún, Jorge, 3
Seneca, 78
Senghor, Léopold Sédar, 2, 31, 100–01, 127
Senmova (2010 film), 98
Septuagint, 42, 60, 148–49
servitude, 156
Shakespeare, William, 15; *Henry V*, 8; *A Midsummer Night's Dream*, 41; *The Tempest*, 13, 49; *Timon of Athens*, 72
Shammās, Anton, 19, 26
Shatner, William, 93–94, 96, 97, 98
Shaw, George Bernard, 77
Shell, Marc, 91
shibboleth, 138, 140
Shklovsky, Viktor, *ostranenie*, 12, 145
Shteyngart, Gary, 3, 14
Sibhatu, Ribka, *Aulò: Canto-Poesia dall'Eritrea*, 131
Sijie, Dai, 3
Siman Act, 136–37
Simic, Charles, 3, 78
Singer, Isaac Bashevis, 5, 42, 46–47, 134; *Der kuntsnmakher fun Lublin*, 136
Sin-liqe-unninni, *Gilgamesh*, 63
Skinner, John, *The Stepmother Tongue*, 5
Sleeping Dictionary, The (2003 film), 37–38

sleeping dictionary, 37–38
Smetana, Bredrich, *The Moldau*, 140
Smith, Ali, 66
Smith, Red (Walter Wellesley), 77
Smith, Sandra, 66
Snyder, Gary, 20
Socrates, 145, 146
Sollors, Werner, 91
Solzhenitsyn, Aleksandr, 10, 46
Sophocles, 15, 69
South Africa, Republic of, 64
Southern Poverty Law Center, 143
Soyinka, Wole, 127
Spanglish language, 29
Spanish language, 52, 137–38, 140, 141–42
Spartacus (1960 film), 89
spatial metaphors, 19, 22–28
Spurr, David, 38
Spyri, Johanna, *Heidi*, 64
Stalin, Joseph, 144
Starnone, Domenico: *Lacci*, 132–33; *Scherzetto*, 133
Stavans, Ilan, 25, 113; *On Borrowed Words*, 80, 87
Steiner, George, 4, 19, 24, 25, 34
Sternberg, Josef von, 89
Stevens, Leslie, 92–93, 97, 98, 99
Stevens, Wallace, 26–27
Stewart, Jon, 158
Strindberg, August, *Le Plaidoyer d'un fou*, 43
subordinate bilinguals, 14
subordinate translinguals, 14
Sumerian language, 4
Super, El (1979 film), 91
Suter, Martin, 20
Suu Kyi, Aung San, 148
Svevo, Italo (Ettore Schmitz), 100

T
Talmud, 149
Tanton, John, 143
Taubenfield, Aviva F., 135–36

Tawada, Yoko, 2, 3, 77
Taylor, Anthony, 92, 95
Tchernichovsky, Shaul, 3, 75
tenorio del harem, El (1931 film), 91
Terence, 78
Thatcher, Margaret, 59
Theroux, Peter, 66
Thompson, Barbara Ann, 98
Thrasymachus, 146
Three Men and a Baby (1987 film), 68
Three Seasons (1999 film), 91
To Be or Not to Be (1983 film), 90
Tomasi di Lampedusa, Giuseppe, *The Leopard*, 66
Toller, Ernst, 17
Tolstoya, Tatyana, 28, 29, 30
torture, 147
translation, 2, 53, 59–76; abusive, 37; and adultery, 34–38, 42; illusionist and anti-illusionist, 60–61; meta-, 69; plagiarism, 65–66; pseudo-, 72–75; and publishing industry, 67; second-degree, 70–72
translator prefaces, 68–69
"translator's invisibility," Lawrence Venuti, 53, 61–62
translingualism as adultery, 39–42, 45
translinguals: ambilingual and monolingual/isolingual, 13; compound, coordinate, and subordinate, 14
treason, 42–43, 59–60
Treaty of Friendship and Commerce, Ethiopia and Italy, 159–60
Treaty of Versailles, 159
Triolet, Elsa, 17, 39
Trois hommes et un couffin (1985 film), 67–68
Trojanow, Ilija, 101
Troyat, Henri, 3
Trump, Donald, 142, 144, 149
Trump, Melania, 142
Tsabari, Ayelet, 77
Tsvetaeva, Marina, 77

Turner, Victor, 18, 23
Twain, Mark (Samuel Clemens):
    Adventures of Huckleberry Finn, 9,
    55; "The Awful Language," 9; *The
    Prince and the Pauper*, 49
Tyndale, William, 42, 60

U
UNESCO (United Nations
    Educational, Scientific, and Cultural
    Organization), 151
United Nations, 31–32, 146–50, 154,
    156
United Nations Covenant on Civil and
    Political Rights, 154
United Nations Covenant on Economic,
    Social, and Cultural Rights, 154
United Nations Human Rights
    Commission, 150, 151
United Nations Human Rights Council,
    149
United Nations Information Centre:
    India, 150; New York, 150; Senegal,
    149–50; Spain, 150
United Nations Security Council
    Resolution, 242, 160
United States, 9
Universala Esperanto Asocio, 150
"Universal Declaration of Human
    Rights," 63–64, 146–63; self-
    translation of, 150
"Universal Declaration of Linguistic
    Freedom," 143–44
Uzun, Mehmed, 3

V
vacanza del diavolo, La (1931 film), 91
Vandervoort, Robert, 143
Vanilla Sky (2001 film), 68
Vasconcelos, José, "la raza cósmica," 30
Vec Vidjeno (1987 film), 99
Vega, Garcilaso de la, *Commentarios
    reales*, 78
Venuti, Lawrence: "domesticating
    translation," 61–62; "foreignizing
    translation," 53, 61–62, 111; "the
    translator's invisibility," 53, 61–62
"verbal hygiene," Deborah Cameron, 29
Verfremdungseffekt, Bertolt Brecht, 53,
    145
Vian, Boris, *J'irai cracher sur vos
    tombes*, 74
vida bohemia, La (1937 film), 91
Vidal, Ramon de Besalú, 78
Vienna Convention on the Law of
    Treaties, 159
Viragh, Christina, 70
Virgil, 15; *Aeneid*, 63
Voltaire (François-Marie Arouet), 72–73;
    Candide, 5, 73
Vonnegut, Kurt, Jr., *Timequake*, 60
Vrioni, Jusuf, 71
Vulgate, 60, 68

W
Walcott, Derek, 107
Walkowitz, Rebecca L., *Born
    Translated*, 5
Walpole, Horace, *The Castle of Otranto*,
    73
Warren, Robert Penn, 10
Waterloo (1970 film), 90
Webster, Noah, 135; *American Spelling
    Book*, 29
Wechsler, Robert, 35
West, Kevin, 36
Wharton, Edith, 9
What's Up, Tiger Lily? (1966 film), 96
Wheatley, Phillis, 78
Whitehead, Alfred North, 153
Whitman, Walt, 22, 30–31, 41; *Leaves of
    Grass*, 140
Wiesel, Elie, 3, 18
Wilde, Oscar, *Salomé*, 7, 43, 130
Wilder, Billy, 89
Williams, P., 76
Williams, R. R., *Dafydd Morgan*, 134
Wittgenstein, Ludwig, 142

Wolfson, Louis, *Le schizo et les langues*, 6, 17
Wood, Ed, 56
Wright, Peter, *Spycatcher*, 59
Wyler, William, 89

X
xenolinguaphobia, 135–45

Y
Yacine, Kateb, 47
Yeats, William Butler, "When You Are Old," 65
Yezierska, Anzia, *Hungry Hearts*, 82–83
Yiddish, hostility toward, 142–43
Yiddishe Koenig Lear, Der (1935 film), 91
Yidl Mitn Fidl (1936 film), 91
Yildiz, Yasemin, "monolingual paradigm," 4, 31, 138
Y tu mamá también (2001 film), 93

Z
Zaimoğlu, Feridun, 8, 127
Zamenhof, Ludwig L., 64, 92–93, 98
Zukofsky, Louis, 79
Zweig, Stefan, 17

About the Author

Steven G. Kellman is author of *The Restless Ilan Stavans: Outsider on the Inside* (Pittsburgh); *American Suite: A Literary History of the United States* (Finishing Line); *Redemption: The Life of Henry Roth* (Norton); *The Translingual Imagination* (Nebraska); *The Plague: Fiction and Resistance* (Twayne); *Loving Reading: Erotics of the Text* (Archon); and *The Self-Begetting Novel* (Columbia). He edited *Switching Languages: Translingual Writers Reflect on Their Craft* (Nebraska); *UnderWords: Perspectives on DeLillo's Underworld* (Delaware); *Torpid Smoke: Stories of Vladimir Nabokov* (Rodopi); and *Leslie Fiedler and American Culture* (Delaware). A widely published critic and essayist, Kellman served four terms on the board of directors of the National Book Critics Circle and received its coveted Nona Balakian Citation for Excellence in Reviewing. He has taught at Tel-Aviv University, the University of California campuses at Irvine and Berkeley, Tbilisi State University, and the University of Sofia. He is professor of comparative literature at the University of Texas at San Antonio.

www.ingramcontent.com/pod-product-compliance
Lightning Source LLC
Chambersburg PA
CBHW061445300426
44114CB00014B/1848